Artificial Intelligence and Large Language Models

Having been catapulted into public discourse in the last few years, this book serves as an in-depth exploration of the ever-evolving domain of artificial intelligence (AI), large language models, and ChatGPT. It provides a meticulous and thorough analysis of AI, ChatGPT technology, and their prospective trajectories given the current trend, in addition to tracing the significant advancements that have materialized over time.

Key Features:

- Discusses the fundamentals of AI for general readers
- Introduces readers to the ChatGPT chatbot and how it works
- Covers natural language processing (NLP), the foundational building block of ChatGPT
- Introduces readers to the deep learning transformer architecture.
- Covers the fundamentals of ChatGPT training for practitioners

Illustrated and organized in an accessible manner, this textbook contains particular appeal to students and course convenors at the undergraduate and graduate level, as well as a reference source for general readers.

Artificial Intelligence and Large Language Models
An Introduction to the Technological Future

Kutub Thakur, Helen G. Barker,
and Al-Sakib Khan Pathan

CRC Press
Taylor & Francis Group
Boca Raton London New York

CRC Press is an imprint of the
Taylor & Francis Group, an **informa** business
A CHAPMAN & HALL BOOK

First edition published 2024
by CRC Press
2385 NW Executive Center Drive, Suite 320, Boca Raton FL 33431

and by CRC Press
4 Park Square, Milton Park, Abingdon, Oxon, OX14 4RN

CRC Press is an imprint of Taylor & Francis Group, LLC

Library of Congress Cataloging-in-Publication Data

Names: Thakur, Kutub, author. | Barker, Helen G., author. |
Pathan, Al-Sakib Khan, author.
Title: Artificial intelligence and large language models : an introduction to the technological future / Kutub Thakur, Helen G. Barker, Al-Sakib Khan Pathan.
Description: First edition. | Boca Raton, FL : CRC Press, 2024. |
Includes bibliographical references and index. |
Identifiers: LCCN 2024000852 (print) | LCCN 2024000853 (ebook) |
ISBN 9781032754819 (hbk) | ISBN 9781032754802 (pbk) |
ISBN 9781003474173 (ebk)
Subjects: LCSH: Natural language processing (Computer science) |
Artificial intelligence--Forecasting. | ChatGPT.
Classification: LCC QA76.9.N38 T43 2024 (print) | LCC QA76.9.N38 (ebook) |
DDC 006.3/5--dc23/eng/20240402
LC record available at https://lccn.loc.gov/2024000852
LC ebook record available at https://lccn.loc.gov/2024000853

ISBN: 978-1-032-75481-9 (hbk)
ISBN: 978-1-032-75480-2 (pbk)
ISBN: 978-1-003-47417-3 (ebk)

DOI: 10.1201/9781003474173

Typeset in Palatino
by KnowledgeWorks Global Ltd.

Contents

Preface

First of all, this is a textbook that can be used for teaching in the classes at the undergraduate or graduate levels. It can also be used as a reference source. This book serves as an in-depth exploration of the ever-evolving domain of artificial intelligence (AI) and ChatGPT chatbot. It provides a meticulous and thorough analysis of AI, ChatGPT technology, and their prospective trajectories given the current trend, in addition to tracing the significant advancements that have materialized over time.

Designed to cater to a discerning audience, this book is meticulously crafted for research practitioners, encompassing a wide spectrum of individuals from erudite academics to seasoned industry professionals who are actively engaged in the vibrant field of AI. Amidst the rapid transformation of the AI landscape, this book proffers a well-structured introduction to the field's future prospects, emerging trends, and the complex challenges it faces. It imparts to the reader a comprehensive understanding essential for skillfully navigating the intricate realm of AI and Chat Robots (chatterbots or chatbots).

The rich content of this book extends its immense value to a diverse readership, encompassing both graduate and undergraduate students, dedicated researchers, and pragmatic industry practitioners, thereby serving as an invaluable resource to a broad array of individuals keen on exploring and mastering this transformative field.

Our book presents cutting-edge insights and developments in the dynamic realm of AI and ChatGPT chatbot, ensuring that readers remain abreast of its ever-evolving landscape. Its distinctive strength lies in its ability to deliver a comprehensive analysis of both AI and ChatGPT, furnishing readers with a holistic grasp of the subject matter. This encompasses in-depth elucidation alongside practical applications, rendering complex concepts accessible.

Furthermore, the book directs its gaze toward the future of AI and Chat Robots, delving into emerging trends, prospective breakthroughs, and the formidable challenges that loom on the horizon. By adopting a forward-looking approach, it equips readers with a prescient perspective on this rapidly evolving field.

What sets this book apart is its innovative pedagogical approach to elucidating the intricate domain of AI and Chat Robots, ensuring an engaging and enlightening reading experience. Also, considering the coverage of the area, this book is up-to-date and extensively illustrative, and thus highly suitable for general readers of the domain.

Kutub Thakur, PhD
University of Maryland Global Campus, USA

Helen G. Barker, DM
University of Maryland Global Campus, USA

Al-Sakib Khan Pathan, PhD
United International University, Bangladesh

About the Authors

Dr. Kutub Thakur (Rony) is Associate Professor at the School of Cybersecurity and Information Technology, University of Maryland Global Campus. He worked for various private and public entities such as the United Nations, New York University, Lehman Brothers, Barclays Capital, Con Edison, Metropolitan Transport Authority, and City University of New York and New Jersey. He received his Ph.D. in computer science with a specialization in cybersecurity from Pace University in New York, an MS in engineering electrical and computer control systems from the University of Wisconsin, and a BS and AAS in computer systems technology from the City University of New York. He has reviewed many prestigious journals and published several papers and books with renowned publishers. His research interests include network security, machine learning, IoT security, privacy, and user behavior. He is currently serving and has previously served as the program chair for many conferences and workshops.

Dr. Helen G. Barker is Department Chair of Cybersecurity at University of Maryland Global Campus (UMGC). Before joining UMGC in 2020, Dr. Barker spent 18 years with Capitol Technology University, retiring as CAO. Prior to her roles in education, Dr. Barker worked for 15 years in the private sector as a management analyst and resource training specialist in the distribution industry in Washington, DC, and 5 years as a researcher with Virginia Tech working in child welfare and economic development analysis. Dr. Barker achieved an MSBA, MS in Information & Telecommunication Systems Management, and Ph.D. in public policy and administration. She received her doctorate in Organizational Leadership. Her research interests include evolving technical areas of cybersecurity, the preparation of the current and future cybersecurity workforce, and neurodiversity in cybersecurity.

Dr. Al-Sakib Khan Pathan is Professor at CSE Department, United International University (UIU), Bangladesh. He received his Ph.D. in computer engineering in 2009 from Kyung Hee University, South Korea, and B.Sc. in computer science and information technology from Islamic University of Technology (IUT), Bangladesh, in 2003. In his academic career so far, he has worked as a faculty member in Independent University, Bangladesh (2020–2021); Southeast University, Bangladesh (2015–2020); International Islamic University Malaysia (IIUM), Malaysia (2010–2015); BRACU, Bangladesh (2009–2010); and NSU, Bangladesh (2004–2005). He has served as General Chair, Organizing Committee member, and Technical Program Committee member in numerous international conferences/workshops like INFOCOM, CCGRID, GLOBECOM, and ICC. He was awarded the IEEE Outstanding Leadership Award for his role in IEEE GreenCom 13 conference. Among various editorial roles, he is currently serving as Editor-in-Chief of *International Journal of Computers and Applications* and *Journal of Cyber Security Technology*, Taylor & Francis, UK; Associate Editor of *Connection Science*, Taylor & Francis; Editor of *Ad Hoc and Sensor Wireless Networks*, Old City Publishing, and *International Journal of Sensor Networks*, Inderscience Publishers; Guest Editor of many special issues of top-ranked journals. He is the editor/author of 34 books. He was named on the List of Top 2% Scientists of the World in 2020, 2021, 2023 by Stanford University, USA. He is Senior Member of IEEE, USA.

1

Fundamentals of Artificial Intelligence (AI)

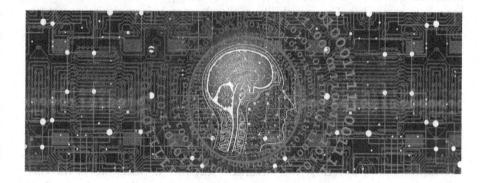

Introduction

Artificial intelligence (AI) is not a new concept or a new terminology in the technological arena, especially in the automation and mechanization of different processes used in our daily business life or even in the field of defense and other governmental as well as private sectors. The core concept of AI dates back to 1940 when the conjunction of automated machines and organic functionalities were considered in the field of cybernetics. At that time, the growth of machines and other technologies based on mechanical automation was at the peak due to emerging competition and global wars, especially World War II, which was one of the most powerful dynamics of developing the advanced cybernetics technologies based on the merger of organic being and mechanical process automation. This era is considered as the starting point of the modern AI.

With the passage of time, the field of AI has passed through numerous phases, which were encouraging as well as discouraging for the advancements of this innovative technology. Today, one of the most advanced applications of AI technology that has emerged in the technological world is the ChatGPT platform. The marvel of ChatGPT is also powered by the advanced technologies under the major field of AI. A wide variety of mechanisms ranging from the mechanical processes powered by hydraulic, electrical, and mechanical machines with the data and feedback from those processes to control and manage the mechanized processes to the most advanced cybernetic devices

DOI: 10.1201/9781003474173-1

in healthcare field as well as in the most advanced unmanned aerial vehicles (UAVs) and even the most advanced cybersecurity systems are powered by this advanced technology of AI and its different branches like machine learning (ML) and others.

The term artificial intelligence stems from the parallelism of human intelligence based on the human brain. The distinctive capability of human brain is to observe and learn from the real-world experience and make the informed decisions based on the learning or understanding of the events and environments around it. This capability makes human beings the most powerful among all animals (humans are considered animals from a biological standpoint) on earth. The AI concept explores and defines the processes and abilities of machines, especially computer systems and software-enabled systems, to develop the intelligence artificially that can somewhat match the capabilities of human intelligence. Thus, the field of technology in which the human-like functions, activities, and behaviors are controlled by the machines is referred to as artificial intelligence.[1,2]

It is very important to note that AI is a wide field of technology that focuses on automated activities controlled by the machines, especially modern computers powered by the advanced software applications at the core of the entire system. This entire process of developing the capability of AI is focused on the major components that can help scientists or engineers to build those advanced capabilities. Those components or fundamental focus areas of AI are as follows:

- Learning
- Reasoning
- Problem-solving
- Perception
- Language understanding

AI is extensively used in a wide range of fields, or it can be said that it is used in almost all fields of modern businesses and lives. ChatGPT is one of those applications, which this book is mainly focused on. The other fields that use the futuristic technology in different forms and manifestations are as follows[1,3]:

- Industrial automation
- Manufacturing industry
- Information and communication technology (ICT)
- Aviation and defense industry
- Cybersecurity and software development industry
- Space technology

- Engineering of all types
- Healthcare and medication industry

There is a whopping increase in the global market value of AI industry during the past few decades. According to the Statista projection, the total market size of AI worldwide will reach a stunning value of over US$1887.5 billion by 2030 from just US$142.3 billion in 2022. The expansion of AI market size is expected to grow 20 times from the market value in 2021 during the next 8 years or so.[4]

The most important areas or industries that are expected to achieve the higher growths include marketing, data analytics, supply chains, robotics, healthcare, computer vision (CV), chatbots, and many others. This substantial growth in this field is driven by a range of benefits that AI offers to the industries. A few very important and desirable benefits that AI technology offers to the industry include the following:

- Saves huge time used in routine tasks
- Offers capability of detailed orientation in all functions and activities
- Enables extensively faster processing of huge piles of data
- Enhances the productivity and efficiency of organizations significantly
- Opens up new domains and areas of business and growth
- Produces the most desired and accurate results
- Round-the-clock activities and consistency in productivity

AI plays a very pivotal role in many modern automated software applications, platforms, and tools, which are providing the advanced levels of capabilities in different processes in all walks of life and business. A few most prominent applications, platforms, or tools that are powered by different forms of AI include the following[2]:

- ChatGPT 4
- All web search engines
- E-Commerce recommendation systems
- Amazon Alexa
- Siri Virtual Assistant
- Self-driving vehicles
- Automated decision-making (ADM) apps
- Web chatbots

Before diving into different aspects of ChatGPT platform, it is imperative to have understanding of the fundamental concepts and technologies working at the core of the platform. The core technologies that realize the idea of ChatGPT platform include AI and its subdomains such as ML and natural language processing (NLP). All those concepts will be discussed separately in the following chapters. In this introductory chapter, the main focus will be on the most fundamental technology working at the backend of the ChatGPT platform referred to as artificial intelligence and its evolution, modern advancements, components, types, capabilities, and other aspects comprehensively.

Short History of Artificial Intelligence

The history of modern AI is as old as the philosophical ideas of automatic machines in different forms and formats on the timeline of human history. Many scientists and researchers believe that some kind of philosophical idea or an abstract or a mythology would always be at the foundation of any invention or scientific discoveries. Thus, it can be said that the history of modern AI can also be divided into two main phases, eras or parts[5,6]:

- Philosophical era
- Scientific era

The philosophical era starts from a very long time ago, even before AD calendar in BCs. This era traces back to the philosophical ideas, myths, and other abstracts written in different fictions, stories, or other literature in the old ages. The most important ideas in those days were focused on the mythological stories and others such as abstract concepts relating to the religions, traditions, and cultures. The scientific era mostly focuses on the practical creation of any such idea, formula, machine, technique, or other entity that is supported by scientific inventions, discoveries, or logic.

The philosophical history of AI can detect traces of the concept of AI in the form of being artificial superman, mechanical man, supernatural things, and other such concepts created by the philosopher through different religious and mythological concepts. They are mostly found in different creations in the field of philosophy, literature, art and culture, psychology, and other social as well as art realms. Initial existence of the concepts of AI surfaced in the creations of fashions, arts, fictions, myths, and other such philosophical inventions. The philosophical era can be further broken into different categories to trace relevant events pertaining to the AI[5]:

- **380 BC–1600** – A large number of human thoughts were created in the form of mechanical men, calculating machines, and other mathematical and numerical systems revolving around the nonhuman being devices acting like a human does. These creativities were mostly philosophical in nature without any solid scientific reasoning or arguments. The main roles that pioneered the concepts of AI in this era included theologians, professors, philosophers, mathematicians, and others.

- **1600–1700** – During this period of initial concepts of AI, the idea of such machines started emerging in different creations that are characterized by somewhat *"all-knowing"* capabilities. Those machines included the names such as "The Engine" mentioned in the novel *Gulliver's Travel* written by Jonathan Swift.

- **1700-1900** – Meanwhile, in another very crucial novel *Erewhon* by Samuel Butler written in 1872 described that the future of the machine would look like that they can possess consciousness that a human brain does. Other than these prominent novels and their respective characters, numerous other such traces can be found in different fashion designs, artistic works, and other scriptures during this era.

- **1900–1950** – This is considered as the middle age of AI concepts and the starting point of modern AI technology. This era consists of numerous fictitious concepts as well as a few proper mathematical derivation-based concepts and creations. The growth of the idea of AI becomes more significant than previous era (during this period). In 1921, the Czech playwright Karel Čapek wrote his science fiction in local language which was translated into English in the name of *Rossum's Universal Robots*. This was the first time when the idea of robot was coined in the fields of both science fiction and technologies. This robot was depicted as a concept of factory-made machine named as robot, which could function like a human brain could do. Later in 1927, a science fiction–based film was released by Fritz Lang. This film was named as Metropolis. In this film, a robotic machine shaped as mechanical girl is featured. This girl attacks the Berlin city and wreaks havoc in the city and damages its futuristic. Later, the Star War Series roles were also the derivatives of the role of a robotic girl. The first robot was built in Japan in 1929 by a biologist, Professor Makoto Nishimura. The name of the first Japanese robot was given as "Gakutensoku". This robot was designed to learn from the natural rules and people. It was first time when the robotic machine could move head and arms and display expressions and other movements. Then comes the year 1939 when a computer appears to solve the problems based on the linear equations, which was invented by a physicist, Professor John Vincent Atanasoff, and his assistant/student Clifford Berry. This machine was named as Atanasoff–Berry Computer (ABC). In 1949, a computer scientist, Edmund Berkeley, drew parallel between the human brain and the computer machines that can become capable of handling huge data and processing information much faster with additional skills or additional features and capabilities. He compared these capabilities and skills in his book *Giant Brains: Or Machines That Think*.

The second phase of the history of AI can be pegged from 1950 when the Turing test was developed. After this point of time, the modern era of AI supported by the scientific reasoning and arguments starts. The chronicle of the modern era of AI history is as follows[5,6]:

- **1950** – The theory of computing machinery and intelligence was introduced by Alan Turing in his book. This book discusses the Initiation Game. This describes the question that machines are capable of learning and thinking. This concept evolved and later on it became the fundamental tool for measuring the intelligence capabilities of a machine and was named as Turing test. The concept of Turing test will be discussed in the next topic separately. This point is also known as the starting point of modern AI technology.

- **1952** – The development of a machine program named as checkers-playing computer program was developed by Arthur Samuel. This program was designed to automatically learn how to play checkers game without human intervention.

- **1955** – The proposal for organizing a workshop on the idea of "AI" was proposed by John McCarthy. This workshop took place the next year and the first-time ever the phrase "artificial intelligence" was adopted after the recognition of the work done by McCarthy in this field.

- **1956** – The first ever AI computer program was created by a team of three people – Allen Newell, Cliff Shaw, and Herbert Simon.

- **1958** – The LISP language was developed by McCarthy. This is one of the most popular and primary languages used for the computer programming in the field of AI and related applications.

- **1959** – A new field of AI was discovered and it was coined as ML field. This was coined by Arthur Samuel.

- **1961** – First time in the history of AI, a real-world mechanized robot was created and deployed in the GM assembly line in New Jersey plant. This robot was named as Ultimate. This robot was invented by George Devol. In the same year, a heuristic problem-solving program was developed by James Slagle. This program was named as Symbolic Automatic INTegrator (SAINT).

- **1964** – Daniel Bobrow developed an AI-based program, which was capable of solving algebra word problems. This was the starting point toward the ML era of modern AI field.

- **1965** – A powerful and interactive computer program named as ELIZA was developed by Joseph Weizenbaum. This program was able to talk with a person in the English language. This proved the starting point of communicating between human and AI-based brains developed in machines.

- **1966** – The first electronic person, termed as Shakey the Robot, was developed by Charles Rosen along with his team of professionals consisting of more than 11 people.

- **1968** – Heuristically programmed algorithmic computer, precisely known as HAL, was featured in a science fiction *A Space Odyssey*. The concept of controlling the spacecraft and communicating with it were introduced in this film. The creation of primary-level NLP computer program SHRDLU was also created this year by a computer science professor, Terry Winograd.

- **1970** – The development of first anthropomorphic robot by Japanese Waseda University. This robot was more advanced in features such as capability to see, limited ability to converse with human, and ability to move with limbs.

- **1973** – The report "State of Artificial Intelligence Research" was presented to the British Science Council by James Lighthill. This report was not encouraging for the AI research and resulted in the reduction of research funds in this field. This era is referred to as artificial intelligence winter in this field.

- **1977** – The film series "Star Wars" was released by George Lucas, director of the film. In this film, a couple of protocol droids (a droid is fictional robot possessing some degree of AI in the film) were introduced that were also able to communicate with the human and perform some other functionalities.

- **1979** – Huge improvement was made in the capability of an earlier developed robot *Stanford Cart*. This robot was originally developed in 1961 by the then engineering student James Adams with limited features. The advancements included a mechanical swivel (or a slider was added), which could automatically move the installed camera on the robot. The enhancement was made by Hans Moravec who was a Ph.D. scholar. This robot successfully crossed a room full of chairs without any human intervention.

- **1980** – The Waseda University students again created a feature-rich robot WABOT-2. This robot was able to play music on digital instruments, read the musical notes, and also communicate with human.

- **1981** – A huge funding of as much as US$850 million was allocated by the Japanese ministry for the research of next-generation computing systems which would be able to perform different human-like activities such as language translation, conversation with human, reasoning like human mind does, and understanding the pictures.

- **1984** – The release of film "Electric Dreams", directed by Steve Barron. This film was based on a love triangle plot among a computer machine, a man, and a woman. The sentient computer was named as Edgar.

- **1986** – First time, a driverless car was developed by Mercedes Benz. This car could drive at a speed of about 55 miles per hour on any road that has no obstacles. This was a big leap forward in the field of modern automotive industry. This car was developed under the supervision of Ernst Dickmanns.

- **1988** – The scientific research report "Probabilistic Reasoning in Intelligent Systems" was published by Judea Pearl. In this same year, first chatbot was developed by a computer programmer Rollo Carpenter. The name of this chatbot (a software application or web interface that aims to mimic human conversation through text or voice interactions) was given as Jabberwacky. This bot was able to simulate the human chatting in very entertaining and humorous ways that became very interesting for people. The same inventor created an advanced version of the chatbot in 1990 – Cleverbot.

- **1995** – Another powerful chatbot ALICE – Artificial Linguistic Internet Computer Entity – was developed by Richard Wallace, a computer scientist and a programmer. He got inspiration from earlier bot ELIZA, developed by Weizenbaum. ALICE was able to collect natural language sample data.

- **1997** – A kind of neural network named as Long short-term memory (LSTM) was developed by Sepp Hochreiter and Jürgen Schmidhuber, who were computer scientists. Also in this year, IBM developed a computer – Deep Blue – that could play chess. Later on, this computer was able to beat the then world champion of chess game.

- **1998** – Pet robotic toy was invented for kids with AI capabilities by Dave Hampton and Caleb Chung. The name given to this pet toy was Furby. It was the first AI-powered toy for kids.

- **1999** – Sony Corporation introduced a powerful robot AIBO – Artificial Intelligence Robot. It was another AI-powered pet dog. It was able to understand and learn from the environment, handlers, and other similar AIBO robots. It was able to perform over 100 commands given by the owner.

- **2000** – A robot KISMET was developed by Cynthia Breazeal. This robot looked like a human face with all organs of a face like lid, nose, lips, eyebrows, and others. This robot was able to recognize and simulate the emotions through its face-like appearance. In this year, another humanoid robot was also released by Honda Company. This humanoid robot was named as ASIMO.

- **2001** – Science fiction film "A.I. Artificial Intelligence" was released. This film was directed by Steven Spielberg.

- **2002** – An autonomous robot vacuum named as Roomba was created by I-Robot Company. This robot was able to clean dust avoiding obstacles.

- **2004** – Science fiction film "I, ROBOT" was released. It was directed by Alex Proyas. This film fictitiously predicts the scientific environment of 2035.

- **2006** – The term machine reading was coined. The definition of this term was also enunciated such as "an unsupervised autonomous understanding of text". The term was coined by Oren Etzioni, Michele Banko, and Michael Cafarella.

- **2007** – The creation of ImageNet database was accomplished. The core purpose of this database was to augment object-recognition research through a large database of annotated images for computer training purposes.

- **2009** – The development of Google's driverless car was a top secret project. Later on, this car passed the self-driving test in Nevada State in the year 2014.

- **2010** – The Kinect game was launched by Microsoft Corporation through Xbox 360. This was the first ever gaming app that could recognize the body motion through different 3D as well as infrared cameras. In the same year, ImageNet launched its advanced version of image database competition – ImageNet Large Scale Visual Recognition Challenge (ILSVRC).

- **2011** – The creation of IBM Watson AI system that was able to support NLP-based question-answering platform. The SIRI was also released this year by Apple Inc.

- **2012** – A huge neural network was trained by Google scientists Jeff Dean and Andrew Ng. They trained a neural network consisting of 16,000 processors with over 10 million unlabeled images of cats through the YouTube videos.

- **2013** – A semantic ML system Never Ending Image Learner (NEIL) was developed by a team of researchers at Carnegie Mellon University.

- **2014** – Cortana was released by Microsoft Corporation. In the same year, Amazon Inc. released ALEXA virtual assistant.

- **2015** – An open letter to ban AI for the development of weapons for war was signed by Elon Musk, Steve Wozniak, and Stephen Hawking.

- **2016** – Android robot SOPHIA was developed. It is also considered as the first robot citizen due to resemblance with humans. In this year, Google Corporation also released a smart speaking assistant named as Google Home.

- **2018** – The first ever bidirectional unsupervised language representation BERT was developed by Google. This would use the transfer learning for performing a wide range of NLP tasks automatically. Samsung "Bixby", a virtual assistant, was also introduced the same year.

What Is the Turing Test?

The Turing test is one of the most fundamental and robust testing systems proposed by British computer scientist Alan Turing in 1950. He researched on AI technology during the 1940s. The test is designed to check if the computer put under testing possesses the intelligence like the human brain. This test is also referred to as the mimicry test in which computer with some kind of intelligence is passed through the Turing test with certain sets of questions to get the response from the computer (that has the expected intelligence). If the computer is capable of fooling the judge terminal, the computer is considered to have AI.

According to the definition of Alan Turing, if the computer is able to mimic the responses like a human being does, the computer is assumed to have intelligence. If a computer program can fool the questioner under specific conditions, the computer program will be declared to have passed the Turing test of AI.[7]

The Turing test consists of three separate locations in which three keyboards and computer terminals will be placed. Those terminals are interfaced through keyboards and screens. Out of those three terminals, one will be operated by the computer program, which is under test; the second one is operated by a human being to respond to the questions put up by the questioner. The third terminal is operated by a human interrogator or questioner. The person operating the third terminal will put up a question to both computers under testing to generate their responses. The respondent terminals would send their answers to the questioner. If the interrogator/questioner is unable to distinguish between the responses received from those two terminals at least half of the times, the machine will be considered to have intelligence. The questions are asked in specific domain limited by certain conditions. The questions will be asked many times to judge the difference. The pictorial depiction of the Turing test is shown in Figure 1.1.

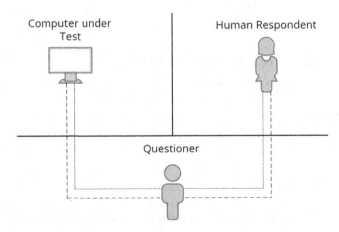

FIGURE 1.1
Turing test environment.

In the depicted environment (Figure 1.1), the questioner asks question in specific conditions that appear on the screens of the rooms. The computer and the human respondent provide the responses to the question. When both answers are received, the questioner decides which response is from computer and which one is from the human being. This process is repeated several times. If the computer has intelligence (as defined), it will try to fool the questioner by providing the responses that can confuse the interrogator (questioner) to decide whether the response has come from a human or a computer.

The prerequisites or capabilities that can make the computer capable of passing the Turing test include the following[78]:

- ML capabilities
- NLP capabilities
- Motor-controlling capabilities
- Knowledge representation capabilities
- CV capabilities
- Automated reasoning abilities

The reverse version of Turing test is also extensively used in the modern security systems based on the AI to check whether the interacting entity is a human or a robot. The most common of such tests used in the modern web environments is known as CAPTCHA (Completely Automated Public Turing test to tell Computers and Humans Apart) test. This test is the anti-Turing test, in which the human interactor is determined through different images, texts, and other signs with an environment-specific question to ensure the interacting entity is not a robot.

The other most common tests extensively used in the modern field of AI are as follows[7]:

- Total Turing test
- Reverse Turing test
- Minimum intelligent signal test
- The Marcus test
- Winograd Schema challenge
- The Lovelace Test 2.0

The alternative tests are designed to overcome the drawbacks and limitations of Turing test. The following are the main limitations of Turing test:

- The limited nature of questions in specific environment
- Narrow field of knowledge

- Extensive use of "yes" or "no" questions
- Conversational answers may create complex environment
- Human–machine interaction is less efficient
- Complex and unintuitive communication interface

There are many computing systems or AI-based computer systems that have attempted the Turing test for passing the exam. A few most important of them are as follows[8]:

- **Parry** – Simulates a person with a mental disorder known as paranoid schizophrenia.
- **ELIZA** – It is an NLP-powered chatbot that simulates the communication between human and machine.
- **Eugene Goostman** – This AI application passed multiple Turing tests and also won a few competitions.

The Objectives of Artificial Intelligence

Since the ancient days of the human history, the machines have been created to make the routine activities of the society easy, efficient, and productive. With the passage of time, new machines were created based on the new invented techniques and scientific discoveries. Those machines enhanced the speed of the process and also the overall productivity because machines do not get exhausted as compared to the normal human being. We need to rather maintain a machine to work properly for our intended purposes, even for long hours continuously.

Initially, the mechanical machines were invented to improve the performance of the activities and processes used in the evolving life and businesses. The mechanical machines were augmented with the electric machines at some stage to make those even more productive than the previous versions. This thirst of efficiency, innovation, and productivity set forth the modern electronic systems, which were used for controlling and automating the systems that were previously operated by human intervention. Today's machine systems are powered by the advanced computing capabilities and many other modern sciences for achieving comprehensive automation in the processes and activities of modern businesses and daily life routines.

Still, people have been the main factor behind all automations, especially in making decisions and other functionalities. At some point of time, people started thinking of the replacement of the human capability of thinking and incorporate that in the machines. This innovative idea is called the artificial intelligence. More and more subdomains of AI technology are gradually emerging for developing intelligence in machines in such a way that many thinking tasks performed by human beings are also accomplished nowadays by the modern machines powered by the somewhat human-like thinking capabilities. Thus, the main objectives of the modern approach toward AI development are driven by the effective use of the power of modern sciences and discoveries to build a machine brain that can control all processes and activities that are performed by human in the traditional life (at least some trials to reach human level!).

The following are the most important objectives that the computer and data scientists want to achieve from the AI[9–11]:

- Problem-solving
- Reasoning
- Learning
- Achieving general intelligence
- Informed planning
- Deeper data insight

The details of these main objectives of AI technology that the scientists want to achieve are described separately in the following sections.

Problem-Solving

Problem-solving is one of the most fundamental objectives of modern AI technology. The solution of all types of problems can be achieved by instilling the power of thinking in the machines so that they can think, learn, and understand from the past experience and environments. The solution of problems by machine intelligence includes the following[9]:

- Building effective computing algorithms
- Developing algorithm-based decision-making capabilities
- Making logical deduction independently
- Simulation of human reasoning
- Applying theory of probability
- Learning from the past experience
- Analysis of data to make decisions

The solutions of problems that are being focused to be solved come from all domains of modern life and businesses. The following are the most important processes powered by AI that can achieve the fundamental objective of problem-solving:

- Industrial process automation
- Automation of communication through chatbots in the form of text, voice, and video
- Supply chain and logistic automation
- Maintenance and operations of systems automatically
- Driverless cars and vehicles
- Unmanned aerial vehicles
- Space and defense

Reasoning

Reasoning is one of the most basic processes in human brain to deduce the results from the given situations, data, facts, conditions, and beliefs. This is an ability of mind in which the decisions are made based on the reasoning process. Similarly, reasoning is the fundamental concept in AI too because it is based on the same ways that human brain follows. The AI-based algorithms make decisions based on the available data or information in the form of facts, statistics, environments, conditions, and others. Thus, it can be rephrased that one of the main objectives of AI is reasoning because it plays a vital role in decision-making based on the available information or knowledge. Reasoning can also be defined as follows: *The general process of rational thinking that results in deducing valid conclusions.*

The following are the main types of reasoning commonly adopted in the AI models and algorithms[12]:

- Deductive reasoning
- Common sense reasoning
- Inductive reasoning
- Monotonic reasoning
- Non-monotonic reasoning
- Abductive reasoning

The deductive reasoning is also referred to as valid type of reasoning, which says that if the conclusion of the argument is correct, then the premises must be correct too. It is extensively used as a type of propositional logic in the field of AI. This is also governed by numerous rules and regulations and facts. The deductive reasoning is also referred to as anti-inductive reasoning or top-down reasoning. This reasoning starts from the general premises and culminates at a specific conclusion. For instance, one premise is that all reptiles crawl and the other premise is that snake is a reptile; the conclusion from these two premises can easily be deducted that snake will also crawl with the help of deductive reasoning. The deductive reasoning process can be divided into four major phases or stages:

- Theory
- Hypothesis
- Patterns
- Confirmation

The inductive reasoning is a type of reasoning opposite to the deductive reasoning. It is also known as bottom-up and cause-effect reasoning. It is basically a type of propositional logic. In this type of reasoning, a series of data are used to achieve a conclusion through generalization process. The conclusion is also referred to as the general statement. The truth of conclusion is not guaranteed by the truth of the premises due to the nature of probability, which is used to find out conclusion in this type of reasoning. The example of this reasoning looks like this: all pigeons that have been observed in all zoos the observer has visited were of white color. This proposition induces that all pigeons are white on the basis of inductive reasoning. The conclusion that has been made in this reasoning is based on the earlier observations of the researcher that everywhere in the zoos, the pigeons were white; therefore, it is assumed that all pigeons in the world are white. This does not guarantee that pigeons will always be white. But there is almost 100% probability that pigeons will be white based on the research and observations achieved through research methodology. But it is possible that the pigeons may have some other colors too. They might be living in other environments, landscapes, or even geographical location, and other factors. The phases of inductive type of reasoning can be classified into four major parts:

- Observations
- Patterns
- Hypothesis
- Theory

In the abductive reasoning, the conclusion is found through the chances of mostly likely conditions. In other words, the conclusion found through abductive type of reasoning is not guaranteed on the basis of the premises. It is also referred to as an extension of deductive reasoning. It is a type of reasoning belonging to logical reasoning domain. In this reasoning, multiple observations are considered to find out the conclusion. For example, one observation says that a ground gets wet when it is raining and the other observation is that the ground is wet. The conclusion from those propositions is that it is raining outside. This does not guarantee that it was raining; it may be a burst of water line which has made the ground wet or perhaps the rain (may be both or one!). Thus, it is said that the conclusion is not guaranteed in this type of reasoning.

Another important type of reasoning is common sense reasoning. In this kind of reasoning, the experience plays a very vital role in deduction of conclusion. For example, if somebody dives into the water, he will get wet. The conclusion of any premises is processed through informal type of observations achieved through past experiences. This kind of reasoning works on the basis of heuristic knowledge and rules for making judgments. The exact logic is not behind this type of reasoning but rather the common sense rules are used for making judgments. The common sense is an ability of human brain to conceive from the past experiences and map them on the existing propositions in such a way that the most likely conclusion is achieved.

The monotonic reasoning, as the name implies, is a type of reasoning that is based on the existing nonchangeable facts that may be added with more information or reduced by cutting the existing information. However, that does not alter the facts that have been deduced from the statement or proposition. For example, earth revolves around the sun is a fact that cannot be changed; more information such as it takes how many days, hours, minutes, and seconds may be added, but you cannot change the basic fact or conclusion. Similarly, moon has no light of its own, which is also a proven truth and cannot be changed. Thus, the monotonic reasoning takes the decision once and it remains the same for always. The following are the main features of monotonic reasoning:

- Conclusion is taken once and used always.
- Information can be added to the conclusion or it may be modified but cannot be rejected.
- The set of premises does not decrease or increase with the additional information provided to the main conclusion.
- It is deduced from the available facts and is not influenced by the new information added to the existing facts.
- The most common use cases of monotonic type of reasoning include the conventional reasoning systems and logical systems.

The most common advantages of monotonic reasoning are mentioned in the following list:

- Once the proof is deduced, it will remain valid always.
- Any new deduction is made from the existing knowledge about the facts; the new conclusion will also remain the same always.

On the other hand, the most important disadvantages of monotonic reasoning are as follows:

- Monotonic reasoning is not effective for describing or expressing the real-world scenarios in any kind of research.
- In monotonic reasoning, it is not possible to express or present the hypothesis knowledge or facts because the conclusion in this reasoning is always valid or true and hypothesis cannot be always correct.
- Addition of the new knowledge or facts from the real-world environment or ecosystems to the existing valid knowledge base cannot be done in the monotonic reasoning because the existing or proven fact is always true and cannot be changed as far as the conclusions of those premises are concerned.

The non-monotonic type of reasoning deals with the type of conclusions that are valid based on monotonic reasoning but with the addition of some more information or facts to the existing premises; the validation of that conclusion changes to invalidate. This type of reasoning is known as non-monotonic reasoning. It is almost contrary to the monotonic reasoning, as the name implies. The following are the most common features of this type of reasoning:

- Adding extra knowledge or facts to the existing valid conclusion may change the validness of the conclusion.
- The most common areas of application of non-monotonic reasoning are either uncertain or incomplete models of logic.
- The human perception about numerous things in the real world is a good example of non-monotonic reasoning.

The following are the main advantages of using non-monotonic reasoning in research studies[12]:

- Non-monotonic type of reasoning is very useful for building logic for robotics in the real-world environments.
- This type of reasoning supports both probabilistic facts and assumptions to make it more effective for numerous other research and logical models.

The following are the most common disadvantages of using non-monotonic reasoning in different research and scientific models:

- The validation of the conclusion is not fixed; so, it is more complex for researchers to use them as valid entities in algorithms or models.
- Not possible to use it for proving the theorems.

Let us have a look at an example of knowledge base and facts to understand the non-monotonic reasoning properly:

- Fish can swim.
- Birds cannot swim.
- Seahorse is a fish.

Based on the above facts, we can conclude that seahorse can swim because it is a kind of fish. If we add more information or modify the information that seahorse is a bird, then the valid conclusion drawn from the same set of knowledge is completely invalidated. This is called the non-monotonic reasoning in the field of research and logic development.

Learning

Learning is one of the most important capabilities of human brain that makes it more powerful than other animals and other creatures in the world. Learning plays a very vital role in natural intelligence because that capability makes human brain understand and learn from the experience or environment. The development of AI was based on the idea that machines can mimic the human brain to perform all activities and functions that a human brain can. Thus, it is one of the most important objectives of AI to develop learning capability in machines. The development of learning in machines is referred to as machine learning.

According to the definition of ML, it is the ability of machines to learn from input such as experience, information, and environments in the form of data and predict an outcome based on the experience and current input without any explicit software programming to predict or make decision.

Normally, the computer programs or software applications are used to perform numerous functions and capabilities automatically through computer machines. In that program, the computer acts like a slave without any thinking capability. The explicit programs are a set of instructions that run the machines to perform certain activities without any input from the machines themselves to learn and make decisions. The decisions are purely based on the instructions, which are normally "if this and then" form. Machines themselves make no decisions per se. In AI, the machines use their capabilities to learn through experience of environments, information, and events. Thus, it is one of the fundamental objectives of AI technology to make the machines learn from experience.

Learning by machines is named as machine learning. There are two basic categories of ML[13]:

- Supervised learning
- Unsupervised learning

The supervised ML is a type of ML in which data ingested into the ML models is labeled or tagged. This is done through the human intervention, by which the machines are made to learn from the input data in the shape of labeled or tagged data in the form of text, voice, video, images, and so on. The machines take that input or information for comparing and deciding any new test data that requires identification, understanding, and decision-making to generate output or prediction. This entire learning through supervised ML algorithms uses the historical data for predicting the future data through different algorithms.

The unsupervised ML uses training data without labeling or tagging in raw formats. The models are not provided any proper information through tags; hence, they try to find out the similar features to group together the similar items based on the resembling features and separating the items or information based on the differences or dissimilarities. Thus, they need huge data to develop the learning through that training data. The features are used to establish the meaningful connection between those items. The unsupervised ML requires huge piles of data for developing learning capability in computer machines.

The practical use of ML categories has respective downsides and constraints. For instance, the tagging and labeling of data through human resources is a costly practice for the companies to hire. But, the results or efficiency achieved through supervised learning is higher than unsupervised learning. On the other hand, the unsupervised learning needs much more training data than the data required in supervised learning. To overcome the drawbacks of the main types of MLs, a couple of other mixed types of learnings are used in the modern algorithms and models of ML:

- Semi-supervised learning
- Reinforcement learning (RL)

In the semi-supervised type of ML, both supervised and unsupervised ML methods are used to train the machines. The training datasets consist of labeled and tagged data in the form of videos, audios, images, text, and other types from sensors to develop learning capabilities. At the same time, the models are also allowed to use algorithms to explore the similar or dissimilar features and develop relationship between those features to predict the output data with more accuracy.

The RL is a type of learning that is used to increase the reward in an AI environment through the actions of an agent in the AI ecosystem. The computer program performs a random action in the given environment and receives the feedback in the form of either reward or punishment of the action. It forces the agent to change state and action in the light of the feedback so that the optimized or optimal reward can be achieved. This method is extensively used in the modern robotics and numerous other applications. The most common features of RL can be summarized as follows[14]:

- The main terms used in this type of learning include AI agent, environment, state, action, reward, policy, value, and Q-value.
- Agent is not programmed or bound through the instructions to take certain action. It takes independent random action in the AI environment and receives the feedback in the form of either reward or punishment.
- The basic principle behind the action of the agent is "hit-and-try".
- The position of the agent in an AI environment changes after taking a hit-and-try action and receiving the reward in the pursuit of increasing the reward.
- The environment used in RL is stochastic, which cannot be predicted and is randomly distributed in terms of probability.
- Different types of approaches are used in RL:
  - Model-based approach
  - Value-based approach
  - Policy-based approach
- Two sub-approaches are used in policy-based RL approach referred to as deterministic and stochastic.
- RL can be further divided into two types:
  - Positive reinforcement
  - Negative reinforcement
- In the positive reinforcement type, the addition of something such as value or behavior can be done for increasing the chances of obtaining the desired outcome again.

Achieving General Intelligence

The thirst for AI started with the objective to achieve the cognitive capability that is either equal to or greater than that possessed by a human brain. Any cognition level equal to or better than human falls under the super AI level. There are three main categories of AI levels[15]:

- Narrow AI
- General AI
- Super AI

The narrow AI is the most fundamental level of AI in which a specific task or group of functions are performed through the machines without any intervention of human. Today, the state of AI refers to the narrow intelligence, in which task-specific decisions are made through machines without human support. The examples of narrow intelligence are the existing chatbots, SIRI, ChatGPT, different recommendation engines, and others platforms. They are highly capable of performing certain tasks after getting trained on huge volumes of training datasets. They are referred to as weak AI because they are far behind the intelligence or cognition level possessed by a human brain.

General intelligence is the second most advanced level of AI. This level refers to the cognition level of machines that is equal to human in performing diverse tasks through comprehensive understanding, learning, and deciding processes. This level of machines is considered faster, more efficient, and productive compared with human capabilities. This level has not been achieved in any form or design as yet. Many scientists believe that this level of ML will not be possible to achieve while some are hopeful (or, at least promote this idea).

The super AI is the idea of cognition or intelligence of machines that surpasses the level of a human being and many term it as doomsday technological level. The idea goes like this that the machines may get out of control. The humans may try to do things more efficiently and employ those machines and today's way of doing things and human surroundings may get completely changed which can cause a completely new era of human existence. Maybe, all human beings would change with the advanced intelligence powered by machines and machines may take over the human race and even destroy the traditional natural life completely. That would be the (predicted or imaginary) era of super intelligence achieved through the merger of advance AI technologies modifying the human brains and merging both.

The initial objective or goal that emerged in the minds of scientists working in the field of AI was to achieve the level of AI equal to human level of intelligence. That goal has not yet been achieved. Continual research and development (R&D) is going on to achieve the desired objective of AI known as artificial general intelligence (AGI). The AGI is also known as strong AI.

Planning

Planning is a very powerful capability of a human brain. The planning deals with different thought processes and activity sequences listed based on those different thoughts emerging in the brain of a human. The thought processes are influenced by the learning through experience. Thus, the scientists and domain specialists set the planning as one of the most important objectives of AI too. Planning is extensively affected by our logic and reasoning. The following are the most fundamental components of planning done by human[16]:

- Setting objectives
- Description of scope
- Identifying task specifications

- Description of goals
- Sequence of actions to be performed

All of the above-mentioned components need cognition or intelligence to identify, define, and perform to achieve the objectives. The following are the most common types of planning used in AI:

- Forward state space planning (FSSP)
- Backward state space planning (BSSP)

Overall, the process of modern planning should be driven by the power of AI to make them more productive, efficient, and fast. It can be achieved through data analysis, learning from past events and experience, forecasting, predictive analytics, and optimization models.

Deeper Insight into Data

Predicting future has always been a major issue for human beings from the ancient ages. People were so anxious to know about their own future or the future of other things around them such as future of countries, future of business, future of animals, birds, and almost everything that is available in the natural ecosystem. They would use various ways to make predictions and imagine the future by using numerology, intuition, astrology, or other mythical ways to predict or have an insight into the future. Majority of those practices were mythical because there was no proper track record of the analysis of the information hidden into the past experience, events, and patterns. Today, having an insight into the future has become another important goal of AI as the research has progressed a lot in this field. Though initially it was not the main goal of AI technology to have deeper insight into the future based on the analysis of the data which is available in huge piles, nowadays some are actively working in this direction.

At present, the information hidden into the events, patterns, and experience has become a fundamental driver of all types of businesses in the modern world. Every business is using the huge volume of data to analyze it from multiple aspects to get the most valuable information from it so that the direction of future plans can be set in such a way that they get the desired objectives perfectly (or, near perfectly) without any doubts or digressions. The majority of the data in the world is available in raw format or unorganized formats commonly referred to as unstructured data. The unstructured data is the biggest type of data generated in the world nowadays. The main formats of unstructured data are available in the shapes of voices, videos, text, numeric, sensor readings, images, and others.

According to the conservative estimates in 2023, the average data created on a daily basis in the world is about 329 terabytes in the form of both structured and unstructured formats. This huge amount of data consists of created, copied, consumed data on the daily basis.[17] With this huge volume of data, if analyzed properly and skimmed for the most valuable information from it, peeping into the future and predicting the status may be possible. Analyzing such a huge volume of data and finding the valuable information can be achieved through big data analytics, which is consumed in the AI as the most fundamental input to predict about the future. The ingestion of such a huge data through AI and ML models can help predict the future of any processes to which these data may be related to. The major portion of this huge hike in the creation of data is driven by the video data followed by the social media and gaming industry. A major portion of the entire traffic on the Internet is contributed by these three domains.

AI is able to provide a deeper insight into the future in terms of processes, activities, and estimations by using the power of big data analytics. The increase in the power of ML or AI is heavily attributed to the ability of modern technologies to handle the big data created by the modern systems in the world.

The relationship between ML and big data can be described as follows. For instance, a huge amount of data is created in the world nowadays in the modern ecosystem of business or day-to-day life activities. The management of that huge data in different formats and forms such as structured, semi-structured, and unstructured is known as big data. This big data would not have hit the market unless the power of modern technologies had not emerged. The big data is extensively handled by the huge computing resources, cloud computing, and the innovative methods of data analytics. The data analytics of big data means collecting, processing, parsing, storing, and managing huge amounts of data with the help of computing, storage technologies, and data transportation capabilities. The processing of this huge data is accomplished through different data analytics models, which provide information as the source for modern AI or ML. Those models mimic human-like brain to learning, reasoning, and predicting the outcomes. Thus, both the big data and ML are very closely related to build an ecosystem that can lead to the prediction of the future or deeper insight into the data to make efficient decisions.[18]

A deeper and meaningful insight into the huge volumes and heaps of structured and unstructured data can be achieved with the help of modern algorithms of AI and ML technology. The main objective of using big data in ML is to achieve the capability to see the future or predict the future in more effective ways as compared to the ancient ways or methods of predictions.

Types of Artificial Intelligence

AI is a broader technology that encompasses numerous methods, functions, capabilities, and models to materialize the core concept of the technology. It has been further divided into a wide range of components, types, classes, categories, models, and subdomains in the modern industries and techno-logical ecosystem. As far as the types of AI are concerned, they are clas-sified into two major categories. These categories are further divided into subtypes. The most important categories to define types of AI are based on both functionality and capability of the technology. The functionality covers the aspects of different functions performed by the machines based on AI. On the other hand, the capability defines the other category of dif-ferent types of AI based on the ability of those machines powered by the AI technologies.

Thus, the following are the two main categories of the classification of types of AI[19]:

- Types of AI based on functionality
- Types of AI based on capability

In the former category, differentiation of AI technology is made on the basis of the functionalities performed by the machines enabled with the AI technology. The latter category consists of different types of AI technologies based on their respective capabilities or features. The details of both catego-ries of AI technologies are described separately in the following sections.

Types of Artificial Intelligence Based on Functionalities

AI technology is emerging and evolving in multiple directions, classes, and categories. Therefore, the classification of different types of technologies in one single domain is not possible. At present, the main types of AI technolo-gies are divided on the basis of functionalities and capabilities. The classifica-tion of AI based on the functionality is also referred to as Type-2 AI category. The types of AI based on functionalities are four in total[20]:

- Reactive machines
- Limited memory
- Theory of mind
- Self-aware

Let us now learn about all these subtypes of AI falling under the category of functionality.

Reactive Machines

The first and most basic type of AI based on functionalities is reactive machines. As the name indicates, this is a type of intelligence of machines that is based on the reaction of an action. In other words, a machine that pro-vides the same result based on certain input data or information is known as reactive machines. For example, an online shopper or visitor interested in purchasing books of his or her choice is used as an input to the computer machine to analyze and provide recommendations that reflect his or her interest shown in the past activities. This result is always shown to the user every time he/she visits a particular website to purchase a book. In this type of AI, the machine is not able to have past memory to show that it has bad or good experience and now it changes the decision based on that experience. It decides only on the basis of data that is fed at the time of decision-making to produce an output.[21]

The following are the most common features and characteristics of reactive machine type of AI:

- It is the most basic or fundamental type of AI.
- It is also referred to as Type-1 AI based on functionalities.
- It does not possess any past experience or memory to streamline the decision with more specific outcome.
- This type of AI is task-specific AI to perform repetitive task based on a set of information to produce an output.
- The machines belonging to this type of AI are extremely limited in numbers for performing task-oriented functionality.
- These systems do not improve or learn based on its past experience. It is just a reactive process–based type of machine that provides output based on the given information for making a decision based on that particular data or information.
- Any experience, time, or practice does not enhance the capability of this machine.
- There is zero concept or understanding of the past in this type of machines.
- The examples of this type of AI machines include the recommendation engines, spam filters, IBM Deep Blue gaming, Google Alpha Go, etc.
- It does not have internal memory to remember and learn for the future decisions.
- The present age of AI has passed the level of functionality of reactive machines types and has advanced to the next level.
- This type of AI uses the static ML models for predicting the outputs based on the given input statically.

Limited Memory

This is an advanced level of AI functionality type in which the modern AI technology is progressing (as we observe at present). The technology has passed the first type of AI named as reactive machines and is trying to perfect this second level of AI functionality type. This type is also referred to as Type-2 AI based on functionalities. The first and second types do exist in the modern technological field in practice while the remaining two types of AI based on the functionalities have not yet materialized. They are just in the ideas or concepts to be materialized in the future. In other words, other than reactive machines and limited memory types of AI, all types of AI based on functionalities are just fictitious.

Limited memory is the ability of machines to store and learn from the past experience to a limited level to make informed decisions based on the past experience or memory. The models used in this type of AI are deployed like the models of reactive machine types, but they are required to have limited memory to learn from the past experience. The following are the most common features of limited memory AI[22–24]:

- These types of AI machines learn from the past predictions and memories to make well-refined future predictions.
- The use of stored data is done for a short period of time or limited time duration for making informed decisions or predictions.
- The most common example of limited memory is the driverless cars that use limited memory type of technology for short period of time for making accurate decisions. In this model, the speeds of the surrounding cars, distances of other vehicles, speed limits, and other navigational information on the road are used to make informed decisions to avoid any kind of accident or mishap that can lead to disastrous outcomes.
- In this type of AI, the machines are still completely reactive machines but add additional short-term memory to process the understanding from that past experience for a very short period of time to make reliable predictions.
- The understanding from the short-term past information is added to the main ML program for generating timely actions or predictions that are more reliable and well-informed in nature so that the information can help the program change the pattern in the reactive machine models.
- This type of AI works in two different ways:
  - The models are trained with the training datasets continuously by a team of specialists to make it understand (make some sense of) from the past experience.
  - The models are trained automatically by the environments, which are created by the developers and specialists. Those environments are updated based on the usage and behavior of the model.

- In-built ML model is required into the machine structures to make them limited memory sustainable models.
- The limited memory type of ML in computers is performed based on six main steps mentioned below. The unified combination of the ML process is known as ML active learning life cycle:
  - Training dataset is the first step to train on the limited memory ML models.
  - The second step is the creation of ML model.
  - The third step is making predictions based on the training of the model.
  - The fourth step in this life cycle is getting the feedback from the ML environment or from the human input.
  - In the fifth step, the feedback is converted into data and stored in the repository as a useful learning.
  - The sixth step is the initiation of this entire process again (repetitively).
- The most important models used for building the second type of AI machines based on the functionalities include the following:
  - **RL Model** – This model works on the basis of *hit and trials*. The errors and trials are used for prediction of the right decision. This model is extensively used in different gaming applications based on AI technologies such as Chess game playing computers, DOTA2, and Go games playing machines.
  - **Long Short-Term Memory** – This model is extensively used for the prediction of sequence. Therefore, it is also referred to as sequence prediction model based on neural network. This model is extensively used in the deep learning (DL) environments for sequence predictions. In this model, the information is stored for arbitrary durations for predicting sequential orders in recurring neural networks. It is also capable of handling the vanishing gradient problem that occurs in most of the neural network models. The most popular application of this model is the language processing, which is influenced by the sequence of the words or the orders of the words for any response. This model works on the basis of single-time step, which consists of three simple steps:
    - In the first step, the model takes the information from the previous timestamp and checks if the information is relevant or irrelevant.
    - If it is an irrelevant information, this model forgets it and if it is relevant, then adds to the new information.

- In the third step, the updated information is passed to the next timestamp data.

This model of ML has two types of memories: long-term and short-term memories for remembering the information timestamp that it receives and marks it relevant. Thus, the most recent information marked as relevant is tagged and stored as the most important information in the sequence while the information pertaining to the past and old is tagged as less important information. This helps predict the sequential information more effectively.

- **E-GAN or Evolutionary Generative Adversarial Networks** – As the name suggests, this is a model that is based on the evolution of the previous paths or predictions. It keeps the information growing through generative evolution. Every time when the model modifies the information, the path or prediction changes slightly for course correction. It is capable of finding and fixing the past errors made by the models. Thus, slowly and gradually, this model enhances the results (i.e., evolutionary).

Theory of Mind

Theory of mind is an advanced type of ML based on the functionality. In this type of AI, the machines can behave like a human mind. It is expected to possess (almost) all capabilities that a human mind does such as understanding sentiments, feeling the behaviors of the opponent person or machine, and make expectations on how to be treated and how to treat the opposite person or machine. Thus, we can say that this type of AI is almost equal to the level of human brain. This type of AI has been drawn from the concept of psychological concept known as theory of mind. In this, it is implied that the human brain has thoughts, feelings, and emotions. Those abstracts can influence their behavior and also these can define the social interactions with the other people in a society. The concept of theory of mind type or level of AI based on the functionality resembles to the theory of mind in the field of psychology. The most common features of theory of mind type of AI are as follows:

- This is also referred to as Type-3 AI.
- There is no existence of such a machine that qualifies for this type of AI in the present-day technological world.
- It is a fictitious or conceptual type of AI.
- Many people are skeptical of achieving this level of AI, while the others are very hopeful of the same with certain apprehensions and fears about the future of the human being and other natural ecosystems.

- This type of machines will be able to understand the feelings of other people and machines or even other entities in the world.
- They will also be able to adjust their behaviors according to the environment, situation, and feelings of the opposite entities.
- They will be able to feel and expect what response should they receive from the opposite entities and also react accordingly.
- The most preliminary projects or machines that may resemble the initial stage of Type-3 AI may be the driverless cars. They are still not able to feel the senses, emotions, or beliefs.
- At this time, a few apps such as SIRI, Alexa, and others can feel and respond to your feelings through just one-way. But they cannot show feelings or generate senses of feelings or beliefs in their behaviors.
- The emergence of artificial emotional intelligence (AEI) is the starting point of the development of this type of AI in the future (may be!).

Self-Aware

Self-aware is the most advanced and top level type of AI. It is referred to as Type-4 AI in terms of functionality levels. Self-aware is that machine or computer system that possesses awareness about the sentiments, feelings, beliefs, and other abstracts that a human can feel not only in self but also in the opposite person. The narrative goes like this that this level of machine will be able to not only feel and understand the sentiments and other emotions of an opposite entity (machine or human) but also feel and manage the emotions and other abstracts within itself exactly like the human brain does. This is called the self-awareness level in which the efficiency and performance of artificial brain will be much higher than a human; hence, it is possible that a machine of this level can start manipulating human into the machines and additional features to transform a human brain to a super intelligent machine. Thus, the existence of the natural human may vanish or mutate to a new system and the natural qualities may get changed badly/irreversibly.

The following are the most common features and characteristics of Type-4 or self-aware types of AI levels[25]:

- It is the nirvana (enlightenment) type of AI when the machines will be superior to human in terms of thinking, feeling, and manipulating capacities.
- This is a hypothetical type of AI level that is far away from the reality in the modern technological field (even given the current trend and achievements).
- Many people or industry experts are skeptical to achieve this level of AI. At the same time, many people believe that this level of AI is

achievable and the results of that achievement will be disastrous to the nature and human existence due to the power of advanced AI mutation.

- Self-aware machines may think of themselves as a separate self-aware entity and start using other entities, including human, for their respective benefits like human does now with other entities and resources of the nature.
- If this level of intelligence is achieved artificially, the existence of mankind may be jeopardized because self-conscious machines may deem human as not-needed entity for the betterment of their businesses and ecosystems.
- This is also referred to as the future of AI.

Types of Artificial Intelligence Based on Capability

AI is getting bigger continuously in terms of many aspects such as capabilities, functionalities, market size, industrial applications, and others. The continual evolution of this technology is opening up new dimensions of its types, domains, and other concepts and criteria. Traditionally, the AI technology has been categorized into main classes and further subclasses under those categories. Among such classification, the types of AI have been divided based on two main criteria – functionalities and capabilities. The types of AI based on functionalities have been mentioned in the previous section. Let us discuss different types of AI that are defined on the basis of capabilities.

Based on the capabilities, AI is divided into the following main types[26]:

- Artificial narrow intelligence (ANI)
- Artificial general intelligence
- Artificial superintelligence (ASI)

The details of all three main classes or types of AI on the basis of their capabilities are mentioned separately in the following sections.

Artificial Narrow Intelligence

As the name implies, this type of AI is based on a narrow range of capabilities of machines powered by the AI. This is a type of AI in which task-specific tasks are performed through AI machines. In most cases, singular tasks are performed through those machines falling under this type of AI capabilities.

The following are the main features and characteristics of ANI type of AI[27,28]:

- ANI is also referred to as weak AI as well as narrow AI; precisely, narrow-AI.
- Singular tasks are the most basic capabilities associated with this type of AI such as facial recognition, search engines, recommendation engines, speech recognition, driverless car, voice assistants, and others.
- This level of AI capabilities has been achieved in the modern real-world applications.
- This type of AI is only capable of replicating or simulating the human behaviors on the basis of a small set of capabilities.
- The most important domain of AI that has achieved the narrow level of AI is NLP, which deals with the language processing in all modern applications.
- This level of AI encompasses the functionalities of both reactive machines and limited memory types of AI based on functionalities. Thus, the machines used in this type of AI have either no or a limited memory to learn from the past data and experience it has encountered during the learning processes.
- The most common applications of processes or machines that possess the capabilities equal to the ANI include IBM Watson, industrial drones, facial recognition, ALEXA and SIRI, spam filters, content recommendations, and other applications.
- Almost all major applications and AI systems fall under this category or a bit higher than the capabilities of this type.
- There is no extensive thinking capability in the machines falling under this category of AI capabilities.

Artificial General Intelligence

AGI is an advanced type of AI with a wider set of capabilities. This is also considered the second stage of AI capabilities set. This level of capabilities includes the thinking and learning like human mind does. This has not been achieved as yet. Thus, we can say that it is under the technology evolution that has not yet matured enough.

The following are the most salient features and capabilities of this type of AI[26–28]:

- The thinking capabilities of this type equals to that of human mind.
- This is hypothetical or conceptual type of AI that has not materialized in the real-technological world.
- There is no real-world example to show that it qualifies to this level of AI capabilities.

- It is also referred to as strong AI.
- The development of this level of capabilities may trigger a race of existence between humans and AI-enabled machines.
- Many scientists believe that this level of AI cannot be achieved in the real-world environment. At the same time, many, including Stephen Hawking and many other contemporary industry experts, believe that this will happen and a serious danger will emerge for the mankind and natural ecosystems with numerous ethical issues.
- Human capabilities are transferred or implemented by a biological slow evolutionary process, which by theory takes longer times, but all these can happen just within a few minutes in AI machines if they become equal to humans in capabilities (ever at all!). At that time, humans will lag behind the AI machines in terms of their speed, performance, productivity, and evolution, which may lead to serious consequences for human beings (as imagined).
- This level of machines will be able to independently think, learn, decide, and respond to situations in the same way or even in the better way than a human brain does.
- Though uphill challenges are there in the way to achieve this level of cognition, scientists are pursuing the course to achieve this uphill task.
- The effective use of facial recognition, gesture recognition, movement detection, and voice recognition are a few prospective technologies that can augment the research and development for achieving the AGI level.

Artificial Super Intelligence

ASI is the most advanced conceptual or hypothetical type of AI in which the capabilities of a machine is expected to succeed the capabilities of a human brain in terms of thinking, learning, deciding, and acting. This level of AI will take over the supremacy of human cognition through machines powered by the super level of AI. The machines of ASI level will definitely supersede human in all regards because of biological evolution and digital evolution.

Human brain and capabilities are based on biological evolution, which takes longer time periods for different activities such as learning a new concept, transferring data from one human to the other one. In fact, developing cognition in children and improving the efficiency of learning through practice are very time consuming and takes longer time periods of months and years. But if the machines can transfer learning to another machine within a few seconds, the improvement can be achieved much faster than biological evolution! That is what is envisioned in this case. The AI capabilities in the form of digital data can be used and transferred to any other machine instantly. The training of the super machines can continuously grow without any interruption or exhaustion.

In terms of all those cases and conditions, if the machines indeed reach the capabilities of human brains, they will definitely supersede the mankind. The most important features and characteristics of ASI are as follows[26-28]:

- The smartest and the coolest cognitive technology in the world.
- It will supersede human capabilities and may enslave the mankind!
- It is a hypothetical or fictitious type of AI that is far away from achieving in the near future.
- Many experts are skeptical to achieve this level of AI or artificial cognition.
- If this level of cognition is achieved, there may arise numerous dangers and apprehensions for mankind, natural ecosystem, ethics, religious beliefs, and much more.
- This level of technology will have much bigger and higher levels of memories, data storages, processing speed, decision-making power, deeper analysis power, problem-solving skills, and many other aspects that will leave the capabilities of humans far behind and will take over all fields and industries simultaneously.

What Is the Structure of an Artificial Intelligence System?

AI system is found in different configurations in different fields and domains. For instance, an AI or AI-based software system running in the form of a chatbots on a website has a completely new ecosystem as compared with a robotic system or a driverless car. Therefore, as far as the structure of an AI system is concerned, it has different components and items. On the other hand, conceptually, an AI system can be divided into two major components:

- Intelligent agent (IA)
- Intelligence environment (IE)

The other components that play the role of communication between the two main components of an AI system are as follows:

- Percepts
- Actions

These two components are directly associated with the IAs to interact with the environments. The first one is percept(s), which is sensed via a device or component that can sense the input from the AI environment and conveys it to the IA to understand and learn from the percepts. Percept is basically the input that an IA is perceiving at any given moment. The actions are the components powered by the physical entities and software program of agent to take action against the percepts that the IA has received. The percepts are analogous to our senses through ear, nose, eyes, skins, and others. Then, the hands, tongue, legs, and other body parts take suitable actions. The percepts and actions are also referred to as the auxiliary components of an AI system that are used for the auxiliary activities to interact between the environment and the agents.

A percept is received through different items in an AI such as camera, voice recording microphone, different types of electromagnetic waves, current, voltage, and other sensory devices. Those devices provide the percepts to the agents to perceive and make a decision based on the intelligence model it uses so that an action can be initiated by the agent. The agent initiates an action through affecters or actuators in different types of AI systems so that the most rational action is provided.[29]

The schematic diagram of AI system consisting of its core and auxiliary components is shown in Figure 1.2.

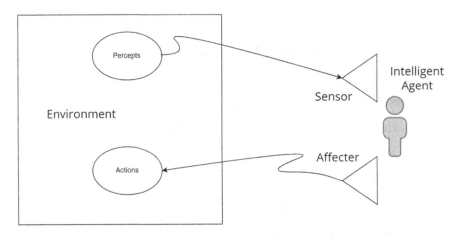

FIGURE 1.2
Schematic diagram of an AI system.

Let us explain the components of an AI system with more details and analogous examples with the human intelligence or natural intelligence.

Environment

Environment is a broader world or ecosystem of different items, spaces, and data in different forms that make an ecosystem other than the agent itself and its entire structure in an AI system is known as environment. This environment of an AI system is the entire world other than the IA.[30]

In other words, the environment is an ecosystem in which one or more IAs can live, operate, and are provided with the setup in which the agents can sense the data and also respond with an action to it.

The following are the most common features and characteristics of an AI environment:

- Some environments are very simple and small consisting of just computer system and its accessories with an agent sitting inside the computer memory.
- Some environments, especially large and complex environments based on both hardware and software, are very complex and detailed.
- An example of an AI environment is Turing test ecosystem.
- The modern software-based e-commerce and other chatbot environments are very complex that take a wide range of data and actions in the forms of percepts and responses in the environment to make it a rational one.
- There are numerous types of environments based on different characteristics. A few very important types of environment in terms of different functions, features, and other criteria are as follows:
  - **Single- or Multi-Agent Environment** – An environment that houses one agent is called single-agent environment and the environment that houses more than one agents is known as multi-agent environment.
  - **Discrete or Continuous Environment** – If the states of an environment are clearly defined with a few distinct features, it is called discrete environment. When there are multiple features and continuous changing inputs, it is known as continuous environment.
  - **Static or Dynamic Environments** – During the course of agent activity, if the environment changes itself, it is called dynamic; otherwise, it is referred to as static environment.
  - **Deterministic or Non-Deterministic Environment** – With the help of current state of the environment and action of an agent, if the upcoming or the next state of the environment is determinable, the environment is called deterministic; otherwise, the environment is non-deterministic.
  - **Fully Observable or Partially Observable** – If an environment is completely evident in terms of its state at any point of percepts and actions, it is known as observable; otherwise, it is partially observable.
  - **Accessible or Inaccessible Environment** – If all apparatus of the sensory system associated with an agent can access the entire state of the intelligent environment, then it is called accessible; otherwise, it is inaccessible.
  - **Episodic or Non-Episodic Environments** – Those environments in which the agents can perform complete activity life cycle in

episodes such as taking percepts and providing actions in an episode are called episodic environments. The next episode of an agent is not dependent on the previous episode. Otherwise, the environment is called non-episodic.

Agent

IA is an autonomous software or system in an AI system that can receive percepts through sensors and make decision on the basis of those percepts and take an action automatically or independently without any intervention from a human. In other words, an IA is capable of perceiving the intelligent environment system through different sensors. It can process them based on its internal capabilities or algorithms and take suitable actions with the help of effective decision-making through its internal intelligent model or algorithms.[31,32]

The following are the main features and characteristics of an IA[30–32]:

- An autonomous or independent entity in the form of either software or hardware or even both to perform different tasks based on the input it receives from the intelligent environment through self-governing decision-making.
- It is capable of learning from the environment continuously.
- IA can carry out two types of functions – perception and action.
- Perception is achieved through different sensors that interact with the environment and agent in an intelligent system.
- The action is accomplished through affecters or actuators.
- An IA may be either a single entity or consisting of multiple sub-agents in an AI system.
- The subagents and agents are hierarchical in structure to perform a sequence of tasks required for a complete intelligent action or response.
- The subagents are mostly designated for performing lower level tasks and the agents are used to perform high-level tasks in an AI system.
- An agent is capable of interacting with many other entities such as human, other agents, environments, subagents, etc. autonomously.
- Exhibiting the goal-oriented behaviors is the core feature of an IA.
- They increase their capabilities through continual learning from the environment and experience.
- An IA is knowledge-based because it uses knowledge of communication, entities, processes, and other environmental information.
- The measurement of the quality of an IA is done through a term known as rationality of an agent.
- The rationality of agent is the measurement of correct judgments, sensibility, reasonability, and responsibility.

- Carrying out the most suitable response or action through effective decision-making is considered the most effective feature or quality of an agent.
- Based on the internal knowledge base and sequence of percepts, an agent can produce the rational results if the expected responses and maximum performance is achieved by the IA under consideration.
- An agent solves a problem in an artificial environment that is characterized by a term PEAS, which stands for performance measure, environment, actuators, and sensors.
- The main factors on which the rationality of an agent depends include the following:
  - Performance measure
  - Prior knowledge about the environment
  - Percept sequence
  - Actions
- An IA is a conceptual entity that may consist of hardware, software, or even both of them. The entire structure of an intelligent agent is given by the following combination along with their definitions:
  - **Intelligent Agent = Architecture + Agent Program.**
  - **Agent Program** = The deployment of an agent function through a software program or algorithm is called agent program.
  - **Architecture** = It is a hardware or software structure on which the IA executes the functions performed by an agent.

The architecture of an IA is shown in Figure 1.3.

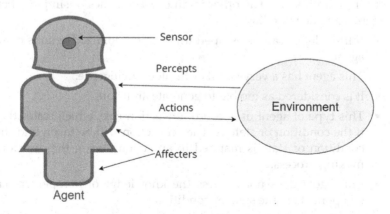

FIGURE 1.3
Schematic diagram of an intelligent agent (IA).

The block diagram of an IA based on the structure is shown in Figure 1.4.

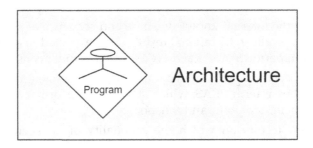

FIGURE 1.4
Block diagram of agent structure.

Types of Intelligent Agents

Agents are very fundamental components of any type of AI system used in numerous industries and technological fields. Each agent has different capabilities, functionalities, level of knowledge, and level of understanding and decision-making power. IAs are categorized in a wide range of classes based on their capabilities and level of intelligence. Among the main categories, the following are a few very important categories[31]:

- **Simple Reflex Agents** – This is one of the simple types of IA. It is commonly used in an observable intelligent environment because there are definite possibilities of developing continuous and infinite loops in partially observable environments. The main characteristic of this agent is that it works on the basis of the present percept and does not remember the past percepts that the intelligent system has observed in history. The other main characteristics of simple reflex agents include the following:
  - Infinite loops can be escaped through randomized actions of an agent.
  - This agent has a very small or limited intelligence.
  - It is considered as too big to generate and store.
  - This type of agent uses condition–action rule, which states that if the condition or state is true, the action will be taken and the condition or state is mapped to an action during the decision-making process.
  - This agent does not possess the knowledge of non-perceptual components of the state or condition.
  - The changes in the intelligent environment lead to the updating of the collection rules too.

- **Model-Based Reflex Agents** – The simple definition of a model-based reflex agent is that it finds a rule whose conditions match the current state. The model of the world is developed by this agent to handle the partially observable environment(s). The following are the other main features and characteristics of this agent:
  - It depends on the percept history for updating state.
  - It continuously keeps on tracking the internal state of it by analyzing and updating every new percept.
  - The existing state is maintained inside the agent that holds a certain structure describing the unseen parts of the world.
  - The state updating requires two main things – how agent action affects the world and how the world emerges from the agent independently.
- **Utility-Based Agents** – As the name implies, those types of agents that are made from the end users or utilities as the building blocks are known as utility-based agents. The other characteristics of this type of agent include the following:
  - The actions chosen by these agents are based on preference of the utility or end-use case in every state.
  - To decide the best one among the multiple options, this type of agent is commonly used in an AI system.
  - This agent helps achieve the most effective, easiest, fastest, and the cheapest way to destination.
  - The happiness of an agent is considered as the core component in measuring the effective action or outcome of an agent.
- **Goal-Based Agents** – In this type of agent, the goal of an intelligent system is the most fundamental issue to consider. The agents use the distance from the main goal or description of the desirable situation for making decision in the ML concept of the intelligent system. The following are the main features of this kind of agent:
  - The action initiated by an agent is designed to reduce distance from the goal.
  - In such a condition, an agent has to weigh and choose one of the most effective possibilities to reach the goal state of the system.
  - The explicit representation of the knowledge is made, which is used for supporting the decision-making process – this makes it more flexible and efficient agent.
  - The knowledge used for decision-making is also easy to modify in different situations, which leads to the change in behavior of an agent easily.

- **Hierarchical Agents** – As the name implies, this type of agents consists of a hierarchy from the higher level to the lower levels. The higher level agents monitor the behaviors of the lower level agents, which are designed to perform lower level actions or functions in an intelligent system. The other main features of hierarchical agents are as follows:
  - Organization of agents is in a hierarchical pattern.
  - The goals and constraints are provided by the higher level agents and the lower level agents accomplish the specific tasks.
  - This type of structure of hierarchical agents is used in those intelligent systems, which are highly complex and consists of multiple tasks and functions to be carried out simultaneously in a system.
  - The most common domains of application of hierarchical agents include robotics, transportation systems, industrial manufacturing, and others.
  - The automated AI-powered solutions where multiple tasks, subtasks, and related inputs are required to be prioritized and coordinated perfectly are the main application scenarios of this type of agent.
  - The order of the agents in hierarchical agent system depends on the complexity of the system.
  - As a simple intelligent system, there may be only two-order agents, high-level and low-level agents as compared to other complex systems.
  - In a complex environment, multiple-order agents are developed in which the higher level agents set the goals and intermediary agents may instruct and monitor the specific tasks of low-level agents.
  - Hierarchical agent system is considered as the most efficient and reliable as compared to many other types.
  - It provides efficient decision-making and improved performance.
- **Learning Agents** – The learning agent, as the name implies, is an IA that is capable of learning from the past experience of dealing with the percept history. The other main features of this type of agent are as follows:
  - A learning agent is normally initiated with a very basic knowledge of the environment and starts learning from the environment through experience.
  - Different ML models are deployed to keep improving the learning process of the agents.
  - Conceptually, the learning agents are divided into four main components:

- **Learning Element** – The ability of the agent to learn from the environment through experience is the responsibility of this component.
- **Critic Element** – This is another important factor of learning agent concept. The main purpose of critic element is to provide feedback to the learning element on the performance of the learning capabilities of learning agents.
- **Performance Element** – The main purpose of the performance element is taking care of the responsibility of external action selection.
- **Problem Generator** – The last component of a learning agent is the problem generator, which is used for suggesting actions. The actions will be suggested in such a way that new and informative experience is achieved.

- **Multi-Agent Systems** – Multi-agent system consists of numerous agents that are able to interact with their respective environments and coordinate with other agents that act collectively to achieve a common purpose or solution. Thus, a multi-agent system is different from the hierarchical system because in hierarchical system, the lower level and intermediary agents are deployed under the influence of the upper agents. In this agent system, all agents are either autonomous or semiautonomous to act and interact with their respective environments and achieve the common goals or contribute to the common goals or objectives. The following are the most important features and characteristics of this system:
  - This type of agent system is also abbreviated as MAS, which stands for multi-agent system.
  - The actions of each agent can be coordinated to contribute to the main cause to achieve an integrated system.
  - Each agent can make its decision, take actions, and perceive its respective environments in either autonomous or semiautonomous state.
  - The most important domains of utilization of MAS system include transportation systems, social media networks, robotics, and others.
  - The other main features of this system include improved performance, extensive flexibility in complex environments, reduced costs, and higher efficiency.
  - The MAS systems can be further classified into subcategories such as heterogeneous, homogeneous, same goal agents, different goal agents, cooperative agent system, or competitive agent system and others.

- Homogeneous agent systems are those in which all agents have similar capabilities, behaviors, and goals.
- Heterogeneous agent systems are those systems in which the agents have dissimilar capabilities, goals, and behaviors.
- Heterogeneous systems are more difficult in terms of coordination but would offer highly flexible and robust capabilities for complex solutions.
- The cooperative agent systems of MAS are those that coordinate and cooperate with each other to achieve the desired common goal.
- In competitive agent systems of MAS, the competitive agents pursue their own objectives to achieve in a broader spectrum of goals.
- A MAS system can also be of competitive and cooperative nature simultaneously under one intelligent system.
- MAS system can be deployed in a variety of models of AI such as game theory, agent-based modeling, ML, and others.
- Strategic interactions between the agents is analyzed by using the game theory; it is also used for predicting agent behaviors.
- The decision-making capabilities of agents are improved by training with datasets in ML.
- The complex systems are deployed with the agent-based modeling to monitor communication between agents and solve the most complex problems in an intelligent system simultaneously.

Sensor

A sensor is an electronic, mechanical, or other device that can sense the change of any particular parameters of an AI environment such as temperature, moisture, light, voice, thrust, and many others and send them to the IA in an AI system. It plays a very vital role in modern AI technology because all types of data in an environment is measured and transmitted to the agent from the environment in the form of percepts. In other words, an IA monitors the environment with the help of sensors by receiving the readings of parameters in the shape of percepts.[33]

Sensors can be classified into numerous categories based on different materials, engineering disciplines, and capabilities. A few of those major categories include the following:

- Electronic sensors
- Electromagnetic sensors
- Light sensors
- Heat sensors

- Mechanical sensors
- Emotion sensors
- Inertial sensors
- Optoelectronic torque sensors
- Mechanical torque force sensors
- Biosensors
- Proximity sensors

The most common types of sensors extensively used in the modern field of AI are as follows:

- Cameras
- Microphones
- Thermometers
- RFID (radio frequency identification) sensors
- Radar systems
- LIDAR
- Sonar
- Ultrasound systems
- Code sensors

A wide range of new circuitries have been developed to sense numerous parameters that can be used in modern AI field such as airflow and pressure, taste, smell, rain, moisture, and many others.

Affecters

The affecters are devices or components that are used in an intelligent system to affect the intelligent environment. The affecters are activated through the action or responses of an IA to influence the environment's components. The following are the most common affecters used in modern AI:

- Artificial legs
- Artificial arms
- Artificial fingers
- Artificial wheels
- Artificial gears
- Air blowers
- Electric nose

Actuator

The mechanical or electromechanical devices that convert energy into motion are called actuators. In other words, the actuators are normally mechanical or electric appliances that are used to transfer physical action through an automated system, especially the robotic entities, to the environment by an IA. The actuators are normally used in robotics and industrial automated processes in manufacturing, logistics, and other fields.[34]

Different Fields of Artificial Intelligence

AI is a highly evolving field, especially during the past few decades; moreover, the future of AI technology is very bright. Such phenomenal growth and future prospects are continuously opening up new domains and fields within this expanding technological sphere. In general, the concept of AI is broader to mimic all functions, behaviors, activities, cognition capabilities, reasoning, decision-making, and other attributes of a human with the help of intelligent machines or computers. To achieve that level of intelligence, many projects and research works are going on in different countries, institutes, companies, and universities simultaneously. With major advancements in language processing technologies, the generative content applications and chatbots have emerged as the major components in the AI field. With the passage of time, new domains and fields are emerging in this broader domain of technologies. A few very important ones are as follows[35]:

- Cognitive computing (CC)
- Machine learning
- Deep learning
- Artificial neural networks (ANNs)
- Computer vision
- Natural language processing
- Expert systems (ES)
- Reinforcement learning
- Robotics

Let us learn about these major domains of AI in the following sections.

Cognitive Computing

CC is a subdomain of broader field of AI. The main purpose of CC is to provide assistance to human in decision-making and thoughts by simulating the decision-making and thinking processes of human brain. This is an assistive technology that helps human brain make well-informed decisions. The following are the most important features and characteristics of CC[36]:

- Both CC and AI are used interchangeably, but in reality they are different.
- CC is a subdomain of AI technology.
- It is an assistive technology based on AI capabilities of machines to help human brain make information-based decisions and enhance human thinking process significantly by simulation techniques.
- The main objective of AI is to replace the human thinking and decision-making with the power of machines, while the core objective of CC is to enhance the thinking and decision-making power of human brains.
- It provides deeper insight into the most complex problems that a human mind cannot dig into to provide a solution, which is highly effective and well-informed.
- Different mind processes are simulated in CC to find out the hidden values into the problem data and come up with the most suitable solution.
- An example of CC is a healthcare application or treatment application that can take all factors such as age, medical history, genetic properties, body type, weight, height, allergies, and other information of a patient into account and make a highly informative outcome for doctor to make a well-informed treatment decision.
- Compared with AI, we can say that CC deals with human thinking augmentation, while AI deals with the automation of the human thinking through machines.
- For choosing the best way out of multiple options, CC is used compared to the AI technology.
- It enables human to effectively work with large piles of unstructured data for finding out the best relationship to augment the human decision-making.
- Final decision is not made by the CC platforms compared with the AI technology in which the final decision is made by the AI technology.
- The other main attributes of CC include interactivity, adaptability, state-fullness, iterative, and contextual nature.
- The analytical accuracy, user experience, process efficiency, productivity, and higher quality of service are a few major benefits of CC.

Machine Learning

ML is a very important and prospective domain of AI technology. It is defined as the field of technology in which the machines are trained with training data to learn and decide autonomously without any explicit programming to perform any certain task or any human intervention. The computers are trained through ML models powered by the ML algorithms written in machine language code. The ML technologies have evolved into many categories and classes and continue to expand significantly across a wide range of industries and sectors. The most common applications that are in use in our daily life and business include the following[37]:

- Search engines
- Recommendation engines
- Self-driving cars
- Social media platforms
- Cybersecurity environments
- E-commerce apps
- Chatbots
- Preventive healthcare
- Image recognition apps
- Voice recognition apps
- Sentiment analysis apps
- Predictive/projective applications

There are numerous subdomains of ML technology itself. Those domains are based on the principle of training machines under certain types of algorithms. The following are the main categories of principles of training the machines:

- Supervised ML
- Unsupervised ML
- Semi-supervised ML

The supervised ML is a type of ML in which the machines are trained by ingesting the training datasets without any tags or labels. In this type of ML, the input and output of an algorithm are predefined or specified. The algorithm is designed to map or assess the input-labeled data with the predefined results or outputs.

An unsupervised type of ML is that method in which the data scientists use unlabeled or untagged data as input to the algorithms to learn by themselves from either similarities or contradictions of feature items or entities. The algorithms are designed in such a way that they find out any connection between two or multiple entities to group them and/or separate them. The trained data and the output are also predefined in this method of ML.

The semi-supervised ML is the middle-way between the supervised and unsupervised ML. The accuracy and reliability of supervised ML is huge, but the overall cost to tag or label huge volumes of data is very high. In the unsupervised ML, the cost is very low but the performance is also a bit on the downside. Thus, the best trade-off between these two models of supervised machine is the mid-way model known as semi-supervised ML.

Apart from the two main ML models – supervised and unsupervised – and one derived model known as semi-supervised ML, there is another type of ML known as reinforcement ML. It has some unique features and characteristics; therefore, it is defined as a separate domain of AI in one of the following sections.

In addition to what is discussed so far, the main features and characteristics of ML are as follows[35,37]:

- ML is performed through algorithms, which define the input and output or results and assess the outcome on the basis of those definitions.

- It does not use explicit computer programming to take certain actions. The program defined through algorithm is written in machine language and installed as the fundamental firmware to achieve the desired level of learning and decision-making on the basis of the training datasets that are ingested by those algorithms.

- The most important functions or activities performed by the ML mathematical algorithms include the following:
  - Regression modeling
  - Different types of classifications
  - Ensemble activity
  - Clustering function
  - Association mining
  - Dimensionality reduction
  - Anomaly detection

- It provides the machines some type of capabilities to translate, understand, execute, and examine the data for solving the most complex problems automatically without any human intervention during the entire process or life cycle.

- It provides the most effective and accurate forecast and behavior prediction in a real-time environment.

- The main domains of businesses where ML is operating for many years now include customer relationship management (CRM), business intelligence (BI) and data mining (DM), human resource information systems (HRIS), virtual assistants, website chatbots, and many other process automation applications.

- This can provide accurate data analysis for bringing out valuable business intelligence for the companies to increase customer satisfaction and business productivity.

Deep Learning

DL is an important type of AI today. Specifically speaking, it is a specialized type of ML that is used to train computers from the data like it comes to human brain to understand and learn from the experience or examples. DL uses large neural networks with multiple hidden layers and huge volumes of data in the form of images, text, voice, and others. DL offers the greatest level of accuracy that even a human brain cannot find in certain cases. The DL structure differs from the normal ML in many aspects such as the number of layers in the neural networks, volumes of data, continual improvement in the capabilities of machines, required processing power, and others. The schematic diagram of a DL neural network is shown in Figure 1.5.

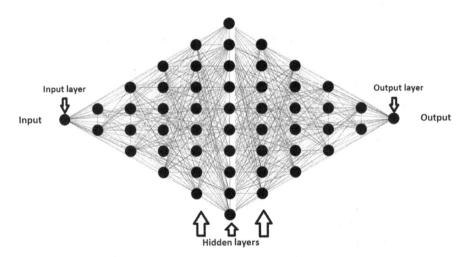

FIGURE 1.5
Schematic diagram of a neural network used in deep learning. (*Courtesy:* Pixabay.)

The following are the most important features and characteristics of DL technology[38]:

- In this model of ML, the machines learn by ingesting huge volumes of labeled data similar to the human brain which learns by examples or experience with the real-world data in the forms of images, senses, text, voice, and others.
- DL models directly learn from the sets of images, voice, and texts through the classification task.

- It offers highly reliable performance and accuracy, even exceeding the performance of a human brain in certain cases.
- Compared with the normal ML, supervised, and unsupervised techniques, the DL models use neural networks with many times greater number of hidden layers – in certain cases, the number may exceed 100 layers.
- It uses huge computing power through high-performance GPUs (graphics processing unit) having parallel structure of computing for accomplishing the required amount of processing power.
- With the advent of cloud computing and clustering techniques (both combined together), a huge amount of time for training the DL models is reduced significantly.
- DL uses millions of images and other forms of data for training purposes. The training datasets are mostly labeled.
- In certain cases, DL models with large number of hidden layers outperform human being in terms of their reliability, accuracy, and efficiency.
- The following are the most important examples of the applications of DL models in the modern industries and businesses:
  - Automated driving and aerospace
  - Industrial automation and medical research
  - Defense and electronics
- In DL, the convolutional neural networks (CNN) or ConvNet are used extensively.
- The automated feature extraction through convolutional neural network replaces the manual feature extraction in normal ML models.
- It is extensively suitable for CV applications due to automated feature extraction, which offers greater accuracy and reliability.
- DL technology is also considered as an end-to-end learning model.
- Contrary to traditional ML techniques with limited hidden layers, the DL technology continuously expands and improves the capability of machines without adopting any shallow convergence, which normally happens in the form of traditional models of ML.
- DL model training process usually follows three main steps or stages:
  - Training from scratch through large amount of data (labeled/tagged)
  - Transfer learning in which the pretrained model is further fine-tuned
  - Automated feature extraction through convolutional neural network

DL models are extensively used in a wide range of AI-enabled applications due to higher flexibility, adaptability, cost-efficiency, robustness, accuracy, scalability, interpretability, and many other aspects. It is considered the most robust and futuristic AI domain of technology that has an extremely bright future.

Artificial Neural Networks

The phrase "artificial neural network" has been drawn from the natural neural network which is the core structure of biological neurons interconnected with each other for processing the signals in human brain. That biological network is called natural neural network and the simulation of that natural neural network for machines is known as ANN.

Like neurons interconnected in a human brain, the artificial neurons known as *'nodes'* are interconnected through wires defined through the weightage, which is equivalent to the synapse in the natural brain. The input of an AI resembles to the dendrites in the natural brain and the output of the AI is equivalent to the axon in the human brain. The node is equivalent to cell nucleus. The architecture of ANN is shown in Figure 1.6.

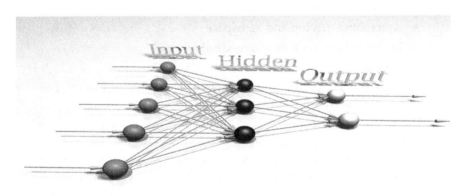

FIGURE 1.6
ANN architecture. (*Courtesy:* Flickr.)

In ANN, the input data is fed into the architecture in the form of training data or test data. The training data is labeled and ingested into the input layer in the form of training dataset, while the test data is fed into the input layer in the form of test data. There is a threshold value set on the input data weightage. If the weight of the input to a node is higher than the threshold value, the signal is further processed to the next node; otherwise, the signal is lost in the node. The weightage is determined on the basis of the importance and relevance of the information. The hidden layers are used to further process and refine the input signals from the previous hidden layer nodes and forward to the next level of layers, either hidden or the output layer. The output of a neuron continues changing with the expanded learning of the input and environments through examples. The more trained the neural network is with the data, the more it behaves robustly and reliably.

The following are the main features and characteristics of ANN[39]:

- A single-node or multi-node layer that is programmed to accept the input data is called the input layer of ANN.
- The input nodes connect to the hidden layers of the network that may consist of multiple nodes in parallel with other layers which are also known as hidden layers, excluding the last node that is connected to the output node.
- All nodes between input and output layers are called hidden layers.
- The weight is calculated as the sum of the inputs and a bias. This whole computation is governed by a formula known as transfer function. The output calculated by the transfer function is forwarded to activation function as an input to produce an output against that input received from the previous transfer function.
- Other main features that come with ANN in the form of advantages include capability of parallel processing, ability of memory distribution, capability of working with incomplete knowledge, storage of data on the whole network, reasonable fault tolerance capability, and many more.
- The most important types of activation functions used in ANN include binary function, linear function, tan hyperbolic function, and sigmoidal function.
- There are two main categories of ANNs:
  - Feed-forward ANN
  - Feed-backward ANN
- ANNs also come with automated control functions to control the computing in the neural network.
- The storage of data is fault tolerant, which means that if the neural network is removed, the stored data is affected very minutely.
- The ANNs can be interpolated as well as extrapolated from the stored data on the networks easily.
- DL is materialized through ANNs perfectly.
- It can be both hardware- and software-based neural network.

Computer Vision

CV is a very important field of AI. This field deals with digital photos, videos, and other images to be used for the purpose of training the computers to learn from those images as the human brain does. Computers are fed with images and videos recorded by cameras to the ML models mostly based on the DL or neural networks to derive the meaningful information from those images so that the computers understand those images and its content and make informed decisions. The main purpose of images and videos used in CV is to make the computers see the world like the human does and learn from those images and make suitable decisions.[40]

The following are the most common features and characteristic of CV subdomain[40,41]:

- CV enables the computers to see images to learn and react to the information available in those images.
- Normally, at the backend of the CV-based ML, there are DL neural network models.
- The start of CV dates back to early 1950s but it accelerated in 1970s, and finally took strong roots in the last couple of decades.
- The accuracy of CV-based applications has reached almost 99% or even more in 2020s.
- The ML models perceive images like the human does in jigsaw puzzle. It distinguishes and separates different contours, edges, and pieces of images and marks them as subcomponents to understand the entire image fed to the CV model.
- The most important applications of CV in modern AI technology include facial recognition, security application, image analysis, and others,
- The DL models are extremely dependent on CV applications in modern technological world.
- The most important fields that are using CV applications include healthcare, e-commerce, defense, internal security, manufacturing, government, and many others.
- The following are the most important processes used in CV programs:
  - Image segmentation and image classification
  - Edge detection and object detection
  - Facial recognition and feature matching
  - Pattern detection and object tracking
- The most important technologies that make the CV field work are CNN and DL.

Natural Language Processing

We are somewhat familiar with NLP but, here, let us know more about it. NLP is a subdomain of AI that deals with the natural language that people speak in the form of text and voice. NLP enables the computer machines to understand, learn, and respond to the natural language that people speak in the form of text or voice. It takes natural language in the form of text and voice and passes through different activities or processes to understand and make decision about what to react in the response to that particular message either in written or spoken form. Understanding all attributes attached to the spoken and written communication in natural language is important in this case.[42]

This entire technological process draws many similarities from the processes involved in natural language conversation done by humans. For example, a human being has ears and eyes to intake natural language communication in the form of voice and text. Computers take the communication or message through microphone, keyboard, optical detector, camera, and so on. Human mind processes communication through capabilities of the brain that it has learned from experience and generates suitable response either through the written text or through the tongue in the form of voice. The computers use the AI techniques to process the input message in the form of text and voice and understand the meaning and sentiments in the communication and respond properly through the same AI model by using the screens or speakers.

The following are the most important features and characteristics of NLP technology[42,43]:

- Understanding and responding to the human language in the form of text and voice is called NLP.
- Uses different sensors for input such as camera, keyboard, optical devices, microphones, and so on, and for output it uses digital screen and speakers.
- It consists of two main phases or stages – data processing and algorithm-building.
- Data processing is accomplished through multiple processes such as tokenization, part of speech tagging, stemming, and lemmatization.
- The algorithms used in language processing models can be categorized into two main classes:
  - **Rule-Based Systems** – In this method, the simple rules based on linguistics and grammatical structures are used for processing the language in both written and spoken formats.
  - **ML-Based Systems** – In this method, the rules are not defined explicitly, but the ML models developed by the scientists and developers are designed in such a way that they develop rules

based on their own understanding and learning experience with the input data in the form of text and voice. The most commonly used techniques in building ML-based systems include DL and neural networks.

- In terms of technical aspects, there are two main methods used in NLP:
  - **Syntax Analysis** – This technique uses the order and arrangement of words in line with the grammatical structures to derive the meaning of a sentence.
  - **Semantic Analysis** – This method applies the meaning and use of words in sentences to learn the meaning of the entire sentence.
- The most important processes used in the syntax analysis of NLP method include parsing, word segmentation, sentence breaking, morphological segmentation, stemming, and lemmatization.
- The most salient techniques used in the semantic analysis of NLP method include the following:
  - Named entity recognition
  - Word sense disambiguation
  - Natural language generation
- NLP is in the market in different forms and its manifestation has been for over 50 years by this time.
- A few most important tool kits used for the development of NLP models include the following:
  - Natural Language Toolkit (NLTK)
  - Gensim NLP Toolkit
  - Intel NLP Architect
- The most common use cases of NLP technology include text classification, text extraction, machine translation, spam detection, virtual agents and chatbots, social media sentiment analysis, text summarization, natural language generation through GPT applications, and so on.
- The following are the modern domains of industries where NLP technology is extensively used:
  - Customer feedback analysis in customer care sector
  - Customer service automation
  - Automated language translation systems
  - Academic research and analysis domain
  - Categorization and analysis of medical records
  - Plagiarism and proofreading problem detection systems
  - Automated market forecasting and trading systems

- Automation of litigation and legal tasks
- Deeper analysis of sentiments

Expert Systems

ES is a subdomain of AI. It is a domain-specific type of AI system, which deals with a particular process for predicting the informed output based on the previous experience and knowledge. The knowledge or experience this system gains is known as the knowledge base of facts. The knowledge base is developed by the industry experts in such a way that the ES can easily learn from that knowledge base by using the specific learning rules that are designed in the module, which is known as inference engine. This type of system was developed by computer scientist Edward Feigenbaum, who was a professor of computer science at Stanford University. He was also the founder of Stanford's Knowledge Systems Laboratory. This was the first such system in history. Presently, there are numerous ES available in the marketplace. The schematic diagram of an ES is shown in Figure 1.7.

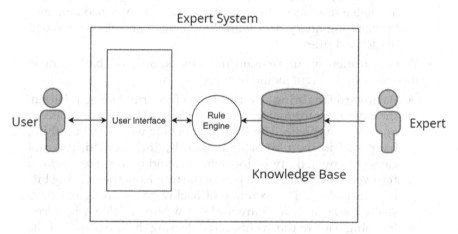

FIGURE 1.7
Schematic diagram of expert system.

The most important features and characteristics of ES are as follows[44]:

- It is a domain-specific process (an intelligent system) that deals with a particular business or activity to predict the output.
- There are three main components of it:
    - **Knowledge Base** – As the name indicates, this is a storage of data or information where the experts of the industry store data that will be used for predicting the well-informed output. This

knowledge base keeps expanding with the passage of time due to experience and addition of more information to it. The detailed information about the subject area is continuously added to it by the experts. This knowledge base has only two interfaces – used by the experts and the rule engine, which is another main component of the ES.

- **Rule Engine** – This component consists of two modules. One module is known as inference module that is a rule-based system for mapping the past knowledge taken from the knowledge to the prespecified rules for making an informed decision. The other module of this component is known as explanation module, which is used to explain the output to the user that how that particular decision was made by taking the data from the knowledge base.

- **User Interface** – The user interface is used to interact or communicate with the user who uses this entire system to achieve the desired output or decisions in a particular field. From this component, the users put the queries to the system to generate a suitable response. The system provides an informed response by mapping query data with the previous knowledge through predefined rules.

- The acquisition of information from the knowledge base is done through two different methods in ES:

  - **Backward Chaining** – In this type of information acquisition, the existing information pieces in different forms are collected and used in the decision tree to conclude why a certain thing happened in the past. This means, by this method, the root cause of any activity or incident is found by reverse-tracking the events or information pieces starting from the existing bits of information. The example of backward chaining is extensively found in healthcare systems where an illness is traced by going back to the events and detecting the root cause of the disease.

  - **Forward Chaining** – In this method, the existing readings and past experience is used to forecast or predict the future events. In other words, this method detects what will happen in the future based on the existing knowledge and past learning. The example of this method is the forecasting of the market behavior applications in trading, financial services, and other fields.

- Other than the three main components already mentioned, there are a few additional parts of this system, which are not considered to be independent parts of the ES. Those components include expert

interface to knowledge base, domain experts who put the information to the knowledge base, knowledge acquisition module, and
internal connectivity between the main components of the ES for
establishing communication.

- ES are commonly applied in specific domain to predict or forecast
the futuristic decisions. The examples of application may include
predicting market behavior, prediction of health conditions, ret-
rospect the root cause from the existing symptoms of a patients,
troubleshooting in manufacturing processes, predicting financial
markets, and many other such types of activities.

- The most important industries where the domain- and task-specific
ES are extensively used include financial services, trading, marketing, telecommunication, healthcare, customer services, logistics and
transportation, and so on.

- The other main features of using ES include higher level of accuracy in the results, effective and logical deduction, informed decision-making, continual improvement in the knowledge base to
improve the decision quality, cost-efficiency, enhanced productivity, and so on.

Reinforcement Learning

RL is a type of ML, but it differs from other types of learning in many areas.
Therefore, it is described as a separate subdomain of AI. In this type of ML,
there is no support from the external data or labeled answers to learn from.
The RL is based on the *hit-and-try* principle in which the learning agent will
try to guess the output in a single step and then checks if it was correct or
incorrect or event neutral (nothing). The successful attempt will be marketed
with positive output or will be given a reward and the unsuccessful attempt
will be awarded with negative feedback or punishment in terms of score.
This process continues to move forward and learn from the previous steps;
thus, an understanding is built based on those results and feedback system,
which continuously updates the output.

The following are the most important features and characteristics of RL[45,46]:

- It is a type of ML which is based on reward and punishment model
of outcome or predictions. If the prediction is desirable, it will be
rewarded and if it is undesirable, it will be punished.

- The main objective of RL model is to maximize the reward by taking the most suitable action that can yield the most desirable results
under the given scenario or environmental conditions.

- The learner is termed as an agent, which is not explicitly trained
through training datasets as is done in other types of ML. In this

learning, the agent is supposed to interact with the environment and surroundings to decide what to do next.

- The entire model of RL consists of four important components:
  - **Policy** – The policy is a core function or behavior of an agent in certain given conditions to act. This policy may be governed by either a simple function or a complex mathematical calculation. The determination of next action is accomplished by following the policy of the model.
  - **Reward** – This is the value in positive or negative in response to an action performed by the learning agent on an environment. The reward may be positive if the outcome is desirable or rewarding and it is negative if the outcome is undesirable or punishing. The main purpose of this model is to maximize the rewards.
  - **Value Function** – It is an overall reward weightage of the actions performed by the ML agent in this environment. The reward function may vary from action to action in this ML environment.
  - **Environment Model** – The environment is an overall ecosystem in which the agent takes actions and gets the outcome in the form of reward or punishment. The environment helps the agent decide what action is beneficial and what will be detrimental to the main objective of this learning, which is maximizing the rewards.
- The agent always learns from the outcome of the past action that results in the form of reward and punishment.
- The workflow of RL is understand the environment, take a trial action, get the result either in negative or positive form, learn from the error, and reposition itself in the changed environment for the next step.
- The applications of RL are limited to certain domains such as gaming, personalized recommendations, resource management, customer management, robotics, and a few others.
- The optimized usage of resource in many enterprise resource management (ERM) software platforms is done through RL. Similarly, in robotics, many tasks that cannot be taught through other forms of training are performed through hit-and-error model of RL.
- The other main domains where RL is adopted include information theory, control theory, operations research, game theory, swarm intelligence, multi-agent systems, simulation-based optimization, genetic algorithms, statistics, and so on.

- The most common algorithms used in RL include the following:
  - **Q-Learning** – It is one of the most commonly used algorithms in RL systems. In this method, the agent is not given policy in advance to learn from; agent has to learn by taking actions itself.
  - **State-action-reward-state-action (SARSA)** – In this sequential algorithm, the agent is provided with the policy to start with. The policy of a RL system is the set of probability in which certain possibilities are projected against certain actions in the environment.
  - **Deep Q-Network** – It is another very important algorithm used in modern RL field. The use of neural networks is the fundamental difference in this algorithm. The action to be taken by the agent in this environment is based on the random samples of the beneficial acts taken in the past.
- The main points and terminologies used in RL are as follows:
  - **Input** – It is the state of the RL model from where the learning activity starts. It is also known as the initial state of the model.
  - **Output** – The output depends on a variety of parameters considered in the model such as positive and negative, wrong and right, desirable and undesirable, and others. The output depends on the type of solution chosen.
  - **Training** – The training is based on the input policy and the output of the actions whether that yields positive rewards or negative punishment. The training continues with the errors or the outcome of the previous action to adjust the next move in such a way that it maximizes the positive outcome. This entire process is called training of the agent in RL.
  - **Expansion** – The increased learning capability with the outcome of the actions of the system is known as the expansion of the capability. The model continuously keeps on learning and expanding its capability.
- There are two types of RL – positive and negative. They are divided on the basis of their outcome values.

Robotics

Robotics is and is not a subdomain of AI. This may be a strange statement but considering the modern AI-powered robots, it is a part of AI or a field of AI that enables the robotic machines to behave like the human does by using their own brain power achieved through the ML capabilities from the environment (without any explicit programming). Again, the traditional robotics, which has been existing in the market for many decades now, is not a part of AI. Before diving into the deeper concepts of robotics, both the traditional and modern ones, let us define the traditional terms of robotics.

The domain of engineering that is the combination of mechanical, electrical, and electronic engineering and computer science or software programming is known as robotics. The robotics field deals with the mechanical or electrical devices that are able to perform specific tasks automatically without any explicit intervention of human beings. The automation is managed by the explicit computer programming, which is installed in the form of a control system program.[48]

The traditional forms of robotics have been in the marketplace for many decades now in a wide range of industries such as logistics, manufacturing, warehousing, agriculture, and other areas where they were used to perform either difficult or repetitive tasks or even both. The traditional robotics does not have brain to think and they make decisions based on the changed environment or in unknown conditions. They are only task-specific machines shaped in different forms such as wheels, arms, legs, and others.

With the passage of time and the advent of modern technologies of AI such as CV, voice recognition, and optical character recognition (OCR), the forms, shapes, and definition of modern robotics have changed drastically. In such changed environment, many people think that robotics and AI are the interchangeable technologies or domains. But, in fact, they are completely separate domains. If we consider the modern robotics, then it is not possible without the use of AI. The modern robots are software-based, hardware-based, and both software-and-hardware-based. The modern robotics is sometimes defined as the *"domain of artificial intelligence that is fully focused on researching and developing the technologies to materialize the concept of intelligent robots"*.[47]

The following are the most salient features and characteristics of modern robotics technologies[47–49]:

- Robotics is a combination of mechanical/electrical engineering and AI in modern technological domain. Traditionally, robotics was just the combination of engineering and computer science to program the instructions.
- Robots are the products of robotics technology that may be based on hardware, software, or both.
- AI gives the brain to the robotic machines to learn and make decisions like the human brain does.
- The future of robotics is intricately associated with the AI because the number of robotic inventions in the future will be more advanced

than the traditional mechanical or electrical robots with a short computer program to instruct the machines to perform specific task without taking any decisions.

- The examples of modern robots that use the power of ML and AI include iRobot Roomba, Robotic kitchens, Moxi, Iron Ox robotics, Mars Rovers, and so on.
- Other than the hardware robots, there are a wide range of software-based robots in the marketplace that are more intelligent than the hardware in many areas.
- The examples of software robots include ChatGPT chatbot (chatterbot), website agents, any other chatbot, customer support agents, virtual assistants, crawlers, and others.
- All these software based agents or robots are fully dependent upon the software engineering and AI technologies.
- Software bots may not be considered as part of robotics in traditional way, but they are termed as robots in modern software field.
- In future, the difference between AI and robotics will keep depleting tremendously.
- A robot consists of numerous components:
  - Power supply and actuators
  - Electric motors and sensors
  - Muscle wires and pneumatic air muscles
  - Piezo motors and ultrasonic motors
- The following are the main sectors and industries where the modern robots are extensively used:
  - Defense and security
  - Aviation and manufacturing
  - Entertainment and agriculture
  - Automobile and drone aviation
  - Logistics and transportation
  - Space and rocket industry
- The following are the most common AI or AI-based technologies that are extensively used in modern robotics:
  - Computer vision
  - Natural language processing
  - Machine learning
  - Complex event processing (CEP)
  - Edge computing (EC)

- Effective computing
- Augmented reality (AR)/virtual reality (VR)
- Mixed reality (MR)
- The following are the most common tasks performed by the AI-powered modern robots:
  - Face detection and object recognition
  - Position estimation and movement detection
  - OCR and gesture detection

What Is the Logic Used in Artificial Intelligence and Its Types?

As we mentioned earlier, reasoning is one of the most important techniques behind the AI technology. Reasoning is achieved by using logic, which is the main parameter for giving any reason for any activity or happening. Thus, the logic can be defined as follows: *"The validation or proof behind any reason of action or activity"*. Decision-making is heavily influenced by the available situation in which the output options to choose from are multiple. Finally, decision-making is based on choosing the most suitable option among the available options in a given situation. Decision-making is accomplished by the IA or simply by an agent in AI system. If the IA is capable of understanding the logic, then it can easily make a decision with the help of reasoning process.[50]

In AI, there are two major categories of logic:

- Deductive logic
- Inductive logic

Deductive Logic

The provision of complete validation or evidence for making any decision is referred to as deductive logic. This logic ensures that all aspects of the given conditions are analyzed and measured in the decision-making process so that no chance of estimated or approximated conclusion exists. The example of such logic is using intelligent systems for suggesting medication to the patients remotely or on-premises.

Inductive Logic

As the name suggests, the inductive logic is the evidence or validation of the reasons in which the decision is made by analyzing bottom-up components of the environment to reach a decision. In this logic, the IA analyzes all parts of an environment from the perspective of individual attributes of the components and then generalizes the outcome and finally makes decision based on that generalized understanding. An example of inductive logic is the reasoning behind NLP systems.

Other Main Types of Logic in Artificial Intelligence

The main branch of AI that enables the machines to learn from the environment or available general knowledge of the real-world ecosystems is ML. ML is the process in which the machines are fed with the knowledge presentation and machines understand that knowledge and make decisions based on the logic system and finally come up with a decision based on the information learnt from the experience. The presentation of knowledge in the format that machine can understand is known as logic.

In other words, it is similar to the machine language used in the computer programming for providing instructions to the computers to carry out specific tasks or actions. The most general categories in which a range of different logics fall have already been discussed in the above topic. Those categories are inductive logic and deductive logic.

The other main forms of logic based on the above-mentioned two categories of logic used in ML are as follows[51,52]:

- Propositional logic
- First-order logic
- Second-order logic
- Third-order logic
- Higher-order logic
- Modal logic

All these types of logic are discussed separately in the following sections.[52,53]

Propositional Logic

Propositional logic is the most fundamental logic of AI to present the data. It uses the Boolean algebra to present the knowledge taken from the real-world environment in the form of natural language. Propositional logic is also known as zero-order logic. The propositional logic is based on two conditions, either TRUE or FALSE. Different conditions are presented with the help of different operators used in the Boolean algebra or presentation. Propositional logic can be further divided into two main categories:

- **Atomic Propositional Logic** – It is based on the knowledge presented in a simple sentence or formula which is easy to present.
- **Complex Propositional Logic** – It is based on the knowledge presented in a complex sentence or formula which is a bit complex to present.

First-Order Logic

The first-order logic is the extension of the zero-order logic, or it can also be referred to as complex propositional logic, which is the second part of the propositional logic. In this logic, more complex sentence or formula is decomposed based on different variables to present the meaning of a proposition completely.

Second-Order Logic

In real sense, the second-order logic is the extension of the first-order logic in which the addition of variables is considered from the basic atom, which is considered for the zero-level or propositional simple logic. Additional feature or property of the object in the environment knowledge is considered in the second-order logic to present the knowledge to machine more accurately so that the machines can understand it properly.

Third-Order Logic

The presentation of knowledge in the form of natural sentences or mathematical formulas is done with the logical symbols to present knowledge in a machine-understandable format. The zero-order logic deals with the atom symbols to present the whole sentence without any additional variables. The first-order logic translates different variables in a sentence and the second-order logic considers the feature of an object in a sentence or formula. The third-order logic considers the additional predicate of the sentence into machine-readable presentation to make the knowledge easy-to-understand to the machines in a ML environment.

Higher-Order Logic

The addition of super-predicate of a formula or sentence in the presentation of knowledge in a logical format is accomplished through higher-order logics. This can increase the orders with the increased number of features and conditions like constants and fixed conditions in general presentation of real-world information.

Modal Logic

Modal logic is extensively used in describing the knowledge in a relative system in which different attributes are related to other systems or relations in proof system for modal logics. This is a more advanced and complex type of logic to present complex knowledgeable scenarios to the machines for easy understanding.

Applications of Logic in Artificial Intelligence

AI is an evolving and expanding field in which a wide range of domains are emerging. The logic is the core component or the foundation of AI technology. Thus, an opportunity for numerous applications of logics in different fields and domain remains. The most important of those applications of logic in AI system include the following[52]:

- **Automated Mathematical Reasoning** – Developing automated systems for performing specific tasks which are developed based on mathematical reasoning.
- **Automated Science Discoveries** – The discoveries of scientific concepts are fully based on reasoning and logic. Thus, the second most important application of reasoning in AI is the discovery of scientific concepts.
- **Inductive Programming** – Another domain or area of application of logics is the inductive programming in which the learners try to understand the computer programs. How they are developed and what logic is used to make the machines understand the knowledge are presented in different formats.
- **Building ML Logical Systems** – Developing logic systems based on modern technologies such as ML so that they can mimic a human brain and act exactly the way human brain functions to learn and make decisions from the given environmental conditions without any explicit intervention of human.
- **Verifying Computer Systems** – The verification or validation of computer systems is also based on the use of logic in an extensive volume. Thus, another main application of logic is the verification and validation of modern computer systems.

Artificial Intelligence Approaches

AI is emerging as the most crucial area in all types of technologies, industries, and domains of our day-to-day life. Every person concerned with any industry or business, especially techies (a person who is very knowledgeable or enthusiastic about technology and especially high technology), wants to know about this modern technology. To learn the concepts and technological aspects of AI, some research is required. While carrying out research in AI, you may come across two main approaches of research[54]:

- Symbolic approach
- Connectionist approach

Symbolic Approach

The symbolic approach of research used in AI is also known as classic AI approach, good old-fashioned AI approach, and rule-based AI approach. Thus, this is the traditional form of approach for conducting AI research. In the symbolic approach of AI research, the human rules based on the behavior and knowledge are inserted into the computer code to make the machine learn the environments that they encounter. Different symbols, characters, and other presentations are used to describe the knowledge or conditions to the computer.

This approach was extensively used in the past for achieving the rule-based automation. It is now decreasing rapidly and new approach of research is emerging, which is known as connectionist approach of research.

Connectionist Approach

This is the advanced-level approach of research in AI. It is more popular in the modern research projects of AI and extensively used in the present-day ML and AI fields. In this model of research, the research mimics the model of human brain to carry out the intelligent activities by the machines. The concepts of brain, neurons, and neural networks are utilized in the modern approach of research. The symbolic approach was hand-coded instructions to the computers for automated tasks, but this approach enables the computers to learn by themselves from the given environments and make their own respective decisions in the most complex and challenging situations perfectly.

SAMPLE QUESTIONS

1. What is AI, and how does it contribute to various fields?

2. What are the objectives of AI, and how do they drive advancements in technology and problem-solving?

3. What are the types of AI, and how do they differ in their applications and capabilities?

4. Can you explain the structure of an AI system and its components?

5. What are the different fields of AI, and how do they impact industries and research areas?

6. How is logic used in AI, and what role does it play in decision-making processes within AI systems?

2

Introduction to ChatGPT

Introduction

ChatGPT is an advanced machine learning (ML)-based conversational platform, which can interact with the users by processing their natural language and generating the most suitable response to the queries raised by the users. The name ChatGPT is derived from the combination of words "chat" and GPT, which stands for generative pretrained transformer. The GPT is an innovative and revolutionary technology in the field of ML that is capable of providing the most advanced responses to the most complex questions or queries asked in a personalized or tailored environment.

ChatGPT is a type of chat robot or chatterbot or chatbot with advanced capabilities. The normal chatbots that are used in different applications on a wide range of websites are task-specific chatbots that generate response to limited number of queries that are preprogrammed to be generated for certain queries or questions. They are not so capable of responding to the personalized and complex queries that really demand (somewhat) skills, knowledge, mind power, and specialization. Those normal chatbots are programmed based on the approach known as rule-based programming with very limited abilities of self-thinking or decision-making in customized situations. They utilize limited resources to provide faster responses that are mapped against the specific questions and queries. On the other hand, the ChatGPT is an advanced platform that uses the latest combination of technologies such as GPT, natural language processing (NLP), neural networks,

DOI: 10.1201/9781003474173-2

reinforcement learning, deep learning, and many others. The ChatGPT is able to generate human-like text and other imaginary as well as artistic presentation in response to your query ranging from simple questions to the most complex questions in almost all domains of industries worldwide.

The main features and characteristics of ChatGPT conversational platform are as follows[55,56]:

- It is a type of artificial intelligence (AI)-based chatbot with advanced features and capabilities to make decisions.
- It is a powerful bot that keeps improving its understanding and accuracy of the results while dealing with new questions.
- The use of NLP and advanced ML algorithms makes it a capable application to accomplish somewhat human-like conversation.
- ChatGPT is able to respond to questions in the form of text and voice and come with the most suitable responses in the forms of text content such as general articles, questions and answers, social media posts, letters, emails, and others.
- ChatGPT is a kind of generative artificial intelligence (Gen-AI).
- It is capable of receiving human-like images, content, text, and videos that are created by AI.
- GPT is an artificial model for processing the input requests and formulating the suitable responses.
- It uses the power of reinforcement learning in the form of human feedback received through star reviews and additional comments.
- The continual improvement based on the reinforcement learning feedback is one of the most important features of ChatGPT that makes it ever-improving.
- It is based on an open-source platform known as OpenAI. This research project is done by a group of entrepreneurs and researchers such as Elon Musk, Sam Altman, and teams from other companies like Microsoft Corporation.
- OpenAI platform has also invented another platform for text-to-art generation known as Dall E Text-to-Art Generator.
- The model used by the ChatGPT is also referred to as GPT-3 language model.
- The advanced features of ChatGPT platform are provided to the users in the name of ChatGPT-4 in the market.
- GPT transformers are specialized in finding out the patterns within the data sequences in the form of plain text or other type of content.
- Out of the transformer neural networks, the human-like text is generated with the help of deep learning, which is a type of ML.

- The transformers are capable of predicting text such as next word, sentence, and paragraph with the help of pretrained datasets.
- The training process of ChatGPT started with the simple training or generative data training and kept expanding with more specific and tailored data. Initial data it used for training was the online text data. Later, the other transcripts were fed to learn the advanced capabilities of basic conversations.
- In other words, the human language was learnt through online data and basics of conversation was learnt through transcripts.
- The improvement of the ChatGPT model is based on the reward and punishment system that is the core concept behind the reinforcement learning through professional or experimental feedback from the trainers and the users.
- Thumbs-up and thumbs-down are two main options for providing feedback about the accuracy and reliability of the response the ChatGPT provides to the user online.
- ChatGPT is capable of providing response to the questions in a wide range of areas or fields such as general knowledge, geography, politics, economics, all other academic fields, computer coding, almost all domains of technologies and engineering, religious matters, history, current affairs, and many more (though all responses may not be accurate, especially about religious issues).
- Until mid-2023, the information provided to the ChatGPT platform for learning purpose was up to 2021. So, the latest knowledge is required to be updated with the current dateline and it is now designed to keep learning from the real-time happenings in the world or any advancements and event occurring in the world.
- In simple words, ChatGPT can provide answer for all types of questions that you ask without any reference to the previous question or so.
- It is capable of remembering the questions that you asked previously while interacting with it; so it is a more attractive start from where you left previously.
- The following are the most common tasks that the people can perform through the ChatGPT chatbot:
  - Playing games and asking entertaining questions.
  - Asking general knowledge questions.
  - Creating emails and other business communication.
  - Creating product description and solving math problems (well, Math solutions are not always correct!).
  - Creating titles for text and producing a social media post.

- Writing articles, blogs, technical reports, and other niche articles.
- Developing new codes for a particular task or modifying the existing code mistakes.
- Composing the music and developing lyrics.
- Summarizing presentations, articles, and other podcasts.
- Answering complex questions.
- The ChatGPT platform is still unable to understand the emotions such as sarcasm, anger, criticism, or irony (at all).
- The answers provided by the ChatGPT chatbot is not cited or provided with any reference to the knowledge it has taken from. Thus, the chances of intellectual property theft and other issues may arise in the future.
- The advanced version of ChatGPT-4 has capabilities and can handle multiple other domains with very accurate and reliable responses.
- The following are the most common alternatives to the ChatGPT software in the marketplace:
  - Google BARD for real-time data processing capabilities through Google search engine training or information
  - ChatGPT Bing search engine of Microsoft Corporation
  - AI-Writer and DeepL Write
  - Open Assistant and ChatSonic
  - Rytr and Perplexity AI
- ChatGPT supports huge level of personalization in generating tailored response for a wide range of queries and questions.
- The human-like communication is possible through both text and voice.
- It can also create response to the tone of the text in certain cases.
- Being able to understand the context or the question or query, the ChatGPT platform is able to generate more sophisticated and personalized responses perfectly.
- The most important use cases of ChatGPT may include virtual personal assistants, mental health virtual support, education support platforms, and others.
- At present, three main versions of ChatGPT have been released: ChatGPT-3, ChatGPT-3.5, and ChatGPT-4 (at the time of writing this book).
- ChatGPT-4 is capable of handling the communication in the form of images too.

- ChatGPT-4 is a multimodal model of AI chatbot that can provide more accurate, highly personalized, and multi-mode communication.
- The advanced version of ChatGPT can perform image analysis along with the captioning abilities and it can also understand humor and sarcasm in the natural language formats.
- Improved ability to create better narrative and story creativity in multiple languages simultaneously.
- Ability to interpret more technical and complex scientific communication and provide the solution to the most complex problems with the help of strong and enhanced reasoning and logical capabilities.
- ChatGPT-3 was trained on the data of as much as 45 TB of text data, which may be equivalent to 1 million feet book shelf space!
- Plagiarism detection is also supported by ChatGPT.

Generative Modeling

Generative modeling is a subdomain of modern generative AI. It is used to develop generative applications with the help of generative models that work on the basis of two main principles referred to as statistics and probability for generating a presentation of the perceived or detected target values or phenomena from the data observations that were learnt through ML models.

The following are the other main features and characteristics of generative modeling:

- The generative modeling is commonly used in unsupervised ML through deep neural networks.
- The basic principles to generate content through generative application is to use the capabilities of probability and statistical analysis.
- The modeling enables the computers to learn from the real-world environment and maps the learning for generating new and unique content based on the test dataset or queries asked by the users.
- The understanding achieved by the computers through unsupervised ML models through deep neural networks is used to predict all possibilities about the subject in consideration from the modeled data.

- To materialize a regenerative model in the field of regenerative modeling, you need huge volumes of real-world data to train on the models from a wide range of parameters of the data so that a perfect matching of the data distribution is accomplished.

- The learned data or distribution is mapped with the queried data to generate a unique set of content automatically.

- The generative modeling is capable of building numerous types of models that can generate content in the form of text, images, videos, voices, simulations, and other presentations.

Generative Artificial Intelligence Models

Generative artificial intelligence or Gen-AI, as the name indicates, is a type of AI that is capable of generating the content or response against any given query or question. This is very imperative to keep in mind that AI is a broader field in which the most important aspect of the domain is referred to as ML. The ML is a technology that enables the machines to learn and make decisions autonomously without any explicit intervention of human resources. Most of those ML technologies are used as predictive models of ML from the input data used as both training and testing purposes. But the generative AI field is a step ahead.

Generative AI is a type of ML model that is used to train the machines to generate response in different forms of content such as text, images, videos, or other designs similar to an expert professional (human) who can come up with a detailed response when he/she is asked to provide the answer to a question. The advanced generative AI models are trained not only on one specific field but also on the entire knowledge available in the world at different sources. The example of such generative AI model is ChatGPT. The earlier ML models such as supervised, unsupervised, or even semi-supervised ML models were trained to predict or estimate the outcome when they are asked or countered with the test data or environment. But they were not able to generate a suitable response in different kinds of contexts that the human can understand about what the machine is saying. The generative models can do that job.

The following are the main features and characteristics of modern generative AI models[57,58]:

- Generative AI models can generate response in the form of a range of content types such as text, images, videos, or others against the queries or questions put up by human to the machine or model.

- A good example of generative AI model is ChatGPT platform.
- It is an algorithm that is able to learn and create new content such as computer code, text, simulations, images, and videos.
- Generative models are used to explore the training data and discover the underlying structure, patterns, and other attributes in the unlabeled data ingested into the generative models powered by deep neural networks.
- It can also understand art, music, and technology and produce the most suitable response to queries like a domain-expert human professional does.
- It can generate art and designs through additional training of the generative models such as DALL-E module, which is also a part of the ChatGPT-4 platform.
- The output of generative models is considered as a bit uncanny and less accurate as compared to the human-generated content.
- Generative AI models can extensively be applied in a wide range of industries such as writing industries, academics, education and training, healthcare, ecommerce, computer coding or software development, marketing, and many others.
- The generative AI models can be traced back to the 1960s when they were tried to implement into the chatbots.
- The building of generative adversarial networks (GANs) in 2014 was the first modern generative algorithm to create authentic images, audios, and videos of real people.
- The GAN models opened up the new domains of positives and negatives in almost all types of industries ranging from content-based industries to cybersecurity.
- The emergence of deep-fake concept has also been triggered with the emergence of advanced generative AI models.
- Two additional models of ML named as transformers and natural language processing models have opened up new areas for generative AI models to produce more reliable, accurate, and meaningful content. Both transformers and NLP models of ML are effectively used in the development of ChatGPT platform to produce the reliable content.
- Transformer technology is a type of ML model that is able to train the machines with extensively huge volumes of content without any explicit labeling on them so that billions of pages of content can easily be ingested into the ML models. They are also able to interconnect or establish connection between different words, pages, paragraphs, and books in all domains of technologies. This capability of transformer is referred to as the "Attention", which is a new notion in this field.

- There are improvements and enhancements in the large language models (LLM), which are also the forms of ML and work to complement the main generative AI models to produce the most accurate text, images, and other content because LLMs support multi-billion parameters of language.
- Another major improvement or advancement in the field of generative AI is the support of multimodal AI, which enables the generative models to produce the content in multiple formats such as text, images, voice, videos, and others.
- The most important use cases of generative AI models include the following:
  - Customer support, technical support, and other customer care domains through online Gen-AI-based chatbots.
  - Deployment of deep-fakes to mimic specific individuals or general peoples.
  - Enhancements in entertainment content dubbing and education presentation and other content fine-tuning.
  - The creation of a wide range of text content such as emails, articles, essays, resumes, papers, social media posts, summaries, and many more.
  - The creation of photorealistic art in customized styles.
  - Discoveries of different types of drug combinations and other healthcare-related improvements in an extensively knowledgeable environment.
  - Enhancement in designing of modern chips and other technological designs based on the extensive knowledge of multiple technologies simultaneously.
  - Designing new products and infrastructures.
- The most important examples of generative tools or platforms in the marketplace at this time are as follows:
  - Text generative tools such as ChatGPT & AI-Writer, Japer, and Lex.
  - Image generative tools include DALL-E, Stable Diffusion, and MidJourney.
  - MuseNet, Amper, and Dadabots are a few examples of music generative tools,
  - GitHub Copilot, CodeStarter, Codex, and Tabnine are good examples of code development tools.
  - Listnr, Descript, and Podcast AI are good tools for voice synthesis.
  - Many more are expected to emerge in the market soon.

Types of Generative Artificial Intelligence Models

The AI models can further be categorized into two major domains in terms of their respective objectives to achieve through machines. Those two main types or categories of AI are as follows:

- Predictive AI models
- Generative AI models

The predictive AI has been on the marketplace for many years now. The main objective of AI models based on the predictive category is to learn from the data ingested in the form of training datasets to predict the outcome automatically. These types of models were not designed to learn from the data and generate the content in different forms to provide response to the users. There were a few preprogrammed tools or software such as chatbots which were able to do this, but their depth or level of response was limited to a few preprogrammed responses. They were not efficient enough to cover all types of communications or conversations of a user in the real-world environment to generate a suitable response. The predictive models are used to learn about the environment and then make decisions based on the prediction estimated out of previous understanding or learning through training datasets. It was not able to perform the following tasks for instance[59]:

- Estimation of probability distribution
- Approximation of generating content
- Covering a wide range of fields

To overcome the problems to understand the most complicated and multi-dimensional data space and estimate the most suitable response in the form of content such as text, image, simulation, video, voice, or other forms of communication, new models of AI were introduced. Those models are commonly categorized into generative models. Almost all generative models used in the modern ML applications or tools are based on the neural networks, which are based on multiple hidden layers to assess and estimate the data to a greater level, commonly referred to as deeper levels. Those generative networks used neural networks with many hidden layers; therefore, they are also referred to as deep generative models. The generative models in the modern and advanced applications are commonly referred to as deep generative models (DGM).[59,60]

There are numerous deep generative models that are used by different ML applications and tools. A few of those main deep generative models include the following:

- Deep belief networks (DBN)
- Restricted Boltzmann machine (RBM)

The deep generative models are largely emerging in the technological sphere for building different types of generative applications in recent years. Providing the full details of all those models here in this book will make it extremely lengthy (also unnecessary). Instead, a few of the most important deep learning models will be described with their salient features, functions, and capabilities in the subsequent sections of this chapter.

From the traditional perspective of ML and AI, the generative models, which are also referred to as the deep generative models in the modern technological domain, can also be further divided into other types or categories. The above-mentioned types of deep generative models fall in those broader categories of generative modeling in AI. The most common categories of generative AI can be classified as follows[59]:

- Probabilistic generative models
- Adversarial generative models
- Normalizing flow-based models

In the next few sections, some discussions on each category of the generative AI models are provided at length along with the types of models used in a particular category for materializing the modern generative tools or applications.

Probabilistic Generative Models

The probabilistic generative models are designed to estimate the data-distribution probability to generate the most suitable or matching response in the form of corresponding content. This uses the sampling from the data distribution to create a new sample. All types of models falling under this category use the probability of data distribution to explicitly model the response. The following are the most common types of generative models falling under this category:

- Variational autoencoder (VAE)
- Gaussian mixture model (GMM)
- Hidden Markov model (HMM)

Adversarial Generative Models

The most common approaches adopted behind these types of generative models consist of two main components or parts:

- Generator part
- Discriminator part

These two components of adversarial generative models of ML compete with each other in the formation of a suitable content response. For instance, the first part of this model tries to form a response that is indistinguishable between the samples of data from which it has mapped the response. The other part, known as discriminator, tries to distinguish or differentiate the content of generated message from the sample data so that a unique text is generated by the adversarial generative model of ML. The name *adversarial* clearly indicates that the model applies two opposite methods in generating the desired content.

The most common types of models that fall under the adversarial generative modeling category include the following:

- Generative adversarial network

Normalizing Flow-Based Models

Normalizing flow-based models are the latest types of models, which are used to overcome the inabilities of main generative models, such as probabilistic model VAE and adversarial model are named as generative adversarial network. Both these models are extensively used in the development of modern generative AI application. Both of them have a major drawback that they are unable to explicitly learn the probability density function of real data ingested into the models. The key concept behind the learning of probability of density function of real data is the complexity of the mathematical function to calculate to reach the conclusion with accurate outcome or output.

Normalizing flow-based model is an answer to overcome that problem of explicit learning of probability density function of real data. It uses the technique of normalizing flows, which is based on a powerful statistical tool for the estimation of density. In this technique, different sequences of invertible transformations are formed to learn the data distribution function. This also leads to learn the loss function of the model through negative log-likelihood.[61]

The other main features and characteristics of normalizing flow-based generative models are as follows:

- The mathematical formula of Jacobian Matrix and its determinant and change of variable theorem are used in this model at the back-end program.
- To reduce the complexity of real-world data distribution, a sequence of invertible transformation functions are used to transform the simple data distribution into complex one and keep transforming till the reliable output is achieved.
- The repletion of the value or variables is done through change of variable theorem to normalize the flow of variables to obtain the probability distribution of the finally targeted variable in the deep generative learning models.

- The most common models for normalizing flow-based modeling are as follows:
  - **NICE** – Nonlinear independent component estimation
  - **RealNVP** – Real-valued non-volume preserving
  - **GLOW** – Extension of NICE and RealNVP models
- A few techniques or methods are used for autoregressive flows:
  - **MADE** – Masked autoencoder for distribution estimation
  - **PixelRNN** – Deep generative model for images
  - **WaveNet** – Deep generative model for audio signals
  - **MAF** – Masked autoregressive flow
  - **IAF** – Inverse autoregressive flow

Introduction to Most Popular Generative Models

A wide range of categories in terms of different features such as functionalities, features, processes, and levels of regenerative models were discussed in the previous section. A large number of sub-techniques or submodels are used for different types of regenerative AI applications. The following are the most common and most popular models used in modern regenerative AI applications:

- **Variational Autoencoder** – VAE is one of the most popular generative models used in modern generative AI applications. It is based on the probability distribution of attributes in the data that means the observed data (ingested through training datasets) is described through probabilistic distribution of latent attributes of the data in a latent space. The latent space is a matrix-like space where the probabilistic value of an attribute of observed data is presented. The output is generated based on the probabilistic distribution of data when encountered with the similar types of queries. The probability distribution is developed for each latent attribute of the data ingested into the machine powered by neural networks carrying out unsupervised ML process. For example, a VAE model is trained for an image with a large number of similar types of images. The model will generate a probability distribution for a wide range of latent attributes such as skin color, lips, width, length, eyes, nose, and many others. A matrix-type latent space is generated for multiple latent attributes of the images. A probabilistic value of each attribute is developed. When a query regarding an image is encountered with the model, it will generate a similar type of image out of those probabilistic attribute values or distribution. The probabilistic distribution is a probability of the attribute distributed over a possibility space; it is not a discrete value that can be calculated through mathematical formulas. Thus, the latent attributes are converted into probability distribution in this model. This model consists of two parts – one part is known as recognition model in which the input training dataset is converted into a probability distribution and the other part of the model is known as the regenerative model, which is used to develop or create an output out of the probability distribution of attributes.[62]

- **Gaussian Mixture Model (GMM)** –GMM in generative modeling of AI field is a probabilistic type of model. It is used to make the machines learn on the basis of the probable values of the latent attributes of the input data. The main assumption of this model is that it considers that all data points are generated from a large mixture of finite number of Gaussian distribution with unknown parameters. In other words, it can be put that the generalization of k-means clustering is used to incorporate the covariance structure of data along with the centers of the latent Gaussians. It uses the expectation–maximization (EM) algorithm for fitting the mixture-of-Gaussian models.[63]

- **Hidden Markov Model** – This is another very important and extensively used generative AI model in the development of modern generative applications like ChatGPT and others. It is a statistical model and commonly used in a wide range of applications of ML projects. This model is deployed to analyze the unobservable events that depend on the internal factors or attributes, which are not directly observables. It describes evolution of observable events to understand the underlying factors of the events. They are used for predicting the sequence of unknown variables from a set of observable events. It is used to observe the Markov chain and find out the probabilistic distribution of the events from the previous sequences of events. This model is extensively deployed in the generative applications that deal with speech recognition, speed analysis, handwriting recognition, sequence classification, activity recognition, machine translation, parts of speech tagging, time series analysis, and many others.[64]

- **Generative Adversarial Network** – The GAN is a type of adversarial models. It is extensively used in image generation, text generation, and video synthesis applications. This model consists of two components in the forms of deep neural networks – one is known as generator and the other one is discriminator. Both are two unstable neural networks that work in competition with each other. The generator network generates a synthetic sample out of the given input, which is taken as the random noise to generate the samples that resemble the original sample of training data and pass it to the discriminator, which tries to distinguish both samples and finds out the dissimilarities in the samples and sends back to generator to create more unique sample. This continuous flow makes the output highly unique and accurate. The discriminator every time tries to distinguish between the real and generated samples. This competition continues till the generator part of the model creates a sample that is difficult for the discriminator to distinguish which is real and which is synthetic sample.[65]

Problem-Solving Scope of ChatGPT

Before diving into the broad scope of problem-solving field of ChatGPT, let us state that ChatGPT is a generative model that provides the response to the queries made through natural language spoken by human. It provides unique and novel response against the query made to the platform rather than just selecting any predefined response from the given list. Therefore, it has a much broader scope in solving a wide range of problems not only in the business spectrum but also in our day-to-day social life. There are many domains of industries and sectors of modern businesses where the problem-solving capabilities of ChatGPT can be utilized. A few of them are as follows:

- Education and training industry
- Mathematics and statistics
- Research and development
- General content generation
- Customer relationship management
- Marketing and sales

The most important aspect of the support provided by ChatGPT is that it can provide you with the most matching response to your query for almost all types of problems and their respective solutions regarding numerous processes and fields of learning. Those responses can provide you with the most suitable answers to difficult questions that require huge level of domain specialization and experience. It is also capable of providing the explanations to the most difficult tasks, scientific facts, concepts, processes, theorems, and other deeper principles of science, arts, culture, politics, and other fields. You can also get detailed suggestions for making any difficult decision. The suggestions provided by the ChatGPT platform will be highly informed and innovative because it has been trained on a gigantic data that cannot be understood by any domain expert or industry specialist. There is no chance of skipping any information that has been ingested and understood by the model. It has huge capability to merge all types of conditions, constraints, experiences, and other areas into a final suggestion. The guidance provided by ChatGPT in the form of text or any other content such as image, video, simulation, formula, or voice is based on the entire understanding of the world about that particular topic. Therefore, the scope of ChatGPT in solving problems of industries and human is huge.

Let us figure out the solutions that it can provide[66]:

- ChatGPT can provide you with the factual answers from history, science, discoveries, geography, politics, sociology, economics, and all other domains that have been established in the field of education and academics.

- It can provide proper explanations for all types of concepts that you are not able to understand properly. You can solve your problem by asking ChatGPT again and again to explain the concepts, definitions, and theorems simply and clearly.

- If you are not able to distinguish between two concepts or domains, you can get help from ChatGPT to solve your problem through simple and categorical differentiation between the two similar looking concepts or things.

- ChatGPT can help you solve your problems of verification of your knowledge or concepts in a clear and intuitive way.

- You can solve a wide range of mathematical problems with the help of ChatGPT by getting detailed and easy-to-grasp explanations of the mathematical concepts, theorems, principles, equations, and other calculations.

- If you are stuck in research work and unable to find the most suitable data for clarifying your assumptions, you can get highly professional-level help from ChatGPT platform.

- Generating different forms of text content is another major area of ChatGPT where it can solve a wide range of issues of users such as creating an article on numerous topics, paraphrasing any existing content, summarizing the bulky content, proofreading the documents, correcting grammatical issues, streamlining the writings with numerous standards, creating banners, marketing content, emails, letters, contracts, and many other types of documents. This is in fact the most powerful capability of ChatGPT.

- If you are lacking in general knowledge and current affairs, ChatGPT is a perfect tool to solve your problem of lacking in general knowledge for a wide range of areas that are common in our day-to-day life.

- The development of creative and innovative content in the field of arts, culture, business, or even in other domains is another major task that ChatGPT can accomplish perfectly to improve the efficiency of a human being.

- Decision-making is one of the most difficult areas, where highly experienced, innovative, and learned human resources are hired for extremely high salaries. ChatGPT is able to help you make the most accurate and informed decisions based on the past data, patterns, outcomes, failures, successes, and many other aspects.

- Developing the most advanced special-purpose applications such as chatbots, social media agents, online education agents, conversational AI systems, customer support agents, virtual assistants, and other similar types of roles and platforms is a major capability or scope of ChatGPT platform.

- Your problem to solve automated tagging, sentiment analysis, part of speech tagging, and other such processes is a notable area of this platform.

- Providing highly personalized and customized solutions to a wide range of roles and domains is a good scope of ChatGPT problem-solving capabilities.

- Enhancing the business settings is another very crucial area of application of ChatGPT to improve the efficiency of business processes, streamlining the business activities, and reducing the cost of processes and activities.

History of Generative Models

The concept of generative models can be traced with the advent of computing machines to accomplish the tasks that a man can do. In the beginning, the generative modeling was very limited in capabilities and features. Those concepts of generative modeling can be traced back to the 1950s and 1960s when the development of chatbots like ELIZA was introduced. That was a very limited type of automated application for generating response to the queries or the questions asked by the users. All those primary applications were rule-based generative models and they would choose the predefined response through software code against the limited number of actions or queries that it could accept. Otherwise, it would reply that it could not understand what the question or instructions are given to the model(s).

This work moved on at a very slow pace and all those applications could not find much business space or use cases in the real-world applications. Different approaches and projects continued for many decades till the year 2014 when the start of a new era of generative modeling emerged. The development of modern GAN was the beginning of modern generative modeling ecosystem. After that point, the growth of generative AI modeling is exponential and new areas of generative AI-based applications are emerging in the marketplace to revolutionize this emerging technology. The history of the development of modern generative AI models can be classified into three main areas:

- Natural language processing field
- Computer vision (CV) field
- Transformer Field

The NLP domain started its journey with the development of ELIZA chatbot, which was rule-based limited-capability bot for materializing the natural language–based human conversation in the practical world. Later on, the advanced version of the NLP application was developed which was named _"N-gram"_. It was an advanced application that could create very short sentences in natural language with many other limitations and constraints. However, it was the primary stage of the data distribution concept. The development of recurrent neural networks (RNN) overcame the limitations faced by the earlier N-gram platform. It could generate longer sentences with greater effectiveness. With the passage of time, the development of long short-term memory (LSTM) and gated recurrent unit (GRU) enhanced the power of attending tokens up to 200 and more. The memory control was possible through gated mechanism in those models. Later on, the transformers made the things even better.

The CV was traditionally in the technological spheres with limited capabilities and features such as texture synthesis and image mapping techniques. The hand-design features would be used in those methods with simple images. With the advent of modern models such as GAN, the CV field took the speed. The advancements in this field continued with the emergence of diffusion generative models and VAE models to generate highly refined images in the field of CV.

The transformer structure models became the most advanced and powerful architectures for not only NLP applications but also for all CV processes. The combination of transformer and NLP is the result of modern ChatGPT platform. Similarly, the use of vision transformers and SWIN transformers (Swift-Window transformer) have taken the CV to new heights nowadays.

The chronicle development or evolution of generative AI modeling is as follows[67,68]:

- **1950s** – The development of HMM and GMM for generating time series and sequential data.
- **1960** – Development of ELIZA rule-based chatbot robot.
- **1970** – The NLP application N-gram was released. It was a statistical language model for performing tasks like speech recognition, text prediction, and others.
- **1980s** – Emergence of numerous artificial neural networks (ANN) and backpropagation algorithms for ML.
- **1997** – Development of LSTM for removing discrepancies in sequence prediction.

- **2000–2010** – The exponential growth of structured and unstructured data that paved the ways for faster growth of ANN for materializing generative AI models in numerous areas.
- **2013** – The release of VAE model for generating new data from the original data distribution but unique in nature.
- **2014** – Development of GRU.
- **2014** – Development of Show-Tell multimodal generative model for the CV field based on RNN.
- **2014** – The release of revolutionary generative model referred to as generative adversarial network (GAN for CV applications.
- **2016** – Another version of GAN model "StackGAN" was developed for the development of an image based on the text description as an input.
- **2017** – Image captioning model "StyleNet" was developed. It was based on neural network architecture.
- **2017** – This year, two major advancements were noticed – the development of transformers and the advanced version of VAE model "Vector Quantized Variational Autoencoder" (VQ-VAE) for vision language field.
- **2018** – StyleGAN and RevNet models were developed for the advanced applications in the field of CV.
- **2018** – The launch of Google BERT platform for NLP.
- **2019** – ChatGPT version 2 was released. It was trained with 1.5 billion parameters.
- **2019** – The release of Visual BERT and ViLBERT (Vision and Language BERT) platforms by Google Corporation.
- **2020** – The release of ChatGPT version 3 with 175 billion parameters.
- **2021** – The launching of image development model DALL-E by OpenAI.
- **2022** – Commercial launch of ChatGPT in November 2022.
- **2023** – The launch of advanced version of ChatGPT-4.

A Glimpse of ChatGPT Statistics

ChatGPT is a highly powerful NLP-based software platform that can understand, learn, and respond to the human communication effectively. Being an innovative and advanced invention in this fast-paced field of AI, ChatGPT is doing great wonders not only in the field of modern business but also in the technological spheres simultaneously. This application, developed by OpenAI group, has set new records in numerous domains in terms of amazing statistics. A few very important statistics of ChatGPT that can boggle your mind are summarized here[69-71]:

- It is the first of its kind platform that grew at over 9900% during the initial 60 days of its launch in the marketplace.
- Reached 1 million users within just five days!
- There were about 200 million users of ChatGPT in April 2023.
- As many as 9600 keywords are used for accessing the ChatGPT chatbot service.
- The United States, India, and Japan are the largest user countries in a descending order.
- It uses reinforcement learning from human feedback (RLHF) as a training method from the responses that are provided by the users to improve the efficiency, accuracy, and reliability of the responses.
- The knowledge base is updated till 2021 (at the time of writing this book).
- The training dataset size consists of over 300 billion of words and over 570 GB of Wikipedia, crawled websites, and books online.
- As of 2023, over 10 million queries are received by ChatGPT.
- The forecast revenue of the platform by 2023 is about US$200 million and about US$1 billion by 2024.
- ChatGPT-4 was launched on 13 March 2023.
- The commercial version for public was released on 30 November 2022. It was the free version named as ChatGPT-3.
- It can generate code in a wide range of computer programming languages for users such as Python, JavaScript, Shell, SQL, C++, C#, Swift, Typescript, Ruby, Java, PHP, Go, and others.
- ChatGPT is available in over 162 countries at present.
- The group behind the development of ChatGPT is OpenAI, which is valued at about US$29 billion in the year 2023.
- The average cost to run ChatGPT service in 2023 is about US$3 million per month that can increase to higher value with the increased number of users.
- ChatGPT Plus service was launched for public with advanced features and capabilities in March 2023 with the initial monthly charge of US$20.
- The main platforms behind the building of ChatGPT are LLMs of families such as OpenAI ChatGPT-3.5 and ChatGPT-4.
- The top masterminds behind the development of ChatGPT include Sam Altman and Ilya Sutskever.
- Thousands of A100 GPUs were used to train the ChatGPT model.

- The total hardware of the ChatGPT model consists of 10,000 GPUs, over 285,000 CPU cores, and a network connection of over 400 Gbps per GPU server.
- The cloud computing platform used by ChatGPT is Microsoft Azure.
- More than 26 languages are supported by the ChatGPT model at this time (at the time of writing this book).
- The allied products of ChatGPT that are developed by OpenAI include DALL-E for images through text, CLIP for text-image connection, Whisper for language translation, and GPT for writing articles, and codes.
- The main challenger or competitors of OpenAI ChatGPT include Google BART, BERT, Microsoft Bing AI, DeepMind Sparrow, Character AI, and others.

OpenAI Conversational Model

OpenAI is an organization that develops the open-source conversational models for processing different types of natural conversation in the form of text, voice, image, and video. The main OpenAI conversational models include GPT-3.5 and ChatGPT-4 models. These models use the following technologies, platforms, and tools:

- NLP model for natural language communication.
- Deep neural networks for training of the models with huge volumes of datasets.
- RLHF training model is used to keep learning from the communication of the users by incorporating the feedback of the users.
- It uses GPT technique for advanced architecture of comprehensive conversational communication based on NLP and CV so that huge volumes of data with billions of parameters can be ingested effectively.

Transfer Learning Model Used in ChatGPT

It is very important to note that it is very difficult to train a ML model, especially in the field of generative AI to create response to the queries of the people in natural language with greater level of accuracy. It costs huge money and time as well. It requires a large amount of data ingested by the model to learn and provide the solution for a particular problem. To save this huge amount of training data and efforts, the transfer learning is used to make the training of the model a bit easier. The transfer learning is the process to transfer the learning of machines to solve a problem with the help of training of large datasets to the other machine as the starting point and adding more training datasets for other problems. This transfer of learning of a problem from one model to anther model is known as transfer learning.

For example, one model is trained for solving a problem A. It has completed the training through huge amount of datasets and desirable results have been achieved. This model can then be transferred to other model to set the starting point of training further from that point. Thus, a huge amount of data, efforts, and time can be saved easily. This method is very useful for fine-tuning the models used in the ChatGPT model. The previous models such as ChatGPT-1, ChatGPT-2, GPT-3, and others were transferred for generating the advanced versions of the ML models in this series. For fine-tuning of ChatGPT, the following main techniques have been used[72]:

- Proximal policy optimization (PPO)
- Trust region policy optimization (TRPO)

Proximal Policy Optimization

This is a technique used in reinforcement learning to establish a balance between comprehension and performance. It is used as a fine-tuning technique in the ML models. It is also known as the state-of-the-art technique in reinforcement learning model. It is referred to as model-less reinforcement learning. PPO was developed by OpenAI for the optimization or fine-tuning of ChatGPT in 2017. This technique is based on competitive type of learning method. Other main features of PPO are as follows[73]:

- It is used for optimizing the loss function in the ML model of ChatGPT.
- As the name indicates, it optimizes the model based on the policy that means only policy is updated and reward model is not changed or modified.
- It is used as policy gradient method in ChatGPT optimization.
- It is similar to TRPO with more stable updates.
- The baseline of PPO is the combination of policy gradient methods such as TRPO and natural policy gradient.

Trust Region Policy Optimization

TRPO is another very important technique or algorithm used for the optimization or fine-tuning of ChatGPT platform. This technique is based on the natural policy gradient algorithms. The main objective of this fine-tuning mechanism is to make sure that updates of the model remain within trustworthy policy area or regions. The other salient features and character-istics of TRPO are as follows[74]:

- It is a type of reinforcement learning algorithm that is developed on the foundation of natural policy gradient algorithms.
- This technique was developed by OpenAI's Schulman in 2015 for optimization of the ChatGPT models.
- It incorporates the previous work accomplished by Amari and Kakade, and others.
- It is considered as the successor of natural policy gradient and pre-decessor of PPO methods.
- It is capable of solving the main problems of natural policy gradient (such as it being unable to determine learning rates and unable to stop overshooting or stalling of the process).
- It is a complex mechanism, which is difficult to understand, or explain its parts and points, deploy the code, debug the problems, and train the model.

Introduction to Large Language Model

LLMs are a type of NLP models that are capable of learning natural language massively with the help of billions of parameters to produce the most accurate text and other content. It is extensively used for the generative AI applications such as ChatGPT platform and others. The LLMs are deep learning models based on deep neural networks. Different types of LLMs are used in the mod-ern generative applications in the marketplace. The main application that uses a type of LLM is ChatGPT. It uses the transformer architecture, which is a type of LLM. These types of models are trained on huge volumes of datasets with multimillion parameters and billions of words and symbols used in the modern natural language. It is a highly capable model that expands the exist-ing capabilities and capacities of numerous generative AI models in terms of their inference, understanding, learning, contexts, and other parameters. As far as the parameters of different NLP generative applications are concerned, the ChatGPT-4 platform is capable of handling over 1 trillion parameters. Thus, it can use the most advanced versions of LLMs more efficiently and effectively to produce the most reliable and trustworthy content.

The main features and characteristics of LLMs and their types are as follows[75,76]:

- The development of modern LLMs was noticed in 2017 based on the transformer neural networks.

- LLMs are also known as the foundation models coined by Stanford University.
- It needs huge volumes of data for training the models such as petabytes of data or so. This is the reason that the LLMs are also known for the ingestion of corpus of data.
- The LLMs are used in different applications for accomplishing the tasks such as text generation, content summary, translation, sentiment analysis, rewriting content, classification of content, and others.
- An example of highly efficient and large LLM is GPT-3, which is the foundation of ChatGPT platform in both freemium and plus versions.
- The LLMs are classified on the following basis:
  - **Zero-Shot Model** – The type of model that is trained on huge volumes or corpus of generic data to produce an accurate and reliable result without any additional training is known as zero-shot model of LLM. An example of zero-shot model is GPT-3 foundation model of ChatGPT.
  - **Domain-Specific Model** – This is a type of model, which needs additional training on the zero-shot model to make it domain-specific or more fine-tuned for a particular area of field. The examples of OpenAI models that run on the foundation of GPT-3 such as Codex and others are domain-specific models.
  - **Language Representation Model** – It is a type of model that is a combination of deep learning and transformer to accomplish the NLP-based regenerative tasks. The example of such model is Bidirectional Encoder Representations from Transformers (BERT) by Google Corporation.
  - **Multimodal Models** – Originally, the LLM was developed for processing NLP in the form of text. But later on additional models were integrated into the LLMs to process both text and images simultaneously. Such combined models are known as multimodal models. The example of such application includes the ChatGPT-4 platform.
- LLMs are based on deep neural networks, especially transformer architectures, which are a type of deep neural networks capable of handling billions of parameters or variables to understand and regenerate the content in terms of wider context, sentimental analysis, and patters of very complex types of language expressions.
- The most important capability of LLMs, especially transformer architecture, used in the ChatGPT platform is the self-attention. The self-attention capability of LLMs is able to weigh all types of words and phrases in a particular or given context. Thus, the language processing model became so capable of handling multibillion context-based

parameters of words, sentences, or phrases in a complex natural language expression.

- Transformer architecture is one of the most fundamental models based on LLMs that is used in ChatGPT platforms. There are three main types of transformer architecture–based LLMs:
  - **Autoregressive Language Model** – This type of model based on transformer architecture predicts the next word based on the previous word. These models are fine-tuned by training through large datasets to maximize the prediction capabilities to predict the most accurate word to come after the given word. The main example of this type of LLM is used in the ChatGPT services, both ChatGPT-3 and ChatGPT-4, which derive their names from generative pretrained transformer.
  - **Autoencoding Language Model** – This type of model learns the capability to generate a fixed-size vector representation for input text by recreating the original input from the corrupt version of the input text. This vector representation is also known as embedding. This model is exclusively trained for predicting the missing words in a sentence through surrounding words and context. This type of model is able to perform a wide range of fine-tuning tasks such as named entity recognition, sentiment analysis, question and answers, and others. The example of such model is the BERT developed by the team of Google Corporation for NLP processing applications.
  - **Combination of Above-Mentioned Models** – The combination of both autoencoding language model and autoregressive language model offers the features and capabilities of both models. This combination is used in T5 model.
- LLMs consist of numerous building blocks. The following are the most important building blocks:
  - **Attention** – This is the most powerful capability of LLM that is used to assign a weight to the words or its parameters in terms of different contexts. This enables the model to choose the relevant word in terms of content to generate a new message and leave the irrelevant parameter to decrease the discrepancies in the output message generated based on the input. The example of attention used in the transformer architecture is self-attention. It is used in the ChatGPT platform.
  - **Tokenization** – The conversion of a sequence of text into sub-words, words, and tokens is known as tokenization process. This splits different words and sentences into smaller parts and tokenize them so that the model can easily understand the message in the sequence of text.

- **Embedding** – The presentation of tokens or words in a continuous vector form that captures the semantic meaning of tokens and words in a high-dimensional space is known as embedding. This building block enables the LLM to capture complex relationship between words, sub-words, and tokens.

- **Transfer learning** – The learning achieved in the previous training process is transferred to the next model as the initial point to save the retraining of a model from the scratch for solving a wide range of problems – this is known as transfer learning. Transfer learning is one of the most important building blocks of an LLM. This component also enables the models to benefit from generic training of machines through general data corpus on the Internet and websites.

- **Pretraining** – The pretraining building block of LLMs refers to the primary training of the model before additional domain-specific training is called the pretraining process. This is given through huge volumes of dataset through either unsupervised or self-supervised training in which the model is enabled to learn relationships between words, language patterns, and other fundamental parts of a natural language.

- The following are the most common examples of LLMs used in different generative AI applications in the marketplace:
  - ChatGPT-3 and ChatGPT-4
  - GPT-NeoX and GPT-Neo
  - Gopher and DeepMind Chinchilla
  - Google MT5 and Switch Transformer
  - DistilBERT and XLNet
  - Google GLaM (Generalist Language Model) and LaMDA (Language Model for Dialogue Applications)

Reinforcement Learning from Human Feedback

RLHF is a type of ML model based on reinforcement learning technique, which uses reward and punishment formula for maximizing the reward value of the model. This model is extensively used in many modern language generative applications. The most important of them is the ChatGPT platform, which uses this model for improving the quality or effectiveness of the responses generated by ChatGPT. It does this by taking the feedback from the human or the users of the application through different categories such as thumbs-up, thumbs-down, and average sign.[77]

In this technique, the reward model of ChatGPT is trained by taking the feedback directly from the users or human interveners. This capability enables the ChatGPT platform to benefit from the expertise of users to assess the response generated by the model by receiving the valuable input in the form of comment from the users. The input is taken from the users through icons located at the top-right corner of the response generated by the application against the query prompted through typing in natural language, as shown in Figure 2.1.

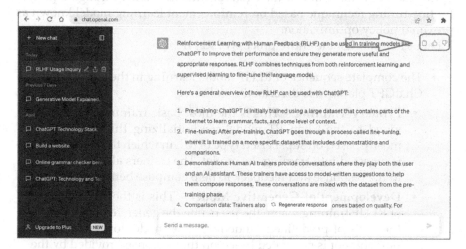

FIGURE 2.1
ChatGPT response area.

Once the user clicks on the icons (marked in Figure 2.1), an additional pop-up window for receiving the additional customer feedback in natural language message appears with proper field to type the desired comment(s), as shown in Figure 2.2.

FIGURE 2.2
Additional human feedback interface on ChatGPT.

The users will be prompted to type in the message regarding their respective experience in the given field and click the submit feedback button to send the input for further assessment and evaluation of the performance of the ChatGPT platform. This entire process is used for taking feedback from the users, and later on this feedback is subjected to automated assessment with the help of modern reinforcement learning model RLHF.

The RLHF model is used as the reward function by ChatGPT for optimization of the response. The maximization of performance process involves the optimization of the policy of the agent of this ML model through a powerful fine-tuning technique based on reinforcement learning model known as proximal policy optimization.

Let us summarize the entire process of RLHF.[77,78]

- The complete sequence of RLHF model learning in the context of the ChatGPT platform is described as follows:
    - **Primary Training** – This is the most basic training that is provided to the ChatGPT model for initializing this model. It is mostly based on supervised type of ML in which the labeled data is ingested into training the model. The trainers also have access to the response and feedback to help compose better responses.
    - **Development of Generative Model** – This is the second phase of RLHF training where the users rate the generated response on the basis of predefined guidelines. The model for rewards and punishment is generated based on the response provided by the users in the form of feedback to assess the behavior and quality of the response generated by the application.
    - **Fine-Tuning** – This stage uses different techniques such as PPO and others to fine-tune the quality of the generated response.
- Thumbs-up impression is used as high reward and thumbs-down is used as low reward in this technique of optimization.
- This technique is able to improve the quality by learning the context, behavior, and other parameters of the user feedback.
- The feedback from the human is used as the loss function for the optimization of ChatGPT model and others of similar types.

Cloud Computing and ChatGPT

Cloud computing has played a vital role in the development of this promising application of OpenAI, from the development through operations. The initial infrastructure used for the development of ChatGPT was the cloud computing platform of Microsoft Azure. On this platform, the entire coding, ML models, and other AI procedures were performed to make it the most amazing product in the present marketplace and technical arena. The role of cloud computing does not end here after the development and launching of ChatGPT platform; there are numerous other options and areas where the relationship of ChatGPT and cloud computing will grow exponentially. It is a new technology that has huge potential to be utilized in different types of businesses, processes, and use cases in the modern industrial world. The new areas of ChatGPT use in the cloud computing environment are evolving regularly. Numerous businesses are exploring the options to use this exciting platform in their respective services.

At the present time, ChatGPT platform has been identified by numerous industries to use for their respective business processes and activities. Some such industries and processes are as follows[79]:

- Translation applications
- Voice to text conversion, and vice versa
- Image development based on text input
- Customer relationship management in natural language
- Virtual assistance for diverse technologies and processes
- Personalization in digital marketing and social interactions
- Handling cognitive-intensive tasks with greater accuracy for complex environments

Software as a Service (SaaS) is one of the most cruising and promising areas in the cloud computing. There are numerous possibilities of ChatGPT to be used as a SaaS product in a wide range of industries, businesses, and markets. As mentioned earlier, ChatGPT is capable of accomplishing the following major tasks:

- Text creations
- Language translation
- Computer code creations
- Code debugging
- Technical document creation
- Video content or image creation

If integrated with numerous types of modern information technologies services and platforms such as cloud platforms for software development, entertainment, performing arts, content creation, human-interaction applications, and others through cloud computing platforms and infrastructure, ChatGPT can prove to be extremely useful for performing almost all types of automation in those kinds of processes perfectly. Microsoft Corporation and other big IT firms are exploring the options to integrate ChatGPT in their cloud services for numerous types of applications for a wide range of businesses and sectors. Thus, cloud computing is expected to become the most crucial component for ChatGPT in furthering the business use cases in which this platform can be used for performing innovative activities and automation.

Application Programming Interface

After the launch of ChatGPT platform for general users, the OpenAI Company decided to launch an application programming interface (API) for developers. This API enables the software developers to integrate the capabilities of ChatGPT into their different types of web-based services such as web applications, websites, chatting software, short message systems, code debugging platforms, and many others. The integration of ChatGPT through developer APIs makes this platform very useful for all types of developers and business people to explore and integrate the capabilities of ChatGPT into their respective business services and products.

For using APIs of ChatGPT, you need unique API key for integrating it into your web environments. Getting a ChatGPT API key is very easy and simple by following the below procedure step-by-step [80]:

- You need to create a free account with ChatGPT platform to generate a unique API key for integrating ChatGPT into your web environment. You can sign up with any Google or Microsoft account. It is important to note that your API key works well for both ChatGPT-3 and ChatGPT-4 simultaneously. Using ChatGPT through APIs is a paid service, which you have to pay for the service that you use.
- Login to your account and choose "API Keys" option. A list of different options appears to choose from.
- Click the "View API Keys" option from the list. The API key creation page with all existing secret keys appears.
- Click the "Create new secret key" option. The system automatically creates a secret API key for you to use in your web environments. *Note:* Keys are secret and unique for your exclusive use, so it should not be shared with any irrelevant person or entity.
- Click the billing option on your account page. The billing interface appears with other options to choose from.
- Choose the "Payment method" option for adding your payment methods and related account number or card number.

- You can check the different details of your account through different options such as limits, billing invoices, payment methods, and others.

Transformer Library

Transformer library is a platform that is used for transferring the pre-trained functions or tasks used in the ML models so that the lengthy and cumbersome work of training the ML model from scratch can be reduced. The most popular transformer library used in the modern ML applications, especially in the NLP field, is the HuggingFace library. A transformer library can support a wide range of modalities and their respective tasks[81,82]:

- **Natural Language Processing** – In the NLP modality, numerous tasks or functions are performed by the transformers to train the new ML model for processing the natural language:
  - Summarization
  - Question-answering
  - Text classification
  - Text generation
  - Named entity recognition
  - Language translation
  - Language modeling
- **Audio Data** – The most important activities that fall under the category of audio data processing that can be performed by the transformers include audio classification, automatic speech recognition, and others.
- **Computer Vision** – A few very important functions or tasks performed by the transformer in the CV modality may include image classification, image segmentation, object detection, and many others.
- **Multimodal** – The multimodal domain is combined or comprehensive modality, which deals with encompassing functionalities. A few of them include the following:
  - Information withdrawal from scanned docs
  - Optical character recognition (OCR)
  - Visual question-answering

- Table question-answering
- Video classification

Transformer libraries provide the API along with other tools for downloading a range of pretrained ML models in the above-mentioned modalities or domains. This capability of transformers reduces the efforts, time, computing resources, carbon footprint, power, and cost drastically for numerous types of ML models. The following are the most fundamental parts or sublibraries of a transformer library used for the modern NLP modality:

- **Transformers Sub-Library** – This sub-library deals with a wide range of functions or pretrained modules of ML that can be downloaded and deployed on your ML models to save initial work of your project. The main functions in this NLP sub-library include information extraction, named entity recognition, text classification, text generation, natural language inference, image captioning, and many others.
- **Tokenizers' Sub-Library** – The assignment of a unique value to the words in a sentence of a document is accomplished through the tokenizer functions. It divides the document into a large number of tokens. The most important algorithms deployed in the tokenizer library include PreTrainedTokenizerFast and PreTrainedTokenizer.
- **Datasets Sub-Library** – This sub-library is used to generalize the datasets for easy understanding through different evaluation metrics. The HuggingFace library supports about 10 evaluation metrics and over 100 datasets.

The transformer technology is one of the state-of-the-art technologies that use the libraries known as transformer library, especially the HuggingFace library. The main features and characteristics of transformer library are as follows:

- It is an open-source library.
- This supports the inoperability among the most popular platforms such as JAX, PyTorch, TensorFlow, and others.
- The supported formats of the code for downloading and deployment in other ML models include ONNX and TorchScript.
- For interference or deployment of the function on a new ML model is done through pipeline () to quickly train with TensorFlow or PyTorch.
- This supports all types of modalities commonly used in the modern ML applications such as NLP, CV, audio, and multimodal domains.
- It is very easy to use onboard and is developed for a wide range of audience such as ML engineers, researchers, scientists, and students.
- It is a state-of-the-art platform or models of libraries.

Python Programming Language for ChatGPT

ChatGPT has a very deep-rooted relationship with Python programming language and its concerned libraries. The core languages that were used for the development of ChatGPT platform included Python, PyTorch, and TensorFlow. Meanwhile, the use of ChatGPT in other types of modern computer programming is also very effective and easy through APIs provided by the ChatGPT platform. ChatGPT offers you with unique APIs to integrate them with your web environment to use the capabilities and power of ChatGPT for performing a wide range of software development tasks[83]:

- Creating code for a specific function through ChatGPT
- Debugging the code issues
- Creating data for testing purpose
- Asking questions to get the correct answer
- Advanced language modeling functions

Neural Network Technology in ChatGPT

Neural network technology is the baseline of ChatGPT platform. ChatGPT is based on the transformer technology, which is a kind of neural network with different layers of neural networks connected to provide comprehensive support for processing the NLP tasks commonly used in the modern ML applications, especially in the generative AI or ML field. The architecture of ChatGPT is a multi-block structure of neural networks that consist of the following components:

- Encoder network
- Decoder network

The connection between the neural networks is based on the hierarchical order of residual transformers, which are neural networks themselves. The main function of encoder network is to process the input data sequence to form contextual representations and the function of decoder network is to produce an output sequence by taking the contextual representations produced by the encoder. A third component known as residual unit, which sits in-between encoder and decoder, is used for two main purposes: generalization and learning.

Both encoder and decoder networks are forms of neural networks that consist of neurons and multiple layers commonly referred to as input layer, hidden layer, and output layer. The neurons generate the values and biases to process the input data to learn from it. They – encoder and decoder – are further divided into two layers known as attention layers and residual blocks. The attention block of encoder attends the input language to create contextual representation and the residual block of encoder establishes the relationship between the representations of encoder and decoder to enable the model to store long-distance information. Meanwhile, the attention layer of decoder deals with the contextual representations created by the encoder and creates new representations; the residual blocks, also neural networks, generate the output sequence. Thus, neural network plays a very crucial role in the materialization of ChatGPT NLP platform.

Deep Learning Technology in ChatGPT

Deep learning technology is the enhanced version of the neural network that can process the input data with hundreds of millions of features. The ChatGPT platform is constructed on the ChatGPT-3.5 architecture, which is a transformer-based highly deep learning model of neural networks. This architecture uses over 100 billion neurons interconnected into 100 layers of deep learning networks of this platform. Thus, deep learning sits at the core of the functionality, architecture, working process, and technology stack of ChatGPT.[85]

Natural Language Processing in ChatGPT

ChatGPT is a platform that is based on one of the most promising domains of AI known as natural language processing. ChatGPT realize the NLP field in practical use through machines by implementing a wide range of technologies into the technological architecture[86]:

- Neural networks
- Deep learning
- Machine learning

The NLP technology is a domain of technology that deals with the training, interpretation, and responding to the queries or communication put up to the machine in a very natural way like a human does. This objective is achieved by processing the naturally spoken and written language through machines in such a way that machines can easily understand the context, sentiments, meanings, and other expressions bound with the natural language that human uses for communication. The machines are also enabled to respond to the messages or communication queries put up by either a human or a machine that can imitate a human being.

ChatGPT is a platform that is developed to provide the most reliable and accurate responses in the natural language by understanding the queries or communication by human. The response should look similar to that generated by a human. ChatGPT platform has succeeded in achieving the most satisfactory response from the users in terms of its capability to provide the most accurate and reliable response to the queries put up by human.

How to Use ChatGPT Bot?

ChatGPT is designed to generate response to all types of queries made by a user in the form of a question or other statement. It works like a very well-informed machine that can provide a suitable response to your queries in all domains of education and knowledge. Using ChatGPT bot is very easy and intuitive. It can provide response in the form of text, image, and voice through the advanced version of the application. To use ChatGPT platform, you need to follow the below procedure step-by-step[87]:

- Register your account with the application. You need to visit https://chat.openai.com/ website to get your account registered. The login interface (or, similar to this) appears as in Figure 2.3.

FIGURE 2.3
Login interface of ChatGPT.

- Click the *Sign up* link. A new page with details on the ways to register for a new account appears, as shown in Figure 2.4. You can choose any one of the following options along with the password to register with the ChatGPT services:
  - Using your email address
  - Using your Microsoft account
  - Using your Google account
  - Using your Apple account

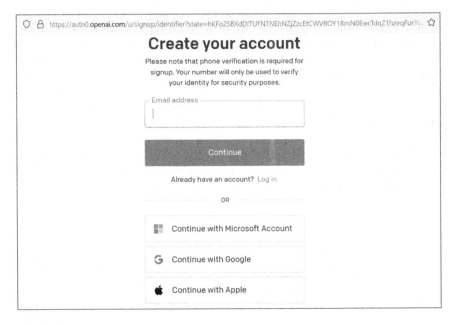

FIGURE 2.4
Creating an account for ChatGPT.

- Confirm a few terms and conditions in a wizard, as shown in Figure 2.5.

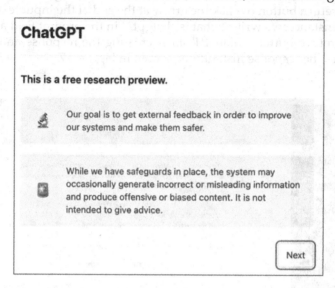

FIGURE 2.5
Declaration of ChatGPT service.

- Once you register with ChatGPT application, a page appears (shown in Figure 2.6) with different information blocks:
  - Examples of queries
  - Capabilities of ChatGPT
  - Limitations of ChatGPT

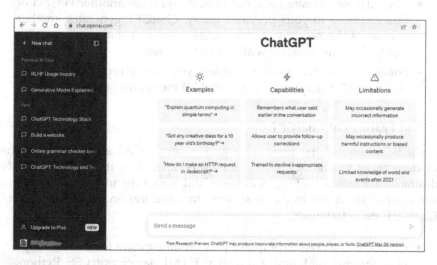

FIGURE 2.6
Different information about ChatGPT.

- Type your query or question in the "Send a message" field and hit the return button or click the arrow at the end of the input text field. For instance, we write "what is chatgpt?" in the prompt field and hit the return button. ChatGPT starts creating the response and completes the response instantly, as shown in Figure 2.7.

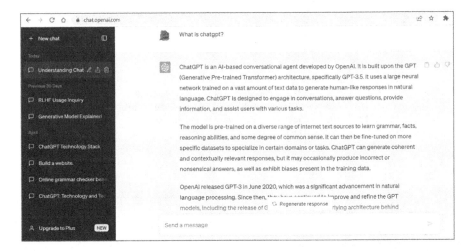

FIGURE 2.7
Response of ChatGPT to our sample query.

- The history of the queries is saved on the left pane with a record of past 30 days in the basic version of ChatGPT-3, as shown in Figure 2.7.
- Click the Regenerate response link, if you want another version of this response to your previous query. ChatGPT generates another version of the response to your query. You can continue repeating this till you are satisfied with the text generated.
- For asking another question or query, you need to type another question in the *"send a message"* field and hit the return button.

Salient Features of ChatGPT

ChatGPT is one of the most advanced generative AI applications in the modern era of technology. It has numerous capabilities that develop highly desirable features for all types of users and across the industrial spectrum simultaneously. A few of the most important features and characteristics of ChatGPT are as follows[88]:

- ChatGPT can create computer programming code for a wide range of programming languages such as HTML, JavaScript, CSS, Python, Java, and others.

- Debugging code in different languages quickly and accurately.
- Creation of marketing content such as banners, flyers, advertisements, slogans, mottos, marketing emails, and others.
- Translation of content from multiple languages such as English, French, Spanish, German, Russian, Hindi, and many others.
- Proposing different recipes for different types of foods popular in all main regions and countries of the world.
- Research content for all types of scientists, researchers, students, marketers, doctors, and other professionals across all domains of industries and knowledge.
- Creating summaries of a wide range of items such as books, websites, movies, stories, thesis, articles, essays, and many others.
- Creation of a numerous types of stories such as fiction stories, horror short stories, child stories, scientific fiction stories, and others.
- Providing general-purpose assistance for resolving certain knowledge-based queries, suggestions, explanations, and other questions in the minds of a common user.
- Understanding complex content in the natural language and providing summarized or rephrased content for easy understanding.
- Feature to maintain context and other abstractions during a multi-turn conversations in a multi-user environment.
- Offers a sentence-level control for different domains such as poetry, step-by-step procedure, formats, summaries, and other patterns of writings pertaining to the control of the sentences.
- Provides knowledge in a wide range of areas of the modern world such as general knowledge, science, engineering, psychology, medicine, healthcare, governmental procedures, legal matters, and many others at a unified one place.

Limitations of ChatGPT

ChatGPT is the most promising, exciting, capable, and highly featured application to deal with all types of queries and questions across all domains of industries and knowledge; nevertheless, it has certain limitations [89]:

- ChatGPT application lacks in common sense that a normal human has. The decisions made by this application is purely on the basis of the understanding of the topic through training datasets related to the real-world information.
- It lacks in generalization of the meaning of the questions due to high sensitivity to the phrases or question text. If you change the phrase with almost similar meaning, the response generated by the application may vary significantly in certain cases.

- It may generate verbose response due to certain limitations of to-the-point understanding of the matters fed for learning purposes.
- The generation of biased response in terms of genders, races, culture, or other areas is possible due to the presence of biases in the training datasets.
- Does not possess capabilities to get the ambiguous input clarified; rather, it tries to guess from the input and generate response based on that assumed input.
- It may generate an offensive or inappropriate response in terms of different cultures and taboos due to the biases present in the training datasets.
- ChatGPT is not able to understand a wide range of emotions and other abstractive context such as sorrows, joys, excitement, empathy, and others.
- ChatGPT is unable to handle multiple tasks at a time
- The ability to generate creative content is limited to a certain level.
- Compared with the human, it cannot operate digital processes like accessing Internet opening websites and other similar types of activities.
- Some certain specialized domains are not properly processed for providing the accurate response to the queries such as medical prescriptions, diseases diagnosis, future projections, gut-feeling based assumptions, and others.
- ChatGPT is unable to express emotions in their response; thus, it creates plain and dull content for using a professional and serious feedback.
- Mathematical problems with higher complexity are difficult to solve through ChatGPT and in certain cases the results may be misleading too.
- There are chances of grammatical, writing, typos, and other errors in the text generated by the ChatGPT application.
- The data incorporated into the ChatGPT is up to the year 2021. Thus, it is unaware of any information after 2021.

Top Services of ChatGPT

The main goal of developing ChatGPT service is to provide all types of services that a human can provide in a digital web environment. A human professional is required in almost all domains of industries to provide numerous services in digital environment, for example, creating digital ecosystems such as websites, developing applications, creating content, providing technical support, creating documents, and many others. ChatGPT also tries to accomplish all those tasks that a human can perform in a digital web environment. It is able to provide some of those services perfectly, while the others are not of that level that a human can provide. A few very important and reliable services and facilities provided by ChatGPT are as follows[90]:

- **Content Creation** – The most important area in which ChatGPT is expert is creation of the content in the form of text, image and voice. The main examples include writing articles, product descriptions, social media posts, emails, summaries, rephrasing of content, blogs, step-by-step procedures, and many others.

- **Education and Training** – It is very useful for e-Learning platforms, general questions and answering applications, domain-specific knowledge, specific explanations of concepts, procedural learning activities, research, and others.

- **Language Translation** – It supports a wide range of languages in which the content can be translated easily with the help of ChatGPT application.

- **Computer Programming** – Numerous types of activities such as creating computer code, code debugging, explaining coding concepts and techniques, generating code snippets, completing code, documenting codes, and refactoring of codes can be accomplished through the ChatGPT platform with professional touch.

- **Customer Support** – ChatGPT can provide services for a range of customer-related applications such as technical support agent, chatbots, virtual assistant, and others.

- **Online Processes** – A large number of online processes such as digital marketing, text checking, writing assessment, research assistant, personalization of customer experience, audience research and feedback processing, handling customer surveys, and others can easily be handled through ChatGPT platform.

- **Miscellaneous** – Numerous other applications can also be performed through this innovative and futuristic application.

SAMPLE QUESTIONS

1. What is the concept of LLMs, and how are they practically applied?

2. List the distinct features of various generative AI models and where they find common use.

3. How does one effectively deploy and utilize the ChatGPT Bot, incorporating practical steps and recommended strategies?

4. Provide a detailed breakdown of RLHF perspective, showcasing its integration of human input into the learning process.

5. What are the diverse technological components within ChatGPT, and how do they contribute to the model's overall functionality?

6. Illuminate the concept of APIs, emphasizing their significance in application programming and outlining their various applications and benefits?

3

ChatGPT Technology Stack

Introduction

ChatGPT is a generative artificial intelligence (Gen-AI) application which is designed on pretrained transformer architecture. The main objective of this platform is to generate human-like texts and responses through machine while communicating in natural language. A large number of technologies, infrastructure, algorithms, models, platforms, programming languages, and computing techniques have been used in materializing this platform.

Generally speaking, the detailed technological stack of ChatGPT is not available in public with comprehensive details and the technological stack and components of this AI platform are continuously evolving and changing. Therefore, it is highly desirable to describe the technological stack of

DOI: 10.1201/9781003474173-3

ChatGPT in terms of different domains and areas. The technology stack of ChatGPT can be divided into two separate categories:

- Hardware technology stack
- Software technology stack

The details of both hardware and software technological stacks are provided separately in the following sections.[91,92]

Hardware Technology Stack

Mostly, the ChatGPT is based on the software platforms, codes, techniques, architectures, algorithms, and tools, but all these software resources reside and work on the hardware technological stack that sits at the bottom of the entire platform. High-performance hardware is required for performing extremely huge computations in deep learning (DL) used as one of the core technologies on the software side. The training of ChatGPT bot is accomplished on the computation-intensive processing units. The overall hardware-based technological stack consists of the following main hardware components and associated infrastructure:

- Graphics processing units (GPUs)
- Tensor processing units (TPUs)
- High-bandwidth memory (HBM)
- Compute unified device architecture (CUDA)

The details of the components and infrastructure used in the hardware technological stack of ChatGPT application are provided in the following sections.

Graphics Processing Units

GPUs are the most powerful computing processors specialized in processing multitasking functions for graphics and compute-intensive applications such as gaming, entertainment, AI, machine learning (ML), DL, neural networks, and other domains. GPU infrastructure for data processing in ChatGPT is one of the most fundamental components or technology of hardware stack. It is a specialized processing unit consisting of a large number of task-specific cores. The material used in GPUs is also same that is used in the traditional CPUs which are the combination of multiple cores to process the data at faster speeds. The most important role of GPU is the processing of graphics and other highly computing-intensive tasks such as DL algorithms.[93]

Tensor Processing Units

TPUs are application-specific integrated circuit (ASIC) developed by Google as a custom-developed hardware. The main purpose of developing TPUs was to accelerate the speed of ML workloads. This is extensively helpful for training your ML models more efficiently through GPUs, which are task-specific combination of cores that perform parallel processing in a demanding workload environment. The design of hardware of TPU is based on a large matrix processing in which it accelerates the processing of GPUs by using the power of processing of large matrices of data in a very short time. It uses a large physical matrix, which is known as systolic array of multiple arithmetic logic units (ALUs) that are used for handling massive matrix of data extensively used in DL of neural networks. It is not designed for processing other traditional data like spreadsheets or any other similar types of data. It consists of HBM and matrix multiplication unit (MUX) to process the data faster.[94]

High Bandwidth Memory

Another very important hardware that is extensively required for processing the data in ML models of ChatGPT is memory. The memory improves the processing capacity and performance of ML significantly. ChatGPT uses the combination of random access memory (RAM) and HBM for better results in terms of performance and speed. HBM is an advanced hardware technology of memory that offers higher speed computer memory interface for 3D stacked synchronous dynamic random access memory (SDRAM). This memory can be used easily in conjunction with graphic accelerators, datacenter AI ASICs, network devices, and other hardware equipment to realize superspeed and performance and huge saving of power and other resources. The advanced versions of HBM are emerging and are being utilized into the hardware stack of highly demanding applications of modern technologies such as ML, neural networks, DL, and others.[95]

Compute Unified Device Architecture

CUDA is a firmware program for parallel computing, but it is integrated into the GPUs for providing additional capabilities of performance and heavy workload processing abilities. Thus, we can add this technology into hardware as well as software stack of ChatGPT platform. This technology is created by NVIDIA for enhancing the capabilities of GPUs. This technology is based on multiple blocks and supports a wide range of computer programming languages in DL algorithms and models in the modern domain of ML applications like ChatGPT.[96]

Cloud Computing Infrastructure

The main technologies that have been discussed in the technological stack are the major components that are associated with the computing infrastructure and allied technologies that help those computing infrastructure increase performance and speed. The computing infrastructures that are used in the modern world are based on the cloud computing infrastructure or models. Thus, the cloud computing infrastructure is one of the most important components of hardware technological stack of ChatGPT. ChatGPT uses Microsoft Azure cloud computing infrastructure for developing a comprehensive hardware technological stack for DL model of the application. At the same time, Microsoft Corporation is also planning to integrate ChatGPT into its cloud services for normal users as well as software developers.

Software Technology Stack

ChatGPT is an AI model for generating response in natural language commonly used by human for communication. Along with the hardware technological stack, a large number of software technologies form this most advanced generative AI model. The software technology is the most fundamental field that is capable of materializing the concepts of modern AI. The algorithms, ML models, data processing networks, communication technologies, and other components all are powered by the software technologies. Thus, the software technological stack plays very pivotal role in the development of ChatGPT application. The software technological stack can further be divided into different domains based on their functionalities, areas of development, and other processes. Therefore, software-based technological stack can further be classified into the following platforms and software technologies used in the development of ChatGPT robot.

- Programming languages
- DL frameworks
- Natural language processing libraries

The details of these major categories of software components are mentioned in the following sections separately.

Programming Languages

Programming languages sit at the core of all modern software-based technologies, including AI and others. The power of computer code has revolutionized the world of technologies significantly. The impact of software or program-ming languages has been pervasive on almost all types of industries and busi-nesses as well as on all areas of technologies, especially the communication and information technology field. There are a huge number of programming languages that are extensively used in different technologies. Some of those programming languages are domain-specific and some are general-purpose languages. ChatGPT is a comprehensive platform that consists of AI engine, training ML models, fine-tuning mechanisms, AI algorithms, front-end web application, and large backend environment powered by main general-pur-pose language such as Python. The most important general-purpose languages used in the development of ChatGPT along with a wide range of libraries and platforms associated with each one of them are listed below:

- Python programming language
- C++ programming language
- CUDA programming language
- HTML language
- JavaScript

The details of these languages used in different domains of ChatGPT are mentioned separately in the following sections.

Python Programming Language

Python programming language sits at the core of ChatGPT application because the entire backend of the ChatGPT application is based on this general-purpose language. Python is a high-level, interpreted, and object-oriented language with dynamic semantics. It was developed a few decades back in 1991. Since then, it is contributing to the high-end programming; in the recent years, it has grown significantly due to the advancements in high workload applications and advanced technologies that are supplementing to this powerful language. The core code of ChatGPT is developed with the help of Python along with many other supportive languages.[97]

C++ Programming Language

C++ is another general-purpose and very powerful language for building high-end applications that are highly featured and complex. Numerous com-ponents, libraries, platforms, and tools used for materializing the profes-sional level services of ChatGPT are developed with the C++ programming language. Meanwhile, the ChatGPT platform is also trained in C++ and many other languages that are supported by this application to provide the code to the developers. The NumPy is one of those platforms that are exten-sively used in the ChatGPT platform. It is developed in C++ programming language. Some libraries used in the Python for creating the core backend of this application such as GPT-3 engine are also developed with C++ libraries. It is an object-oriented, multipurpose, and high-end programming language. This language belongs to the C language family.[98]

CUDA Programming Language

CUDA is a parallel computing programming platform that helps the compute-intensive applications such as ML neural networks used in ChatGPT and other applications to increase the speed by harnessing the power of parallel computing systems to the GPUs used in NVIDIA processors. CUDA is developed by NVIDIA for its GPUs consisting of thousands of cores. It is firmware-level software that is integrated into the GPUs of NVIDIA and extensively used by the neural networks of ChatGPT application. This programming platform is extensively used in many other compute-intensive applications too.[99]

HTML Language

ChatGPT is a comprehensive application involving a complete backend and front-end environments and connections among numerous subdomains of this generative AI web application. HTML is one of the most fundamental codes extensively used in the web interfaces for interacting with the common users. The ChatGPT platform also uses this fundamental front-end technology for its front-end design and application interface.

JavaScript

JavaScript is extensively used for interactive web interfaces in the modern web development. ChatGPT is trained for providing support to the developers who want to learn JavaScript or want to build codes in this scripting language. ChatGPT uses different libraries that use JavaScript codes at different levels in both front-end and backend development.

Deep Learning Frameworks

DL through deeper or multilayer hidden neural networks is the core of AI and compute-intensive generative AI applications. The foundation of ChatGPT is based on the following main architectures and platforms:

- Pretrained transformer
- NLP training model
- Inference model

All these models and architectures are based on deep neural networks. DL is the most fundamental power used by ChatGPT to mimic the learning like a human does. The implementation of DL technology in the development of ChatGPT is accomplished through different platforms[104]:

- PyTorch platform
- Keras platform
- TensorFlow
- Theano
- NumPy
- Anaconda

The details of these platforms used in ChatGPT DL technology, especially in transformer architecture, are provided in the following sections.

PyTorch Platform

PyTorch is one of the most powerful and commonly used DL platforms extensively used in the modern ML applications and other compute-intensive ML generative AI applications. This platform is based on Torch library. It was developed by Meta AI; subsequently, it has become a part of Linux Foundation. It is an open-source software platform. It was launched in 2016 by a team of developers such as Adam Paszke, Sam Gross, and others. This platform has been developed with the help of different computer programming languages such as Python, C++, CUDA, and others. ChatGPT uses this Python library for ML applications extensively in its different architectures and models.[100]

Keras Platform

This is a powerful API developed by Google for the deployment of neural networks in different types of ML and AI application. It is developed in Python and works very effectively on the TensorFlow framework. A majority of works regarding the implementation of neural networks in ChatGPT platform are done through PyTorch but TensorFlow platform and Keras library have also been implemented in the development of ChatGPT application.[101]

Keras platform is used to deploy the most complex problems of DL by breaking them into smaller parts and implementing through neural networks with the help of Keras library. The following are the main features of Keras neural network library:

- It is a high-level DL API.
- Both ChatGPT and Keras are developed in Python; therefore, they are easy to deploy and work in collaboration smoothly.

- Keras supports numerous backend neural network computations.
- The interface of Keras is very user-friendly.
- It is easy to learn and use with a minimum and straight learning curve.
- It is conformable with numerous other neural network implementation platforms and frameworks such as TensorFlow, Theano framework, Microsoft Cognitive Toolkit (CNTK), MXNet platform, PlaidML, and others.
- TensorFlow uses Keras as its official high-level API.
- The prototyping time of Keras API library is much smaller compared with many other neural network platforms.
- Keras API is very fast in running because it works on the top of TensorFlow platform.
- Bigger research community and it is growing at a very fast speed.
- Many big companies and organizations use Keras as neural network deployment API for their respective services.
- Keras is equally capable of running on both GPUs and CPUs efficiently.
- Keras library supports almost all types of neural network models used in the modern ML projects.
- Keras is modular in its structure; thus, it is very flexible, scalable, cost-effective, and innovative for different types of AI research projects.
- The development of Keras-based neural network model involves the following main steps to implement in the process:
  - Different layers of neural network models are defined at the first step known as network definition stage.
  - The second step of AI model development through Keras is network compilation in which the code is compiled to make it machine-understandable.
  - After compilation, the model is made fit for the data that we are going to use for training of the ML model.
  - The next step is the assessment or evaluation of the neural network in which the errors of the model are checked and identified.
  - The final stage of Keras model-building is making predictions, which is accomplished through testing data on the model after training it for making predictions.

TensorFlow

ChatGPT uses PyTorch at the core of ML models. It also uses TensorFlow framework and Keras for implementing certain ML modules in the neural networks for materializing the DL processes. TensorFlow is a comprehensive or end-to-end framework for the implementation of DL models of ML. It is an open-source framework. TensorFlow ML framework was developed by Google Corporation back in 2015. This platform has numerous additional features, which make it one of the most liked ML platforms for neural networks. The following are the most important and attractive features and characteristics of TensorFlow platform[102,103]:

- It is an end-to-end comprehensive ML platform in the marketplace.
- It offers additional support for documentation and training.
- It is very simple and easy to learn and implement.
- It uses a powerful API library known as Keras on the top of it.
- It supports different options such as scalable production, deployment options, and multiple abstraction levels.
- It supports different OS platforms, including the Android.
- It is a very powerful symbolic mathematics library extremely useful for neural networks.
- It is capable of effective deployment of dataflow programming across a wide range of tasks and activities.
- It supports multiple abstraction levels for both training and building the ML neural network–based models.
- It offers a large community resource, comprehensive ML ecosystem, huge library, and a range of tools for ML model development and deployment simultaneously.
- It uses Keras library as the official API on the top of its foundation.
- It is equally useful for both expert and beginner developers.
- It is useful for Windows, Android, Mobile, Web, and Cloud platforms.
- It supports a wide range of data tools to process, consolidate, clean, and ingest the data efficiently for different ML models.
- It is capable of dealing with different data processing and other activities such as standard datasets, preprocessing data layers, validating and transforming large datasets, data pipelining for data loading, and others.
- It supports distributed training, effective debugging, immediate model iterations, and much more under one single roof.
- It supports the capabilities of fine-tuning the ML models through conformable tools such as TensorBoard, model analysis, and others.
- It is able to deploy ML models in clouds, on devices, in web environments, on-premises, on CPUs, on GPUs, on advanced TPUs, on FPGAs (field programmable gate arrays), in the browsers, and other hybrid environments simultaneously.
- It is also able to deploy the industry best practices, model tracking, performance monitoring, data automating, model re-training, and others used in the different activities of ML operations or MLOps.

Theano

Theano is another major Python library that is extensively used by different DL models. ChatGPT also uses this Python library for some optimization and evaluation of mathematical expressions, which involve multidimensional arrays of matrices. It is the foundation library that is very popular in many neural network and DL environments due to the ability of this library to support different functions related to convolution neural network as well as recurrent neural networks simultaneously. The other main features and characteristics of Theano Python library are as follows[105]:

- It is a highly efficient library to deal with the fastest numerical computations in the DL models.
- Theano can be implemented on both GPUs and CPUs effectively.
- It is considered the key foundational library for DL models.
- It is an open-source library released under BSD license.
- The name Theano is given after a well-known Greek mathematician.
- This library is developed by LISA group, which has been renamed as MILA.
- It is also used as the compiler of mathematical expressions for Python language.
- The syntax of Theano library expressions is symbolic.
- Theano supports major platforms such as Windows, Linux, OS X, and others.
- It is capable of taking structures and converting those structures into very effective code, which uses the NumPy and some other native libraries.
- It is especially designed for handling large DL algorithms and models effectively.
- Theano library offers stable optimization, faster execution speed optimization, and symbolic differentiation efficiently.
- Basic purpose of developing Theano Python library is to define, optimize, and evaluate mathematical expressions perfectly.

NumPy

Another software platform used in the software-stack of ChatGPT application is NumPy Python library. It has been used in ChatGPT for working with the matrix arrays. This platform works in connection with the TensorFlow and Keras more effectively for defining, evaluating, and optimizing the complex arrays of features and attributes. The most important features and characteristics of NumPy are as follows[106]:

- The name NumPy has been derived from the combination of Numerical and Python.
- It is another effective Python Library used for dealing with the arrays.
- The main functions of this library can deal with numerous mathematical areas such as Fourier transform, matrices, linear algebra, and others.
- The author of NumPy is Travis Oliphant.
- The NumPy library was released in 2005.
- NumPy Python library is an open-source platform that is free for everyone to use and contribute to the library freely.
- It offers more than 50 times faster speed than traditional Python list of array objects.
- The processes can effectively access and manipulate the NumPy functions in any Python environment for ML or DL projects. This accessing and manipulation of functions is known as locality reference in computing field.
- The majority of the source code in which this library has been written is in C and C++ for providing faster speeds and greater performance. However, some parts and functions of this library are also written in Python language.
- It is also very well-known for scientific computation in the field of modern AI and ML.
- The use of Fortran language is also a very important characteristic of this library to provide the power of mathematical programing.
- It is very easy to use Python library due to high-level syntax of this platform that makes it more accessible and productive.
- It supports a wide range of other libraries, platforms, and environments to offer most flexible and productive environment for computation-intensive applications.
- Other than DL, NumPy can be effectively used in numerous other domains such as space, physics, sport analysis, and others.

Anaconda

Anaconda is a powerful platform for writing and executing codes in Python and R programming languages. Along with many other main software platforms, Anaconda Python development platform is also used in ChatGPT. It is a very efficient platform for data scientists. The main purpose of this platform is to achieve the simplification of package management and deployment of code professionally with full ease and efficiency. The other main features and characteristics of Anaconda Python development platform are as follows[107]:

- It is an open-source distribution platform of R programming and Python languages for data science software development.
- The writing and execution of code in Python and R language is the core objective of this data science platform.
- It offers simplification of package management and deployment.
- Anaconda supports multiple platforms such as Windows, Linux, MacOS, and others.
- It has over 6000 Python libraries and counting and also more than 2000 interoperable R packages.
- Supports DL and other next-generation applications that are computation-intensive and complex in nature.

Natural Language Processing Libraries

Natural language processing (NLP) is a type of AI to deal with the communication by machines in natural language like the human does. NLP uses different models, techniques, technologies, development platforms, libraries, and tools for the development of NLP models like ChatGPT. A wide range of NLP libraries are available in the marketplace that can be used for building an NLP model of ML. Numerous NLP libraries are used in the development of ChatGPT chatbot:

- Hugging face transformers
- SpaCy (spelled often, "spaCY" with small "s") platform
- NLTK library

The details of the above-mentioned NLP libraries are described in the following sections.

Hugging Face Transformers

Hugging face is one of the most powerful NLP libraries with thousands of functions available for free to use for your ML models or even play with different computers that are powered with ML. All those functions are available for free at the central space of HuggingFace transformer known as Hugging Face HUB client library by Hugging Face Inc. It is an open-source platform to access and modify or customize different models in line with your desired objectives of ML models. The following are the most important features and characteristics of HuggingFace transformer library[108,109]:

- It is a specialized platform for ML professionals, creators, and collaborators to develop modern NLP models.
- A large number of pretrained models and datasets are available to access, copy, transfer, and use in matching NLP applications.
- It is perfectly conformable with Python computer language.
- HuggingFace transformer is the core framework that is designed for building DL projects and applications.
- It offers APIs for downloading and integrating models for your applications and projects.
- It supports a wide range of NLP-based domains such as computer vision (CV), audio, multi-modal applications, and other NLP domains.
- A very few powerful models are already available in ready-to-use condition such as text summarization, sentiment analysis, and others.
- HuggingFace offers three main domains of services such as model hub for trained models, transformer pipelines for interface to NLP tasks, and NLP transformer libraries for downloading NLP functions and tools for the optimization and fine-tuning of your NLP models.

SpaCy Platform

SpaCy (or spaCy) is another popular NLP library that is extensively used in building modern NLP applications. It has numerous additional capabilities than a simple library; those capabilities make it one of the most liked platforms for building NLP-based projects. It is capable of processing huge volumes of text for NLP so that the text can easily be utilized for NLP-based ML projects effectively. The main features and characteristics of SpaCy platform are as follows:

- SpaCy platform is an open-source platform free to be used and modified for every developer, contributor, and community.
- It is a Python library that supports not only NLP models but also numerous additional features to process large volumes of texts for NLP models.
- It is extremely helpful for building a wide range of applications dealing with numerous activities such as text analysis, document analysis, chatbot capabilities, and others.

- You can also build specialized NLP models with the help of this valuable Python language library for NLP field.
- This platform is developed by Matthew Honnibal and Ines Montani and was released in 2005 in open-source and BSD license.
- It supports a large number of other natural language processing tasks due to its support to many plug-ins and other advanced integrations.
- It has become one of the most popular and the mostly used Python library with a huge supporting community in the world.
- The most advanced use cases in diverse industrial environment powered by SpaCy Universe include Prodigy, Rasa NLU (Natural Language Understanding), Kindred, SpaCy-PyTorch-Transformers, Blackstone, Mordecai, and many others.

SAMPLE QUESTIONS

1. Explain the different parts that make up the hardware technology stack and how they work together.
2. Describe the basics of cloud computing infrastructure. Why it is important in modern computing?
3. Provide an overview of popular software technology stacks and what each component does in building software?
4. Explain in simple terms the purpose and functioning of deep learning frameworks in developing advanced machine learning models?
5. Introduce commonly used natural language processing libraries and briefly explain what they are used for in processing human language?
6. Describe how natural language processing libraries contribute to tasks involving human language, making them more understandable and manageable in various applications?

4

Natural Language Processing (NLP): Foundation Building Block of ChatGPT

Introduction

Natural language processing (NLP) is a subfield of artificial intelligence (AI). It is very important domain in modern applications that deal with the communication in the natural language form that humans do. The NLP enables the machines to understand, analyze, and manipulate the natural language communication in the form of text, voice, and video and enabled the computers to generate suitable responses to the communication in natural language like the humans usually do.

It is very crucial to note that in the modern IT systems, the majority of raw data is generated in the form unstructured data such as voice, videos, images, and other sensory data. A large ratio of that data is pertaining to the natural language communication on a wide range of social platforms, normal websites, blogs, web applications, mobile applications, business process applications, governmental service websites, and many others. All those portals deal with the natural language communication used by common human users. The response to those users is required to be provided by

DOI: 10.1201/9781003474173-4

the human resources on the other side of the communication. This provision of response to the queries of human users was done through different call centers and other services centers where a large number of support representatives would provide the answers to the queries of the users. This entire process is extensively costly, time-consuming, less-productive, and prone to different mistakes due to the involvement of human interference. In such circumstances, the businesses want to use machines to understand the communication used by human and provide suitable response to the queries and other messages similarly like a representative sitting in a call center does. Building computer machines capable of understanding the communication by users, processing the meaning, manipulating the suitable response to the communication, and providing in a suitable format is an issue of technology that is known as natural language processing.

NLP has been in the field for many decades now in one or the other form and manifestation, but the older versions of automation in natural language communication was extremely limited to certain predefined response against predefined queries or questions. This type of automated communication by machines was completely based on rule-based communication. In that rule-based communication, predefined answers would be fed to the computers through explicit computer programming that would instruct the machines to invoke certain types of predetermined response against a predefined question or query. It was not like the modern NLP that is completely based on machine learning (ML), which is another type or subdomain of AI technology.

If you look at a wide range of modern applications that are very common in modern communication with machines as well as users themselves as listed below, you will come up with the conclusion that NLP has become pivotal in modern automated communication in natural language. These applications are as follows:

- ChatGPT version 3 and version 4
- Voice assistants such as Alexa, Siri, and others
- Automated translation applications
- Online grammar and writing mistake checking applications
- Questioning and answering chatbot applications for specific domains
- Automated customer support service platforms
- Customer relationship management applications
- Virtual assistants and recommendation engines
- Auto-completion of online forms and fields
- Business intelligence BI applications
- Unstructured data analysis applications
- Sentiment analysis applications

All of the above-listed applications are based on the modern NLP technology, which utilizes the ML techniques such as neural networks (NN) and deep learning (DL). ChatGPT is also a powerful machine-generative AI application that uses DL and NN for understanding the natural language communication used by humans and provides suitable response to the meaning of the communication message or query. With the help of NLP technology, modern industries have achieved numerous benefits[111]:

- Efficient use of hidden information in piles of unstructured data, which was almost impossible with traditional way of automation based on rule-based and explicit computer programming mechanism.
- Substantial reduction in numerous business processes due to the process automation through NLP-based applications such as customer support, technical support, customer relationship management, and others.
- Automated correction of huge volumes of text through grammar correction application online without any substantial cost or time.
- Simplification of text manipulation such as building summary, simplifying complex sentences, creating explanations, and others.
- Identifying the tone and rating of the text along with the plagiarized content in any text created for online posting or research purposes.
- Classification of text, extraction of text, translation of content in multiple languages, customer feedback analysis, and many other applications are other major areas of attraction or use in modern business ecosystems.
- Categorization and analysis of medical records, stock forecasting, financial trading estimation, talent recruitment in human resources, and many other applications.

As far as the ChatGPT is concerned, it is known as NLP-based generative AI application in which the NLP technology sits at the core of the entire platform. It uses numerous platforms, libraries, tools, and infrastructure associated with ML, NN, and DL, which materialize the NLP through different techniques. Without having a proper overview of NLP application, it is not possible to understand the core building blocks and functionalities of ChatGPT technically. Therefore, let us have more information about NLP next.

What Is Natural Language Processing?

NLP is a field of AI that makes the machines capable of understanding, assessing, and manipulating the communication in natural language used by human and produces a matching response to the query or message originated from a human. In other simple words, NLP deals with the natural language that is spoken by human in computer environment and enables the machines to play with natural language similar to that the human does.[112]

Let us have a look into the technical aspects of NLP technology with summarized points to understand the processes and techniques running at the backend of this technology, especially in the ChatGPT application[111,112]:

- Domain of technology that helps machines understand and respond to the natural language that humans use for communication.
- It is based on ML techniques powered by NN and DL technologies.
- Technical phases of NLP consist of the following:
  - Data preprocessing phase
  - Algorithm development phase
- Technological field-wise NLP is depicted in the Figure 4.1.

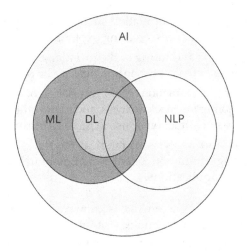

FIGURE 4.1
Pictorial view of NLP in terms of technological context.

- Data preprocessing is a set of techniques that are used to clean and customize the unstructured data into the formats that are easy to understand for the NLP algorithms. The most important activities that include data preprocessing are as follows:
  - **Tokenization** – Breaking of words into smaller units.
  - **Stemming and Lemmatization** – The words used in natural language are squeezed and connected to their roots.

- **Stop Word Removal** – The most common words in the sentences are removed to reduce the sentence to a compact and meaningful size and sense.
- **Part of Speech (POS) Tagging** – All words are marked with their identities in terms of POS grammatically.
- The algorithm building phase may consist of two main principles – the traditional rule-based system and machine-learning-based system. The former method is not used in modern applications like ChatGPT and others. The latter method is used in modern NLP applications like NLP and others. The second type of algorithm development is mostly based on the modern AI technologies such as DL through NN and normal ML approach that also uses different types of NN.
- The processing of neural language data in NLP is accomplished through two major areas or types of analysis:
  - Syntax analysis
  - Semantic analysis
- Syntax analysis uses the grammatical rules such as arrangement of words in sentence, identity of words in grammar, and other grammatical things. The following are the most important techniques used for the syntax analysis:
  - Parsing the sentence into different POS and other identities of words in a sentence under analysis.
  - Segmentation of words is another technique in which the words are separated from the other words through proper marks.
  - Sentence breaking is also a technique used in syntax analysis in which the sentences are broken through different marks such as full stop and other signs.
  - Aligning the words to their respective roots is called stemming. It is another important technique in syntax analysis for NLP.
- Semantic analysis is the second most important technique used in the NLP technology. The main principle behind this technique is to consider the meaning and usage of the words in the sentences. The main processes that determine or analyze the sentence in this technique are as follows:
  - Named entity recognition (NER)
  - Word sense disambiguation
  - Natural language understanding
  - Natural language generation

- The most important tools used for NLP application in modern technological domain are as follows:
  - Natural language toolkit (NLTK)
  - Intel NLP architect
  - Gensim Python library

There are some other techniques that are commonly used in accomplishing the NLP through NN-based DL technology.

How Does Natural Language Processing Technology Work?

The working procedure of NLP technology is very complex due to the involvement of numerous algorithms, techniques, technologies, tasks, activities, and phases of actions. The basic working principle of NLP is similar to the entire process of listening, processing, understanding, manipulating, and responding to the communication message by a human to another human in naturally spoken or written language in our daily life. NLP uses different components, tools, algorithms, and techniques for every step, activity, and process that involves natural communication between two people. From ear to listen to a message to an eye to see a signal movement and from understanding sentiments to sensing other abstracts in human are accomplished through different hardware and software devices and tools, respectively. The internal processing of the listened data is done through natural NN and a response is manipulated within that central processing through NN. In NLP, all those activities are performed by artificial neural networks (ANN). Thus, we can say that there is no a straightforward static methodology controlled by any computer programming instructions; rather they involve numerous platforms, tools, technologies, and methods at different phases to accomplish the entire process of interaction of machines with other machines or human through natural language communication.[113]

The main phases of NLP technology are mentioned below with the details to show how this technology works in real-world environment[113,114]:

- **Lexical Analysis** – This is the first phase of NLP in which the morphology of the words is accomplished. The relationship among the words in a sentence is also established and tagged in this phase. The other main functions of this phase are as follows:
  - Conversion of sequence of characters into sequence of tokens.
  - The combination of parser and lexer (a computer program that performs lexical analysis) is used for this purpose in programming and web environment analysis.
  - An instrumental process in the early stage of NLP to segment sounds or text into different words and other units

- **Syntactic Analysis** – In this phase, the meaning of a natural language sentence is perceived through grammatical analysis of groups of words, not the individual words in a sentence. It is a very vital phase in NLP working process. This is similar to the process used in the computer programming for analysis of string of symbols.

- **Semantic Analysis** – The process in which the meaning of the words is discovered through lexical and grammatical meaning. The entire meaning of natural language is achieved here in this phase for further processing. It is another very critical phase in the entire working process of NLP. The main objectives of this phase are as follows:
    - Capturing the meaning of sentence by considering the context of the text, structure of the logic of the sentence, and grammatical roles.
    - Semantic analysis is done through two types of analysis – compositional semantic analysis and lexical semantic analysis.

- **Discourse Analysis** – The next very important phase of working process of NLP is discourse analysis in which the motives of the communication in a text are achieved or analyzed. The historical and social contexts are considered at the core of understanding the discourse of the text effectively.

- **Pragmatic Analysis** – Last but not the least, pragmatic analysis deals with the meaning of the words for extracting the actual meaning of the text from different perspectives considered in the above phases of the analysis. It is the most crucial phase to find out the meaning of the text under the analysis of NLP technological model.

All of the above-mentioned phases of NLP working process perform a wide range of activities to accomplish the main objectives of those phases. The most important activities and functions performed under those phases are as follows[114]:

- Tokenization function to break down the words into smaller tokens.
- Lemmatization process is performed to link the words to their respective root words.
- Stemming process removes the prefixes and suffixes of the words to simplify the words that can be easily linked with the roots through lemmatization function.
- POS tagging activity ensures all words belonging to any part of words (grammatically) are marked properly.

- Bag of words is an activity to create a matrix of words in a particular excerpt to depict the frequency of the words in a body of the text.
- Stop-word removal function removes all those words having no significant meaning in the sentence such as articles, prepositions, and others.

Branches of Natural Language Processing

In terms of domains of academics, the NLP technology can be categorized as the combination of computer science, mathematics, and linguistics. There is a very minor difference between the mathematical formulas used in the form of equations in computer science through different programming languages; therefore, they are commonly considered in a single combination of areas of academics. Thus, the NLP technology can be categorized into two main branches of education or knowledge[115]:

- Linguistics branch
- Computer science

The pictorial representation of the categories or branches of NLP is shown in Figure 4.2 for easy understanding of the concept.

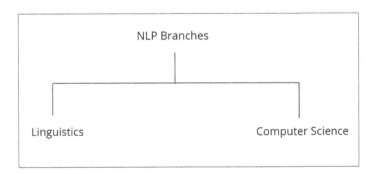

FIGURE 4.2
Branches of NLP.

These two branches are extensively considered in terms of the development of NLP applications such as ChatGPT and others. The entire computation of the NLP project is handled by the computer science domain, which deals with the general coding as well as mathematical coding in any computer programing language. The combination of mathematical expressions and other coding is merged into computer science domain. The other area of NPL is the natural language that human speaks for communication. The knowledge of natural language is called linguistics. Thus, the second major branch of NLP is linguistics to process the language in the form of text and voice.

The main focus of linguistics is on the ways to analyze the text or voice messages or paragraphs by using different scientific techniques. Computer science deals with the methods that can analyze the text or voice to process the input text or voice and generate suitable response in naturally spoken languages as used by humans.

Historical Eras of Natural Language Processing

The history of NLP can be traced back alongside the traces of AI technology. The traces of AI can be found around seven decades ago in the 1950s. The start of the AI was also the starting point of NLP because the first test that established the starting point of AI was Turing test, which is also based on the communication with machines through different inputs in simple symbols and signals.

The entire history of NLP can be divided into different phases or eras based on the techniques or technologies that governed this field of AI. The most important eras or phases of history of NLP are as follows[116]:

- Symbolic NLP era
- Statistical NLP era
- Neural NLP era

The details of technologies, scientific work, progresses, discoveries, and inventions in each era are mentioned with timeline in the following sections.

Symbolic Natural Language Processing Era

The symbolic NPL era is spread over the period between 1950s and early 1990s. The starting point of AI works was Turing test. The other activities with timeline are mentioned below:

- **1954** – Successful development of Georgetown experiment that translated a few Russian sentences into English.
- **1964** – ELIZA was developed by Joseph Weizenbaum at MIT.
- **1966** – Automatic Language Processing Advisory Committee, precisely referred to as ALPAC report, was published that depicted a

very gloomy picture of NLP applications. This report resulted in reduced research and development for language processing applications across the world.

- **1968** – Development of SHRDLU rule-based natural language understanding program for computers developed by MIT professor Terry Winograd. This platform used PDP-6 operating system, DEC platform, and programming languages Micro Planner and LISP. This program is considered as one of the primary programs in NLP.

- **1970s** – In this entire decade, the development of NLP or AI applications was slow due to the ALPAC report and other steps taken by different countries to reduce funding in this field. A few chatterbots like PARRY and other conceptual ontologies were created by different professors and researchers in this decade.

- **1980s** – During this decade, numerous activities and creations took place. The main focus of those research activities was on rule-based parsing, morphology, semantics, and other areas of researches. A few of them include the following:
  - Head-driven phrase structure grammar or HPSG generative grammar computational application
  - Two-level morphology
  - LESK algorithm
  - Centering theory
  - Rhetorical structure theory
  - Development of RACTER chatterbot
  - Jabberwacky chatterbot

Statistical Natural Language Processing Era

The first era was mostly focused on the rule-based NLP techniques. The next era of NLP development focused on the statistical techniques. This era was spread between 1990s and 2010s. The advancements in the field of computer power, i.e., computing processing power and other information technologies, pushed focus of the research toward ML algorithms for language processing. The main activities, inventions, and discoveries that transformed the NLP from rule-based to statistical techniques include the following:

- **1990s** – The development of NLP applications, especially in the domain of language translation, such as IBM alignment model and other ML models.

- **2000s** – The substantial growth in web ecosystem, increased raw data, and computing power lead to the development of different ML methods such as supervised ML, unsupervised ML, and semi-supervised ML algorithms for processing the natural language communication, etc.

Neural Natural Language Processing Era

The neural era of NLP refers to the phase of NN that resembles the human brain network consisting of neurons. This era starts from the early 2000s and continues even today. Numerous types of NN were developed that would work similar to the human brain and would process the natural language similar to the natural brain. The most important activities, discoveries, and development in this era are as follows:

- **2003** – The development of first language model based on artificial NN based on multilayer perceptron. It had one hidden layer and context length of several words. That model was trained on about 14 million words with a CPU cluster. This model was capable enough to outperform the best n-gram statistical models. This was developed by Yoshua Bengio.
- **2010s** – Numerous NLP models and algorithms were developed based on representation learning and DL. They used numerous hidden layers to produce highly reliable and amazing results. Those models were extensively used in healthcare and medical record reading systems.

Applications of Natural Language Processing

NLP is expanding significantly due to its scope in a large spectrum of businesses and industries. There are many areas in which the power of NLP is used for achieving the most desirable objectives such as business productivity, time-saving, cost-saving, customer support, replacement of costly human resources, process automation, and many other things. This is possible due to the power of modern NLP models and applications that offer highly reliable results, faster turnaround time, reduced cost, and much more. There are numerous applications of NLP technology[117-119]:

- ChatGPT
- Domain-specific chatbots
- Language translation
- Speech recognition
- Text processing
- Spam filtering

- Sentiment analysis
- Predictive recommendation
- Smart assistants
- Data analysis
- Grammar checker applications
- Personalized marketing
- Social media monitoring

Let us know more about all these major applications.

ChatGPT

ChatGPT is one of the most powerful and advanced applications in the field of NLP. This application can be used in numerous fields and industries. It uses the advanced DL-based transformer ML models and it has got huge traction in diverse domains with the launch of the initial version, ChatGPT-3. The advanced version of ChatGPT-4 offers even more reliable and additional features that can be used in numerous domains such as software development, linguistics, and other knowledge-based queries. The following are the most important functions of ChatGPT:

- Answering questions related to almost all knowledge areas in the world
- Developing, testing, debugging, and explaining the computer coding in numerous programming languages used in modern software development
- Implementing general-purpose chatbots in education and training fields
- Text creation, modification, summarization, grammar checking, and many other processes associated with the text processing
- Social media monitoring, text analysis, customized and personalized marketing, and many other areas in modern digital marketing

Domain-Specific Chatbots

Domain-specific chatbots are special-purpose software applications that deal with answering services for a specific application, service, product, or area. The examples of such domain-specific chatbots include the bots used on the websites of different services, products, and applications. The most common areas or sectors where domain-specific chatbots are extensively used include healthcare, IT and telecommunication, travel and hospitality, retail, ecommerce, and many others. According to a latest forecast, the global market size of chatbots is expected to reach US$21.08 billion by 2028 from just US$5.8 billion in 2023 with a whopping growth of over 29.18% over the forecast period. Thus, the scope of this application is also huge.[120]

Language Translation

Language translation is another big domain in which NLP technology is used extensively. For many decades now, the researchers have been trying to achieve the desired results in the translation field with the help of numerous types of techniques; they got reliable success with the help of modern NN-based ML tools such as Google Translate, numerous online translator apps, and others. The translators based on NLP models are able to handle the differences of sentence structures in different languages properly and produce the correct results. The previous rule-based applications were not so useful and accurate to deal with the sentence structure and other grammatical issues in different languages. Translation applications are extensively used in numerous fields such as education, government, social media, websites, digital marketing, advertisements, and many other areas.

Speech Recognition

The conversion of spoken message or speech into text by the computing models or computer applications is called speech recognition. Numerous NLP applications are capable of performing this functionality perfectly. This function of speech recognition is used for many different purposes:

- Transcription function
- Text-to-speech function
- Translation function

The example of voice input on Google search, talking to chatbots, and other similar types of applications are examples of speech recognition.

Text Processing

Text processing is one of the most important applications of NLP. It is a very powerful and fundamental part of NLP. NLP deals with the computers to learn, analyze, and provide response to the input question. This is huge and comprehensive procedure, while the text processing is the limited version of the application of NLP in which different functions of text processing are utilized for a particular business activity. A large range of text processing activities can be accomplished through text processing function[121]:

- Analyzing text for different purposes such as sentiment analysis, negative and positive attributes for reviews, grammatical analysis of text for correct language, correction of punctuation, rectification of text spelling issues, extraction of valuable business information for business intelligence, and much more.

- Manipulating the text through different activities such as headline correction, tokenization of text, stemming, and others.
- Generating text is another main function of text processing mechanism in which a response is generated based on the input query or test data put up by a human user or even an intelligence computer machine.

Thus, we can define text processing (application) as the analysis, manipulation, and generation of text against a given input. This process is extensively useful for numerous business applications:

- Targeted and personalized digital marketing.
- Recommendation and suggestion for better user experience on websites, retail, and ecommerce applications.
- Achieving better customer feedback and reviews through survey response analysis from the end users of products and services.
- Summarization of text and creating the most effective copies and extracts of long and complex copies of texts.
- Deeper insight of huge unstructured text-based and other data.
- Correction of text and detection of plagiarism to make content more accurate and freer from any kinds of plagiarism or copyright infringement.
- Automated customer support and trouble-ticket management through the text processing of the trouble ticket generated by the customers.
- Classification of the language and detection of intentions are other two major functions that are useful in modern business applications.

Spam Filtering

Spam filtering is a very crucial type of application of NLP. The capability of natural language is to classify the text and analyze it to understand the intention and context of the text to make it happen accurately. Spam is one of the main sources of malicious activities on the Internet to spread viruses, spywares, phishing, fraudulent activities, and many other malicious activities. The total number of spam emails sent out on the Internet is on average about 122.33 billion emails per day. The average share of spam emails on the Internet is about 56.5% of all emails sent out on the Internet.[122] Stopping such a huge volume of spam emails from reaching into your legitimate inbox can save you and your company huge time and subsequently huge money because *"time is money"*. It can also save you from any kind of malicious attack and phishing activities. Phishing is basically a form of social engineering and scam where attackers deceive people into revealing sensitive information or installing malware.

NLP enables the computers to detect the potential spam emails and filter them to the spam folder or trash folder easily. It uses different techniques associated with its main part known as natural language understanding (NLU) to accomplish this task[123]:

- Understanding the structure of text
- Assessing the meaning and context of the text
- Weighing the weightage of words and sentences
- Implementation of tokenization, detection of lengths and number of words, and others

There are numerous traditional spam detection methods such as rule-based filtering, signature matching technique, heuristic method, challenge and response system, DNS blacklisting technique, and Bayesian filtering technique. The Bayesian is one of the most advanced spam email filtering techniques used in the modern NLP applications. It uses a matrix based on the Bayes rule to detect a wide range of characteristics of a piece of text through multidimensional analysis of words, sentences, paragraphs, context, subjects, meaning, and other factors.

Sentiment Analysis

Sentiment analysis capability of NLP technology is very useful for numerous applications in modern online business processes. The most important of those functions that produce the desirable business bottom line include the following:

- Effective feedback from users
- Rectification of marketing course
- Enhancement in online purchases
- Better user experience and others

Sentiment analysis is also referred to as the mining of the opinion of the end users or stakeholders in any business service or products. By using the capabilities of NLP technologies, the businesses can benefit in different ways to achieve the above-mentioned desirable business objectives or goals in different business processes.[124]

Predictive Recommendation

A well-trained natural language process model is capable of processing the input data in real-time environment. For example, a user types a few words or even a few characters; the machine helps out to provide the most suitable possible recommendations in search engines in real-time environment. Similarly, on the basis of the customer behavior analysis and previous interests, NLP-enabled models can suggest the most matching and relevant products to the users online. There are other such applications that modern businesses are benefiting from:

- Search engine suggestions in real-time environment
- Products or service recommendations on any website or social media sites
- Auto-filling of forms and other fields in purchase orders, online applications, and others

All of the above-listed functions are powered by NLP technology through its predictive recommendation power. It has been found in the real-world online business ecosystems that the use of online suggestions or recommendations on numerous online platforms, especially ecommerce platforms, increased businesses significantly.

Smart Assistants

Smart assistants or virtual digital assistants are the software applications powered by the NLP technology to analyze, understand, and respond to the voice queries put up by a user or client. It is another very important application of NLP in modern businesses. If you have ever interacted with the Google Assistant, SIRI, or ALEXA, you have already interacted with virtual assistants for your queries. They are highly trained ML applications that are capable of processing your voice as input by using the speech recognition capabilities and convert it into the machine understandable text by performing many other sub-functions so that they can understand the meaning and context of the question put up by the users. Once they understand the meaning of the question or query in the voice format, they provide a suitable response in the voice by reversing numerous processes used in converting the speech to text. And yes, all these forward as well as reverse processes of conversion of voice to text and then creating suitable response and then converting it into a voice message again take place in real-time environment without any substantial delay, hitch, or any other discrepancies.[125]

The basic working flow of a smart assistant or virtual digital assistant consists of a few main steps in sequential order[126]:

- User inputs a voice message through a microphone to the NLP-powered software application.
- Application converts the voice message into text by using some of the most popular voice-to-text conversion models such as hidden Markov models (HMM).

- It compares the smallest units of speeches in millisecond to prere-corded speeches it has understood in its memory.
- The application breaks the words into its different characteristics such as POS and other main attributes.
- The context of the speech is determined after breaking and tagging the words by using different grammatical as well as other algorithms.
- Finally, a response is generated after understanding the input message or query by adopting the reverse functions of the forward flow.

This application of NLP saves huge money in all types of online businesses by replacing the costly human representatives and assistants with virtual ones.

Data Analysis

Data analysis has been revolutionized after the advent of modern applications powered by ML and NLP technologies. The volumes of data have already increased significantly during the past few decades. That huge data, most of it, is in unstructured form, which is very difficult to process by traditional rule-based software applications. Some advanced power of computing was required to peep into the valuable information hidden in those huge volumes of data. The ML technology comes as survivor in such situation.

NLP-powered applications like ChatGPT and other task-specific applications can learn from huge amounts of data and also process the unstructured data in bulk and find out the valuable information by performing data analysis of those volumes of data through the power of NLP algorithms. The most important activities and tasks performed by natural language applications in data analysis include the following[127]:

- NLP has enabled broader data interaction within organizations, extending beyond data analysts and data scientists. Its conversational approach makes data exploration more natural for nontechnical team members while providing essential insights. Surveys offer valuable insights, but as data size increases with a large number of responses, it becomes impractical for a single person to read and draw conclusions. Leveraging NLP, companies can manage survey results and gather insights more accurately and efficiently than humans. Machines excel at analyzing vast amounts of language-based data without bias, inconsistency, or fatigue. By automating data analysis, text and speech data can be comprehensively and rapidly analyzed.
- Business intelligence and analytics products are incorporating NLP capabilities, enhancing natural language generation for narrating data visualizations. This improves the accessibility and understanding

of data visualizations for diverse audiences. Narration not only enhances storytelling but also reduces subjective interpretation of data. NLP applied to social media enables monitoring of topic awareness, responses, and identification of key influencers.

- To apply ML, well-curated input is crucial. However, sources like electronic health records often contain unstructured text. By employing NLP on electronic health records, organizations can gather clean and structured data for advanced predictive ML models, eliminating costly manual data annotation.

- NLP revolutionizes the speed of data exploration. Visualization software can generate and answer queries as fast as they are presented verbally or typed. Understanding human language is challenging due to variations in verbal and written expressions, languages, dialects, grammar, syntax rules, accents, and slang. NLP resolves language ambiguities, provides structure for textual analytics and speech recognition, and aids in understanding.

- NLP finds applications in investigative discovery, enabling pattern recognition in written reports or emails for crime detection and resolution. Text mining, powered by NLP, converts unstructured text into structured data, facilitating analysis and utilization in ML algorithms, data warehouses, databases, and dashboards for various analytical analyses.

- Keyword extraction algorithms reduce large bodies of text into key ideas and keywords, allowing the identification of main topics without reading the entire document. Text statistics visualizations offer insights into sentence length, word frequency, and word length, presented through histograms or bar charts. NER extracts specific entities such as places, dates, or names from the text.

- Sentiment analysis, a fundamental NLP function, analyzes words in text to determine the overall sentiment, categorizing results into positive, negative, or neutral. Negative numbers indicate negative tone, while positive numbers indicate positive sentiments within the text.

Grammar Checker Applications

Grammar checker applications may include punctuation and spelling checkers, grammatical error correctors, sentence structure checkers, POS identifiers, active and passive voice finders, and many others. All those modern applications to analyze the natural language through computer applications are powered by computer science and linguistics. This combination is also referred to as computational linguistics in academics or in the educational field. The main purpose of such applications is to check and detect the text in natural language in terms of syntax and semantics to make it look completely natural and similar to the text created by humans. The most important areas of applications of NLP in grammar checker systems are mentioned in the following list with full details[128]:

- Analysis and classification of simple, complex, and compound sentences in terms of voices, narrations, tenses, POS, and other aspects of grammar.
- The detection of the most common grammatical mistakes from the text to make it free from all grammatical mistakes:
  - Punctuation mistakes like misuses of commas, semicolons, colons, braces, quotations, exclamation marks, periods, and others.
  - Detection of spelling errors in terms of different versions of English language and other languages in the world.
  - Finding verb–noun disagreements, noun-adjective disagreements, disagreements in phrases, clause-level mistakes, active and passive voice errors, misplaced modifiers, unclear referencing of pronoun to the related noun, and others.
  - Identification of incomplete sentences, run-on sentences, sentence fragments, other various sentence structural issues, and comma slice errors.
- NLP algorithms can assign appropriate POS tags to each word in a sentence, such as nouns, verbs, adjectives, etc. This information helps identify errors related to incorrect word usage or agreement.
- NLP-based dependency parsing helps analyze the grammatical relationships between words in a sentence, such as subject–verb relationships or modifiers. By understanding these dependencies, grammar checkers can identify errors like subject–verb disagreement or misplaced modifiers.
- Grammar checkers incorporate rule-based systems that utilize linguistic rules and patterns to identify common grammatical errors. These rules cover aspects such as subject–verb agreement, verb tense consistency, pronoun usage, punctuation, and sentence structure.
- NLP models can consider the context of a sentence and surrounding text to provide more accurate grammar suggestions. They can take into account factors like the intended meaning, discourse coherence, and the writer's style to offer appropriate corrections.
- Advanced language models, such as transformer-based models, can be trained on large amounts of text to learn grammar patterns and improve the accuracy of grammar checking. These models can identify subtle errors, improve suggestions, and handle more complex linguistic phenomena.

- NLP-based grammar checkers generate suggestions for correcting errors by leveraging language patterns and grammar rules. They can propose alternative words, rephrase sentences, or recommend changes in punctuation or sentence structure to improve grammatical accuracy.
- NLP-powered grammar checkers can learn from user interactions and feedback. By collecting data on user corrections and incorporating it into their models, grammar checkers can continuously improve their accuracy and offer more relevant suggestions over time.

Overall, NLP plays a vital role in grammar checker applications by providing the underlying linguistic analysis and pattern recognition necessary to identify and correct grammatical errors in written text, helping users improve their writing skills and produce more accurate and polished writings or texts.

Personalized Marketing

The marketing has always been very pivotal in any kind of business; but, with the advent of the modern information technologies, the shape of marketing has changed drastically. The personalized, extremely focused, and featured types of campaigns have become very commonplace in modern domain of digital marketing due to the advancements in the modern ML capabilities, especially NLP technology. This became possible due to the following capabilities powered by NLP[129]:

- Understanding the customer data
- Finding the customer preferences
- Uncovering the customer sentiments
- Analyzing the customer feedbacks and reviews
- Real-time analysis of customer behavior
- Benefiting from the predictive insights
- Understanding the customer needs properly
- Targeting the customers with personalized type of messages and ads
- Suggesting additional products of his/her interests
- Clustering the different customers into different categories and classes
- Extraction of names, locations, reviews, interests, products purchased in the past, interests shown in categories of products, and other such information through NER technique of NLP
- Persona creation and customer polling assessments
- Interacting through chatbots and virtual assistants with personalized communication to establish trustful relationship

- Extracting informal information from social media sites to get a deeper insight into the personal behavior of the customers
- Analysis of voice commands passed through voice assistants

Social Media Monitoring

NLP or NLP-powered tools are a very effective way to monitor social media for gaining deeper insight into the user' behaviors to streamline the marketing and advertisements to achieve the most desirable business goals. NLP plays a crucial role in social media monitoring by enabling businesses to extract actionable insights, understand customer sentiment, identify trends, and engage with their target audience more effectively. By leveraging NLP-powered social media monitoring, businesses can make informed decisions, improve brand perception, and enhance their overall social media presence.

NLP is widely used in social media monitoring to analyze and extract valuable insights from the vast amount of textual data generated on social media platforms; a few of those activities are as follows:

- **Analysis of Sentiments** – NLP techniques enable sentiment analysis, which involves determining the sentiment or emotion expressed in social media posts. By analyzing the language and context of user-generated content, businesses can understand the overall sentiment associated with their brand, products, or specific topics. This information helps understand customer's opinions, identify trends, and measure brand reputation.
- **Trend/Topic Identification** – NLP algorithms can identify and extract key topics and trends from social media conversations. By analyzing hashtags, keywords, and contextual information, businesses can monitor the most discussed topics, emerging trends, and public interests. This insight helps in understanding customer preferences, identifying potential opportunities, and adapting marketing strategies accordingly.
- **Customer Feedback Analysis** – NLP enables businesses to listen to and analyze customer feedback and conversations on social media. By monitoring mentions, comments, and reviews, NLP algorithms can extract valuable information regarding customer's opinions, suggestions, and concerns. This feedback analysis helps businesses improve products, services, and customer experiences.
- **Influencer Finding** – NLP techniques can be used to identify influential individuals or key opinion leaders in social media conversations. By analyzing engagement, follower count, and content relevance, businesses can identify influencers who can help amplify their brand messages and reach a wider audience.

- **Multiple Social Network Analysis** – NLP algorithms can analyze the connections and relationships between social media users to perform social network analysis. By examining patterns of interactions, mentions, and shared content, businesses can identify influential communities, user clusters, or potential brand advocates. This information assists in targeting specific user groups and optimizing marketing campaigns.
- **Preempting Product Crisis** – Social media monitoring powered by NLP can detect and track conversations related to potential crises or issues surrounding a brand. By monitoring keywords, sentiment, and sudden spikes in social media activity, businesses can quickly identify and respond to potential crises, minimizing their impact and managing brand reputation effectively.

What Techniques Are Used in Natural Language Processing?

Understanding human natural language by machines is a very complex and intricate process that involves numerous techniques, algorithms, technologies, and platforms simultaneously. The following are the most important techniques to understand, manipulate, and generate text in NLP-powered applications[130,131]:

- POS tagging
- Tokenization
- Named entity recognition
- Sentiment analysis
- Summarization
- Topic modeling
- Text classification
- Keyword extraction
- Lemmatization and stemming

The details of each technique used in the NLP technology are provided in the following sections.

Part of Speech Tagging

POS tagging is a process in NLP in which each word of a given text is assigned with a grammatical POS. The goal of POS tagging is to determine the syntactic category or grammatical role of each word in a sentence, such as whether it is a noun, verb, adjective, adverb, pronoun, conjunction, or other POS. It helps understand the relationships between words and enables subsequent analysis and processing tasks. For example, in text parsing or information extraction, knowing the POS of each word helps identify noun phrases, verb phrases, subject–verb agreements, and other syntactic patterns. POS tagging is typically done using either rule-based approaches or statistical models. Rule-based taggers rely on predefined grammatical rules and dictionaries to assign POS based on patterns, word suffixes, or context. Statistical taggers, on the other hand, learn from annotated training data to predict the most likely POS for each word based on its surrounding context.

The most common tagsets used in NLP technology are as follows:

- Penn Treebank tagset, which consists of tags like NN (noun), VB (verb), JJ (adjective), and many others.
- Other tagsets may include additional fine-grain categories to capture specific linguistic features.

The POS tagging is very pivotal in NLP to analyze and understand the grammatical structure of text, enabling subsequent processing and analysis tasks to be performed more accurately and effectively.

Tokenization

Tokenization is a very critical method of NLP used for processing the natural language for making it understandable for machines. The breaking of text into smaller units or parts referred to as tokens is known as tokenization. The most commonly used tokens in NLP include the following:

- Individual word tokenization
- Sub-words tokenization
- Character tokenization such as punctuation and other signs
- Other attributes based on the model or algorithm

Tokenization process or technique is implemented at the initial stage of the NLP model. It paves the way for other main techniques such as POS tagging, NER, sentiment analysis, and others that further help the ML models to understand the text more efficiently.

Named Entity Recognition

The extraction or marking of the most important information from the text such as location, companies, names, events, places, topics, themes, monetary values, time, percentages, and other important information based on the governing algorithm is known as named entity recognition in NLP technology. It is one of the most fundamental components in numerous types of NLP projects such as chatbots, search engines, recommendation engines, sentiment analysis tools, and others.[132]

Sentiment Analysis

Sentiment analysis is another very important technique used in NLP technology. By this process, the emotion or an opinion of a user is analyzed in terms of different categories such as good, bad, or neutral. In real-world applications, this technique analyzes the text and finds out the emotion or view hidden within that text description of a speech. The most common attributes, which are used for categorizing sentiments or view of the text include positive, negative, and neutral.[133]

Sentiment analysis, also known as opinion mining, is a subfield of NLP that focuses on understanding and extracting subjective information from the text. It involves analyzing textual data to determine the sentiment or emotional tone expressed within the text. Sentiment analysis can be applied to various types of text data, such as product reviews, social media posts, customer feedback, news articles, and more. It helps businesses and organizations gain insights into public opinion, customer satisfaction, and brand perception. The most common steps that are involved in this NLP technique are as follows:

- **Presentiment Processing** – This step involves a couple of processes, which are the most fundamental for almost all other techniques used in NLP. Those processes include the text classification, POS tagging, and cleaning of the text from irrelevant signs and words.

- **Sentiment Classification** – ML algorithms or pretrained models are employed to classify the sentiment of the text. Common approaches include supervised learning, where labeled data is used to train a classifier, and unsupervised learning, which relies on techniques like lexicon-based analysis or clustering.

- **Post-Processing and Analysis** – Once the sentiment classification is obtained, post-processing techniques can be applied to refine the results. This may involve handling negations, intensifiers, or addressing context-specific challenges.

Summarization

Another very important technique implemented in the NLP or NLP technology is summarization of the text. This process finds out the most relevant summary or precise gist of a long text that does not lose the meaning, fluency, and accuracy of the original text. The most important features and characteristics of text summarization technique used in NLP are as follows[134]:

- It is used to achieve effectiveness of indexing, lesser biased text, personalized touch, increased accuracy, and short reading time of the text.

- There are three main types based on the objectives:
  - **Based on Input** – In this type of summarization, either one or more than one documents are used for summarization. If one document is used as input, it is called single document and if more documents are inputs, it is called multi-document input summarization type.
  - **Based on Output** – This category uses the types of outputs as the main differentiator. It is further divided into two more types such as extractive summary and abstractive summary.
  - **Based on Purpose** – The main objectives to achieve in the summary is another discriminator to categorize different types of summarization based on purposes. The main subtypes of this category include generic summary, query-based summary, and domain-specific summary.
- The following are the most fundamental steps of this technique:
  - Data cleaning and other preprocessing activities
  - Tokenization of sentences
  - Tokenization of words
  - Word-frequency table-building
  - Summarization of text
- The summarization of text in NLP can be based on numerous approaches:
  - **Statistical Approaches** – These methods rely on algorithms such as graph-based ranking, sentence scoring, or clustering techniques to identify important sentences or phrases for the summary.
  - **ML Approaches** – ML algorithms, such as decision trees, support vector machines (SVM), or DL models like recurrent neural networks (RNNs) or transformer models can be trained to learn patterns in the data and generate summaries.
  - **Transformer-Based Approaches** – State-of-the-art models like BERT (Bidirectional Encoder Representations from Transformers) or GPT (generative pretrained transformer) have shown promising results in abstractive summarization by leveraging their contextual understanding of language.

Topic Modeling

As the name indicates, topic modeling deals with the identification and separation of topics based on different criteria in ML models governed by NLP or NLP technology. Topic modeling in NLP is a technique used to uncover the main themes or topics present in a collection of documents. It is an unsupervised learning method that analyzes the patterns of word usage within the text to identify coherent topics that frequently occur together. The goal of topic modeling is to automatically discover the latent (hidden) topics in a large corpus of documents without any prior knowledge or explicit labeling. It allows for exploratory analysis of textual data by organizing documents into meaningful clusters or categories based on their shared thematic content. The most common algorithm used in NLP models are as follows[135]:

- Latent semantic analysis (LSA)
- Latent Dirichlet allocation (LDA)
- Probabilistic latent semantic analysis (pLSA)
- Nonnegative matrix factorization (NMF)
- Pachinko allocation model (PAM)

Topic modeling technique is deployed in a wide range of modern business applications to achieve the most desirable business bottom lines. The following are a few of the most important applications of topic modeling in NLP:

- **Document Clustering** – For categorizing different types of documents in separate categories for efficient management and processing.
- **Information Retrieval** – The information extraction from texts stored in different systems based on different criteria is accomplished through this application.
- **Sentiment Analysis** – Another main application is the opinion mining of the users' reviews through negative, positive, and neutral attributes.
- **Content Recommendation** – The recommendation of content, products, services, and other items of interests through topic modeling in NLP.
- **Keyword Extraction** – A major business application of topic modeling is the extraction of keywords for effective search engine optimization.
- **Trend Analysis** – The analysis of different trends in businesses, technologies, marketing, products, services, and many other areas can be done through this technique of NLP field.

Text Classification

The categorization or classification of text documents based on the content of that particular document is called text classification. It is one of the most important techniques extensively applied in NLP applications. It involves training a ML model to learn patterns and relationships between the textual features and target classes. Text classification is a supervised learning task where a labeled dataset is used to train a classifier that can predict the class or category of unseen or new text data. Text classification has various applications in NLP, including sentiment analysis, spam detection, document categorization, topic classification, intent recognition, and many others. It enables automated organization and analysis of textual data, allowing for efficient information retrieval and decision-making based on the content of the text. The typical steps involving this technique of NLP are as follows:

- **Text Preparation** – The text data is preprocessed by cleaning and transforming it into a suitable format for analysis. This may involve removing punctuation, stop words, and special characters, as well as performing tokenization and normalization.
- **Feature Extraction** – The most relevant features or representations are extracted from the preprocessed text data. This can involve various techniques:
  - Bag-of-words
  - TF–IDF (term frequency–inverse document frequency)
  - Word embedding (e.g., Word2Vec or GloVe)
  - More advanced techniques like BERT
- **Training Dataset Development** – The labeled training data is prepared, where each text document is associated with a known class or category. This requires human annotation or labeling of the data.
- **ML Model Training** – ML algorithms or DL models are trained on the labeled training data to learn the patterns and relationships between the text features and their corresponding classes. Common algorithms used for text classification include Naive Bayes, SVM, decision trees, random forests, and NN.
- **Model Evaluation** – The trained model is evaluated on a separate test dataset to assess its performance and generalization ability. Evaluation metrics such as accuracy, precision, recall, and F1 score are commonly used.
- **Model Prediction** – Once the model is trained and evaluated, it can be used to classify new, unseen text documents into the predefined classes or categories.

Keyword Extraction

The process of mining the most relevant or most important words or phrases that are relevant to the piece of text or article is known as keyword extraction. This is an automated process of NLP technology. It is another very important technique used in the NLP projects. The main examples of the applications of this technique are the tools used in search engine optimization of different websites or webpage. There are a large number of keyword extractions tools available in the marketplace to automatically extract important keyword expressions and single words.[136] Keyword extraction techniques can be combined or customized based on the specific requirements and domain of the application. The extracted keywords provide a condensed representation of the document's main topics or concepts, facilitating various downstream tasks and enabling efficient information retrieval and analysis.

The most common approaches applied to keyword extraction technique of NLP include the following:

- **Graph-Based Approaches** – Graph-based keyword extraction methods involve representing words or phrases as nodes in a graph, where the edges represent relationships between them. Algorithms such as TextRank or PageRank can be applied to rank the nodes based on their importance. The top-ranked nodes are considered as keywords.

- **ML Approaches** – ML algorithms, such as supervised classification models or unsupervised clustering algorithms, can be used for keyword extraction. In supervised approaches, labeled training data is used to train a model to predict whether a word or phrase is a keyword or not. In unsupervised approaches, clustering algorithms are applied to group words or phrases into keyword clusters based on their semantic similarity.

- **POS Tagging** – It can be used to identify the grammatical category of words in a sentence. By focusing on specific POS, such as nouns or adjectives, keywords can be extracted based on their relevance to the document's content.
  - **Statistical Approach** – Statistical approach can be used as a keyword extraction tool in NLP projects. For instance, TF-IDF is commonly used to extract keywords. Other models can be built on top of that.

Lemmatization and Stemming

In the NLP field, lemmatization and stemming are two very important techniques that are closely related but slightly different techniques. This is the reason that they are mostly expressed together. These techniques are used for normalizing the text in ML projects. With the help of these two techniques, the root words are found against the derived or inflected words in any text.

The most common type of tool used for lemmatization and stemming technique is known as NLTK.STEM. There are also many other tools available in the marketplace for this purpose.[137] They help standardize words, reduce vocabulary size, and improve the accuracy of text analysis tasks by treating related words as a single entity. Let us have a look at the definitions of those two important techniques used in NLP:

- **Lemmatization** – Lemmatization aims to determine the base form or lemma of a word by considering its POS and applying morphological analysis. Unlike stemming, lemmatization ensures that the resulting lemma is a valid word. For example, lemmatization converts words like "running", "runs", and "ran" to the lemma "run".

- **Stemming** – Stemming is the process of removing suffixes from words to obtain their base or root form, known as the stem. It involves applying heuristic rules to truncate or remove the ends of words. The resulting stems may not always be valid words themselves, but they are used to group words with similar meanings together. For example, stemming converts words like "running", "runs", and "ran" to the stem "run".

The most common differences between stemming and lemmatization are as follows:

- Stemming is faster than the lemmatization techniques.
- Lemmatization processes the word to meaningful entity known as lemma, while the stemming strips both ends of the word, i.e., prefixes and suffixes, and forms the root of the word, which may have no meaningful context.
- Lemmatization uses heavy computation compared with the stemming process or technique.
- Stemming is beneficial for large datasets to maintain high performance while the lemmatization provides more accuracy compared with the performance.

SAMPLE QUESTIONS

1. What is NLP?
2. How does NLP technology function in processing human language?
3. What are the primary applications of NLP?
4. Which specific techniques are commonly employed in NLP?
5. How is NLP applied in the context of sentiment analysis?
6. What challenges are associated with the implementation of NLP in real-world applications?
7. In what ways does NLP contribute to the advancements in AI and ML?

5

Deep Learning Transformer Architecture

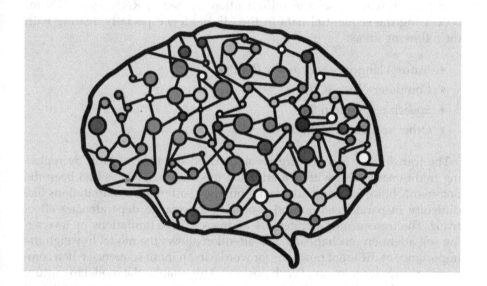

Introduction

ChatGPT is a platform that is based on the transformer architecture. The transformer architecture is built out of deep learning (DL) artificial intelligence (AI) networks. In the previous models of machine learning (ML), the use of recurring neural networks (RNN) was the core component in building the advanced ML models for different types of sequential data processing dealing with timestamps, positioning of the variables, and other such types of items. Thus, the most popular choice for the data scientists was to use RNN for processing the sequential data in ML models. Those RNN were short in a couple of areas that were known as the basic downsides of this network. Those limitations suffered by RNN networks are as follows:

- Lacking in parallelization of sequential data processing
- Effective detection of long-range dependencies

DOI: 10.1201/9781003474173-5

The above-mentioned discrepancies were addressed through another mechanism known as self-attention. The self-attention was introduced by Ashish Vaswani and his team of computer scientists in the field of AI, who published a research paper "Attention is all you need" in 2017 for overcoming the limitations of RNN and CNN neural networks.[138] Previously, the sequence-to-sequence modeling was based on the RNN or the convolutional networks. Vaswani et al. introduced a new technique known as transformer, which uses the self-attention instead of RNN and CNN for processing the sequential data in the ML models especially dealing with the following areas:

- Natural language processing (NLP)
- Computer vision (CV)
- Speech recognition (SR)
- Other sequential tasks in ML

The transformer architecture revolutionized the field of NLP by replacing traditional RNNs with self-attention mechanisms. RNNs had been the dominant choice for sequential tasks, but they suffered from limitations like difficulty in parallelization and capturing long-range dependencies effectively. The transformer architecture addresses these limitations by leveraging self-attention mechanisms. Self-attention allows the model to weigh the importance of different positions (or words) in an input sequence when computing the representation of each position. This enables the model to capture contextual dependencies effectively without any recurrence or convolutional operations.

The DL transformer model sits at the core of the ChatGPT platform to provide the power, performance, speed, reliability, and accuracy. In this chapter, all aspects of DL transformer technology or architecture will be discussed. The importance of DL transformer in modern AI models will also be discussed at length in the following sections to shed more light on this futuristic AI technique or architecture.

Importance of the Deep Learning Transformer

The DL transformer is the most advanced technology in the AI technology for processing the sequential inputs or data. It is becoming the most popular architecture for advanced NLP, CV, and other applications. ChatGPT has used this model at the core of its platform to overcome the limitations that were associated with the earlier models such as RNN and convolutional neural networks (CNN). The importance of DL transformers is characterized by the following factors[141]:

- **Higher Performance** – The transformer architecture has achieved remarkable performance on a wide range of NLP tasks. It has surpassed previous models, such as RNNs, in tasks like machine translation, text generation, sentiment analysis, and question-answering. The transformer's ability to capture long-range dependencies and its parallelizable nature has contributed to its success.

- **Efficient Context Modeling** – The transformer architectures excel at capturing contextual relationships within a sequence. The self-attention mechanism allows the model to weigh the importance of different elements based on their contextual relevance. This ability makes transformers well-suited for tasks involving understanding, generating, or processing sequential data, including text, speech, and time series data.

- **Parallelization Capability** – Unlike recurrent neural networks, which process sequences sequentially, transformers can process the entire sequence in parallel. This parallelization significantly speeds up training and inference times, making the model more efficient and scalable. It also allows transformers to leverage computational resources more effectively, making them suitable for large-scale applications.

- **Capability of Pretraining and Transfer Learning** – Transformers have been successfully employed in transfer learning scenarios. Pretraining a transformer model on a large corpus of data, such as the BERT (Bidirectional Encoder Representations from Transformers) model, allows the model to learn general language representations. These pretrained models can then be fine-tuned on specific downstream tasks, requiring less labeled data and achieving better performance.

- **Versatility** – While initially developed for NLP tasks, the transformer architecture has shown its versatility by being successfully applied to other domains, including CV and SR. For instance, Vision Transformers (ViTs) have demonstrated competitive performance on image classification tasks, showcasing the broad applicability of the transformer model beyond NLP.

- **Perfect Interpretability** – The attention mechanism in transformers provides interpretability by revealing which elements of the input sequence contribute more to the model's predictions. This interpretability can be crucial in understanding the model's decision-making process, debugging, and analyzing the model behavior.

- **Continual Improvement** – The transformer architecture continues to evolve and improve. Researchers have proposed various extensions and modifications, such as incorporating additional architectural elements, adapting the model for specific domains, or combining transformers with other models. This ongoing research ensures that the transformer model remains at the forefront of AI advancements.

There is a huge scope of this futuristic technique in all futuristic NLP projects as well as in other ML projects such as CV, SR, and many others.

What Is the Transformer Model?

The Transformer model is one of the most advanced ML-based models for NLP applications. This model has been used in ChatGPT platform for processing the natural language communication. It is based on neural networks with multiple hidden layers to process the sequential input data to transform it into another form of sequential output in NLP applications. The most important use case of transformer model is the automated translators based on the DL transformer architectures.

The most important features and characteristics of DL transformer model are as follows[139,140]:

- A sequential data processing model that is extensively used for NLP, CV, and other sequential data processing tasks.
- This model supports parallelization of processing presentations of sequential data to make it a high-speed and relatively quicker model compared with the traditional neural network models such as CNN, which could process sequential data in serial and would not support the parallelization.
- It is capable of processing entire sequence of the data in the text for an NLP application and also for other sequential applications.
- The transformer model's architectural design has proven to be highly effective in various NLP tasks, including machine translation, text summarization, sentiment analysis, and question-answering. Its ability to model context, process sequences in parallel, and capture long-range dependencies has made it a powerful and widely used architecture in the field of DL.
- This DL transformer model is based on the encoder and decoder architecture for sequential data processing.
- It uses the self-attention mechanism for learning sequence in the presentation of the data in input and converting it into the output presentation.

- It does not depend upon the recurrence or convolution processes in processing the sequential data because it uses the concept of attention for the same.
- In other words, the transformer model deals with the mapping of the input sequence to the sequence of continuous presentation and then that presentation is fed into the decoder part of the transformer for generating the output.
- There are numerous components of DL transformer model:
  - **Encoder** – The encoder takes an input sequence (e.g., a sentence) and generates a sequence of contextualized representations for each element in the input. Each element's representation is computed by attending to all other elements in the input sequence using self-attention. This allows the model to capture dependencies and relationships between elements effectively. In the transformer model, the encoder is one of the main components responsible for processing the input sequence and creating a rich representation of it. The encoder's role is to encode the input sequence into a set of high-dimensional representations, often referred to as "contextualized embedding" or "hidden states". The encoder consists of a stack of identical layers, and each layer typically contains two subcomponents: the multihead self-attention mechanism and the position-wise feed-forward neural network.
  - **Decoder** – The decoder, often used in tasks like machine translation or text generation, generates an output sequence based on the encoded input representations. It employs self-attention and incorporates attention over the encoder's outputs to capture relevant information from the input sequence. Similar to the encoder, the decoder consists of a stack of identical layers. Each layer in the decoder typically contains three subcomponents: masked multihead self-attention, encoder–decoder attention, and position-wise feed-forward neural network.
  - **Self-Attention** – This is a revolutionary concept that overcomes the limitations of the previous procedures such as recurrence and convolutions. Self-attention is a mechanism that computes the importance or attention weights of each element in the input sequence relative to other elements. It allows the model to focus on different parts of the input when generating representations, enabling the capturing of long-range dependencies.
  - **Multihead Attention** – Multihead attention is the use of multiple parallel self-attention layers within the model. Each layer attends to different parts of the input sequence, allowing the model to

capture diverse relationships and improve performance. All the main steps used for accomplishing single self-attention process are repeated multiple times to complete the multihead attention task. These steps are taken in parallel to enhance the speed of the process.

- **Positional Encoding** – Since transformers lack the inherent notion of position or order in the input sequence, positional encodings are added to provide information about the relative positions of elements. This encoding helps the model understand the sequential structure of the input.

- **Feed-Forward Neural Networks** – Transformers include feed-forward neural networks applied to each element's representation independently, enabling the model to transform and refine the representations further.

- **Residual Connections and Layer Normalization** – Residual connections facilitate the flow of information through the model's layers, while layer normalization helps stabilize the training process by normalizing the representations.

- The encoder component of the DL transformer model consists of the N number of identical layers (where $N = 6$). Each of those six layers consists of two more sublayers that handle two other important processes such as multihead self-attention and feed-forward neural network, which consists of two linear transformations with rectified linear unit or ReLU activation between them.

- The first sublayer of six identical layers are tasked to implement the multihead self-attention mechanism.

- Multihead self-attention is a key component of the transformer model, which is a DL architecture commonly used in NLP tasks. Self-attention allows the model to weigh the importance of different words or tokens within a sequence when encoding or decoding information. In the context of the transformer model, "multi-head" refers to the idea of performing attention computations multiple times in parallel, each with its own set of learned parameters. By using multiple attention heads, the model can capture different relationships between words or tokens.

- The multihead self-attention process can be further divided into the following sequential steps for better understanding. The first four steps are taken to accomplish single self-attention process, and repeating this for multiple times is known as multihead self-attention process:

  - **Presentation of Input Data** – Each sequence of words is first transformed into three vectors: query (Q), key (K), and value (V). These vectors are obtained by multiplying the input sequence with learned weight matrices.

- **Calculation of Attention Score** – In this step, for each token in the input sequence, the attention scores are computed by taking the dot product between the query vector of the token and the key vectors of all other tokens. This measures the relevance or importance of the token to the other tokens in the sequence.

- **Calculation of Attention Weights** – The attention scores are scaled by a factor of the square root of the dimension of the key vector to prevent the gradients from becoming too small. Then, the soft-max function is applied to obtain the attention weights, which represent the relative importance of each token in the sequence.

- **Calculating Representation of Context Value** – The attention weights are used to weigh the value vectors of all tokens. These weighted value vectors are then summed up, resulting in a weighted sum representation, which captures the context or information from other tokens in the sequence.

- **Repetitions of Above Steps** – The above-mentioned steps are used to conduct one single self-attention process. To obtain the multihead self-attention, this entire process is repeated multiple times, typically with different learned weight matrices, to obtain multiple sets of attention weights and weighted sum representations. These sets of representations are then concatenated or linearly combined to produce the final output.

- The encoder of transformer consists of two sublayers and the decoder consists of three sublayers of neural network.

- The main sublayers of encoder are as follows:

  - **Multihead Self-Attention** – This component allows the model to capture the dependencies between different words or tokens in the input sequence. It employs the concept of self-attention, which calculates attention weights for each word or token based on the relationships between all the words in the sequence. The multihead aspect refers to performing self-attention multiple times in parallel, allowing the model to capture different types of relationships between words. The attention weights determine how much each word should contribute to the representation of other words in the sequence.

  - **Position-Wise Feed-Forward Neural Network** – This component provides a nonlinear transformation of the representations obtained from the self-attention mechanism. It applies a fully connected feed-forward neural network to each position in the sequence independently. This network has two linear layers with a ReLU activation function in between. The purpose of this component is to add more complexity and expressiveness to the representations and enable the model to learn more sophisticated patterns in the text data.

- The main sublayers of decoder are three in number:
  - **Masked Multihead Self-Attention** – This component allows the decoder to attend to the previously generated tokens in the output sequence, ensuring that each position can only attend to the positions before it. This masking prevents the model from seeing future tokens during training, which ensures the autoregressive property required for generation. By attending to the preceding tokens, the decoder can capture the dependencies and relationships within the output sequence.
  - **Encoder–Decoder Attention** – This component of decoder enables the decoder to attend to the encoded representations generated by the encoder. It helps the decoder access the information from the input sequence and align it with the current position in the output sequence. The encoder–decoder attention mechanism allows the decoder to focus on relevant parts of the input sequence while generating the output.
  - **Position-Wise Feed-Forward Neural Network** – Similar to the encoder, the decoder also employs a position-wise feed-forward network to add nonlinearity and increase the expressiveness of the representations at each position.
- For enhancement of training stability, overall performance, and gradient flow of the transformer model, two important techniques are used:
  - **Residual Connections** – Residual connections, also known as skip connections, are connections that bypass certain layers and allow the flow of information from earlier layers directly to subsequent layers. In the context of the transformer model, residual connections are used to mitigate the vanishing gradient problem and make it easier for the model to learn effectively. This technique helps propagate gradients more effectively through the network, making it easier to train deep models. It enables the model to learn incremental changes rather than completely replacing the original input. Residual connections are a key factor in allowing the successful training of DL transformer architectures. In each layer of the transformer, a residual connection is introduced before applying the layer normalization. The residual connection is a simple element-wise addition operation that combines the input to the layer with the output of that layer. This means that the original input to the layer is directly added to the transformed output of the layer, allowing

the model to learn residual functions. Mathematically, it can be represented as follows:

Output = Layer Normalization (Input + Sublayer (Output))

- **Layer Normalization** – Layer normalization is a technique used to normalize the activations or outputs of each layer in the transformer model. It helps address the internal covariate shift problem by reducing the distributional shift of the data and improving the stability of training. Layer normalization is applied after the residual connection is applied in each sub-component of the transformer layer, such as the multihead self-attention and position-wise feed-forward network. It normalizes the activation by subtracting the mean and dividing by the standard deviation across the hidden dimensions of the layer. The layer normalization operation is performed independently for each training instance and each hidden dimension. It helps reduce the dependence on the scale of the inputs and makes the model more robust to varying input distributions. By applying layer normalization, the transformer model benefits from improved training dynamics, faster convergence, and better generalization. It also helps alleviate the impact of vanishing or exploding gradients, which can occur in deep neural networks.

- **Positioning Encoder** – It is another important component of transformer architecture. It is a technique to inject the positional information into the input data or sequence. Unlike recurrent or CNNs, which inherently capture sequential information, the transformer model relies solely on self-attention and does not have an inherent notion of order or position in its input. Positional encoding is introduced to address this limitation and enable the model to consider the sequential order of the tokens in the input sequence. The positional encoding is added to the word embedding of the input sequence before being fed into the transformer model. It provides a representation that encodes the relative or absolute position of each token in the sequence. The positional encoding is designed to be a fixed and learnable representation rather than being updated during the training process. It consists of a set of sinusoidal functions of different frequencies and phases, defined based on the position and the dimension of the embedding. The positional encoding is added element-wise to the word embedding, which carry the semantic meaning of the tokens. This combined representation of word embedding and positional encoding provides input to the transformer model, allowing it to have access to both the semantic information and the positional information of the tokens.

- **Feed-Forward Network** – This is an important component of transformer architecture that is available both in encoder and decoder deep neural networks of transformer model. It is a type of fully connected neural network that introduces nonlinearity and adds complexity to the model's computations. The feed-forward network is applied independently to each position in the sequence within the self-attention sublayer of the transformer layer. It consists of two linear transformations with a nonlinear activation function applied in between them. The purpose of the feed-forward network is to introduce nonlinear transformations to the representations learned from the attention mechanism. It allows the model to capture more complex patterns and relationships within the data.

- The most important applications of transformer network include ChatGPT, DALL-E, Microsoft Copilot, Google Search, and others. They are normally implemented in the large language model (LLM)-based applications.

What Is a Pretrained System?

A pretrained system is an AI or AI-based module that can be trained on a huge corpus of data and can also be improved by adding the modules that have already learned from the large corpus of data. The continual fine-tuning and enhancement is possible in pretrained ML projects or models. In other words, a pretrained system refers to a ML model or system that has been trained on a large dataset using a specific task or objective. The pretraining process involves training the model on a vast amount of labeled or unlabeled data to learn general representations or patterns within the data. The most important applications of pretrained models come from NLP, CV, SR, and others. Such most popular applications are as follows:

- ChatGPT – Derived from GPT
- Bidirectional Encoder Representations from Transformers

The goal of pretraining is to enable the model to capture rich and meaningful features from the data that can be further fine-tuned or utilized for specific downstream tasks. By training on a large corpus of data, a pretrained system can learn useful representations that can generalize well to new, unseen examples. These models are trained on vast amounts of text data from sources like books, articles, and the web. Once a model is pretrained, it can be further fine-tuned or adapted for specific downstream tasks. Fine-tuning involves training the pretrained model on a task-specific dataset with labeled data. By fine-tuning, the model can specialize its learned representations to the specific task at hand, which often leads to improved performance. The advantage of pretrained systems is that they can leverage the knowledge and representations learned from a large dataset, which might not be feasible to train from scratch on limited resources. Pretraining helps in capturing general knowledge and patterns, which can be transferred and utilized for various downstream tasks, saving time and computational resources.

The other main features and characteristics of pretrained AI-based systems are as follows[142]:

- These models save significant time, computation, and other resources for the development of powerful ML applications.
- They are task-specific models with capabilities to continual improvement and fine-tuning through labeled datasets for a specific task.
- Pretrained models are very well aware of the main objectives from starting point to achieve through fine-tuning and other tweaking processes.
- These models are also referred to as reusable pretrained models.
- In the NLP field, they are mostly based on DL and pretrained transformer architectures.
- These models support transfer ML for both starting a new project or fine-tuning the existing models.
- These models enable the systems learn both the lower level and higher level features of natural language perfectly.

What Are the Main Types of Pretrained Systems?

The pretrained systems are the advanced AI systems that are trained on large corpus of data for fine-tuning and improvement of the existing models that can be transferred from one model to another one. The modern pretrained systems are mostly based on transformer and associated technologies.[143]

Compared with numerous types of embedding models, transformer-based models are able to support transfer learning. By virtue of this, it has become possible to develop new ML projects faster, cheaper, and in a more efficient way. The most important transformer-based pretrained ML systems are as follows[144]:

- Bidirectional Encoder Representations from Transformers
- Generative pretrained transformer
- Text-to-text transfer transformer (T5)
- Attention mechanism and transformer
- Universal Sentence Encoder (USE)

The above-mentioned transformer-based pretrained ML systems are dealt with in detail in the following sections.

Bidirectional Encoder Representations from Transformers

BERT is a highly advanced ML-based program dealing with the natural language. It was developed by Google Corporation in 2018. This NLP model is based on transformer DL technology. It is a pretrained program on a huge corpus of training dataset that supports transfer learning for building new projects by transferring the pretrained modules and improving them through further ML training. This model uses large amount of unlabeled training datasets to learn the powerful language representations.

The architecture of BERT builds upon the original transformer model, which introduced the concept of self-attention mechanisms to capture relationship between words in a sentence. The transformer model consists of an encoder and a decoder, but BERT focuses only on the encoder part. The encoder in BERT processes the input text by transforming it into a set of contextualized word embeddings. It has significantly advanced the field of NLP and has been influential in various NLP tasks, such as text classification, named entity recognition, question-answering, and more. The key innovation of BERT lies in its pretraining strategy. BERT is pretrained in a masked language modeling (MLM) task and a next sentence prediction (NSP) task. During pretraining, BERT learns to predict missing words in a sentence given the context of the surrounding words (MLM), and it also learns to determine whether two sentences appear consecutively in a document (NSP). This pretraining process allows BERT to capture deep contextual relationships between words and sentences.

Once the pretraining is completed, BERT can be fine-tuned on specific downstream tasks with smaller labeled datasets. Fine-tuning involves adding a task-specific layer on top of BERT and training the model on the labeled data for the target task. This fine-tuning process adapts the pretrained BERT model to the specific task at hand, making it highly effective for various NLP tasks. The following are the main features of BERT system:

- It is trained on both sides, which is opposite to the GPT model of NLP.
- It is an encoder-based AI-based language model.

- There are two main versions of BERT:
  - BERT_BASE
  - BERT_LARGE
- The first version, i.e., BERT_BASE version, is of the size of GPT, while the BERT_LARGE is a larger model with more than 24 transformer blocks and over 340 parameters.
- This model is trained for two tasks such as NSP and masked language model with the help of English Wikipedia and Books Corpus.
- **Masked Language Model** – This is used to achieve bidirectionality in the model. One of the key advantages of BERT is its ability to capture contextual information bidirectionally. Unlike previous models that rely on left-to-right or right-to-left contexts, BERT considers both directions when encoding a word's meaning, allowing it to better understand the nuances of language.
- **Next Sentence Prediction** – NSP is one of the two tasks used during the pretraining phase of Google BERT model. NSP is designed to help BERT learn the relationship between pairs of sentences or document structures. The NSP task involves training BERT to predict whether two given sentences appear consecutively in a document or not. During pretraining, BERT is provided with pairs of sentences from a large corpus of unlabeled text. For each pair, there is a 50% chance that the second sentence is indeed the consecutive sentence to the first sentence, while the other 50% chance is that the second sentence is randomly chosen from the corpus.
- The encoding of inputs of BERT models in specific ways consists of the following three main parts:
  - WordPiece tokenization embeddings
  - Segment embeddings
  - Position embeddings
- All the above three components are element-wise added together to provide the model with a large input vector of 768-dimensions.

Generative Pretrained Transformer

GPT is developed by OpenAI. This model was first proposed in 2018 dubbed as GPT-1. Later on, numerous other GPT models or versions were introduced by OpenAI. The foundation of state-of-the art ChatGPT application is based on the series of different GPT versions developed by OpenAI. The main objective of building this NLP model was the pretraining of a general language model for using it directly for multiple tasks simultaneously. GPT models are based on the transformer architecture, specifically the decoder portion of the transformer, and have been influential in advancing the field of NLP and text generation. The GPT models are trained in an unsupervised manner on vast amounts of unlabeled text data from the Internet. The objective of training is to predict the next word in a given sequence of words. By learning from this task, the models acquire a deep understanding of language patterns, syntax, and semantics.

The original GPT model, GPT-1, was introduced in 2018. It consisted of a single-layer transformer model with 117 million parameters. GPT-2, released in 2019, was a more significant breakthrough. It had 1.5 billion parameters and demonstrated remarkable capabilities in generating coherent and contextually relevant text. GPT-2 was so powerful that OpenAI initially refrained from releasing the full version due to concerns about potential misuse. Subsequently, GPT-3, introduced in 2020, became the largest GPT model with 175 billion parameters. The GPT-3 platform demonstrated even more impressive language-generation capabilities, allowing it to perform tasks such as text completion, translation, question-answering, and even creative writing to some extent. The GPT-3 version showed that larger models could produce high-quality, context-aware text, but they also raised concerns about ethical considerations, computational resources, and environmental impact.

The other main features and characteristics of GPT model are as follows[144,145]:

- GPT is a type of DL neural network.
- They are used for learning, manipulating, and creating the human-like text or voice for communication similar to the communications done by humans.
- The most important tasks performed by GPT include answering questions, creating text from voice and vice versa, generating codes, summarizing text, and creating numerous types of articles used for different purposes.
- GPTs support the transfer learning and fine-tuning through additional training for molding the model for special purposes.
- Before GPTs, the creation of text was accomplished through RNNs and long short-term memory (LSTM) neural networks.
- The transformer technology was first used by Google in 2017 for just learning the natural language. It was not able to generate the language.
- OpenAI developed multiple versions of GPTs and used it for the generation of human-like text in different applications, especially in ChatGPT version 3 and version 4.
- The most important versions of GPT developed by OpenAI include GPT-1, GPT-2, GPT-3, GPT-3.5, and GPT-4.

- For the purpose of producing input embeddings, the first version of GPT uses 12 decoders through encoding of sequence inputs by using byte pair encoding (BPE) mechanism.
- For training on two tasks, i.e., text classification and text prediction, the GPT uses BookCorpus, which includes over 7000 unpublished books.
- The fine-tuning of GPT is accomplished through four supervised tasks:
  - Natural language inference
  - Question-answering and common sense reasoning
  - Two types of classification
  - Semantic similarity

It is worth noting that GPT models are generative models, meaning they generate text based on the patterns they have learned from the training data. However, they do not have a built-in understanding of the real world or true comprehension of the generated text. They rely solely on statistical patterns learned from the training data to generate text that appears coherent and contextually relevant.

Universal Sentence Encoder

The encoding of text sentence into multidimensional vectors is accomplished by using USE. It is developed by Google Corporation and used for various purposes[146]:

- Text classification
- Clustering
- Semantic similarity
- Other NLP tasks

Building multidimensional numeric vector is very important for measuring the distance between two vectors so that the position of the word can be assessed for achieving the above-mentioned tasks. Converting data into vectors is one of the main fields in which the data scientists are more interested in working on to achieve the advanced capabilities in many fields of ML such as NLP, CV, SR, and others. It is designed to capture semantic information and produce meaningful sentence embeddings that can be used in a wide range of NLP tasks. Unlike word embeddings, which represent individual words, the USE generates embeddings for entire sentences or short paragraphs. The model takes advantage of DL techniques, specifically deep neural networks, to learn meaningful representations of sentences. The advantage of using the USE is that it provides a simple and efficient way to capture the semantic meaning of sentences, regardless of the specific task or domain. The pretrained model is trained on a large corpus of data, making it capable of encoding sentences with a wide range of meanings and contexts. Overall, the USE offers a powerful tool for encoding sentences into fixed-length representations, enabling easier comparison, analysis, and understanding of textual data in various NLP applications.

Additional features and characteristics of USE are as follows:

- The architecture of USE is transformer-based neural network developed by Google.
- It is available with two versions:
  - **Universal Sentence Encoder Lite** – This version of USE provides a smaller and faster version of the USE. It offers good performance while being suitable for resource-constrained environments.
  - **Universal Sentence Encoder Multilingual** – This version of USE is designed to handle text from multiple languages. It is trained on a multilingual corpus and can encode sentences in different languages into meaningful representations.
- The USE model encodes sentences into fixed-length numerical representations.
- Transformer-based USE model of Google Corporation consists of six transformer encoders on the top of each other.
- Technologically speaking, Google developed two versions of USE: one is based on transformer encoder and the other one is based on deep averaging network (DAN). There is a trade-off between those two types of models. The main factors pertaining to trade-off include computational resources and accuracy of the results. Transformer encoder uses more computational power and produces higher accuracy while the DAN-based model uses lesser resources of computation and produces a little lower accuracy.
- A few major uses of USE based on transformer encoder are as follows:
  - Effective use as an embedding layer at the beginning of DL models
  - Avoiding the nuisance of duplicate sentences or phrases before analysis
  - Accomplishing text classification task by identifying the semantically similar sentences
- Numerous tasks related to NLP, CV, SR, and other functions of NLP can be accomplished through USE based on transformer encoder model.

Text-to-Text Transfer Transformer

T5 is a state-of-the-art DL language model architecture. This versatile model is developed by Google Corporation in 2019. This language model architecture was introduced by Google through a research paper "Exploring the Limits of Transfer Learning with Unified Text-to-Text Transformer". The model architecture is highly useful for NLP field to develop DL models for various tasks:

- Text generation
- Question-answering
- Text summarization
- Language translation

The training process involves pretraining T5 on a large corpus of publicly available text from the Internet. The model learns to predict the output for a given input by leveraging the vast amount of knowledge contained within the training data. It uses transformer architecture, which is a type of DL model specifically designed for sequence-to-sequence tasks. T5 differs from previous models like GPT-3 in that it is trained using a "text-to-text" framework. Instead of training separate models for each NLP task, T5 is trained using a unified framework where different tasks are cast as text-to-text transformations. In this framework, both the input and output are text strings, allowing for a more generalized and flexible approach to handling various NLP tasks. The architecture of T5 consists of an encoder–decoder setup with multiple layers of self-attention mechanisms, enabling the model to effectively capture the dependencies and relationships within the input text. It also employs techniques such as MLM and sequence-to-sequence training to enhance its performance.

Other main features and characteristics of T5 are as follows[147]:

- In T5 model architecture, the input and output are text strings. Those strings enable the system to handle numerous NLP tasks effectively.
- Multiple layers of self-attention are used for capturing the relationship and dependencies within the given input text.
- A range of NLP tasks can be accomplished through this model by fine-tuning the pretrained models with specific datasets and are transferred as a transfer learning technique.
- It is considered as one of the most flexible model language architectures in the modern NLP field.
- All tasks in the NLP domain are reframed into unified text-to-text format (text strings at both input and output).
- This model was pretrained on C4 model, which stands for Colossal, Clean, Crawled, and Corpus. This C4 pretrained structure consists of cleaned version of over 700 GB size of common crawl dataset.

- The fine-tuning of this model was done through domain-specific training of text summarization, sentence similarity detection, language translation, and others.
- The following are the most common fine-tuning steps involved in T5:
  - **Formulation of Specific Tasks** – The specific NLP task is formulated in a text-to-text format. This involves defining the input and output text representations for the task. For example, for translation, the input could be a sentence in one language, and the output could be the translated sentence in another language.
  - **Fine-Tuning Dataset Preparation** – A dataset is collected or created for the target task. The dataset should consist of input–output pairs that align with the text-to-text format defined in the previous step. The dataset is usually labeled or annotated with the correct outputs for training.
  - **Tokenization** – The input and output texts in the dataset are tokenized, which involves breaking them down into smaller units such as words or sub-words. Tokenization ensures that the model can process the text efficiently.
  - **Setting Up Training Architecture** – The pretrained T5 model is initialized, and the dataset is split into training datasets and validation datasets. The training set is used to update the model's weights, while the validation set helps monitor the model's performance during training.
  - **Fine-Tuning Process** – The model is trained on the task-specific dataset using techniques such as backpropagation and gradient descent. The weights of the model are updated based on the loss between the predicted outputs and the ground truth outputs from the dataset. The model goes through multiple training iterations or epochs to improve its performance.
  - **Evaluating on Test Datasets** – After training, the fine-tuned model is evaluated on a separate test set or benchmark dataset to assess its performance. Metrics such as accuracy, precision, recall, or BLEU score (for translation tasks) are commonly used to evaluate the model's quality.
  - **Repetitive Refinement** – Depending on the evaluation results, further iterations of fine-tuning and evaluation may be performed to improve the model's performance. This iterative process helps optimize the model for the specific NLP task.

Attention Mechanism in Transformer

The attention mechanism enables the model to focus on relevant parts of the input sequence when generating an output in the transformer architecture in

NLP models. Transformer architecture is a type of DL model that leverages attention mechanisms for efficient and effective sequence processing.

The attention mechanism allows models to assign different weights to different parts of the input sequence, emphasizing or attending to more important or relevant information. It helps the model capture dependencies and relationships between different positions within the input sequence. The key idea behind attention is to calculate a weighted sum of the input representations, where the weights indicate the importance or relevance of each input position. The self-attention mechanism in the transformer allows each position in the sequence to attend to all other positions, capturing dependencies across the entire sequence. It calculates attention scores by comparing the input representations of each position with representations of all other positions using dot products. These scores are then used to calculate the weighted sum of the input representations, resulting in the attention output. By leveraging attention mechanisms and self-attention, the transformer model enables efficient and effective processing of sequential data, leading to significant improvements in various NLP tasks such as machine translation, text generation, and sentiment analysis.

What Are Large Language Models?

LLMs are types of DL algorithms in the field of AI. These models are trained on huge or large corpus of data that consists of numerous sources on the Internet. The main objectives of LLM models is to make machines learn through training on massive datasets in such a way that they can generate human-like text automatically against the queries or requests of humans or other intelligent machines that can somewhat understand and generate automated responses.

The most salient features and characteristics of LLMs are as follows[148]:

- LLMs are also known as foundation models for AI projects based on DL neural networks.
- The concept of LLMs emerged in 2017 when the first transformer model or architecture of languages based on transformer neural networks was developed.
- LLMs are cable of learning from human conversational data in the form of text and voice and can generate suitable response against any query asked in the natural language format that the humans speak.
- The most common objectives of using LLMs are as follows:
  - Language translation
  - Text generation

- Content rewriting
- Text summarization
- Sentiment analysis
- Classification and categorization
- The most common examples of LLMs are as follows:
  - GPT
  - Bidirectional Encoder Representations from Transformers
  - Text-to-text transfer transformer
- LLMs are characterized by their extensive size and capacity, often containing billions or even trillions of parameters. These models are normally trained on large language datasets consisting of diverse text sources, such as books, articles, websites, and other textual data available on the Internet.
- LLM-based transformers leverage attention mechanisms to capture relationships and dependencies between different words or tokens within a sequence. This allows the models to understand context, syntax, semantics, and even generate coherent and contextually the most relevant text.
- The following are a few common categories of LLMs:
  - **Autoregressive Language Models** – Autoregressive language models generate text by predicting the next word or token in a sequence given the preceding context. Models like GPT fall into this category. They are trained to predict the next word based on previous words, enabling them to generate coherent and contextually relevant text.
  - **Transformer-Based Models** – Transformer-based models, such as GPT, BERT, and T5, utilize the transformer architecture as the backbone. Transformers use self-attention mechanisms to capture dependencies between different positions within a sequence, enabling effective representation learning and contextual understanding.
  - **Encoder–Decoder-Based Models** – Encoder–decoder models are commonly used in sequence-to-sequence tasks, such as machine translation and text summarization. These models consist of an encoder that processes the input sequence and a decoder that generates the output sequence. Transformer-based architectures, like the transformer model itself and T5, often serve as the basis for encoder–decoder models.
  - **Pretrained Language Models** – Pretrained language models are models that are initially trained on large amounts of text data in an unsupervised manner. These models learn to represent

language effectively and capture linguistic patterns. Examples include GPT, BERT, and T5. Pretrained models can be fine-tuned on specific downstream tasks to achieve state-of-the-art performance with less task-specific data.

- **Multilingual Models** – Multilingual language models are designed to understand and generate text in multiple languages. These models are trained on multilingual text data and can handle various languages without language-specific fine-tuning. Multilingual versions of models like GPT and BERT have been developed to support a wide range of languages.

- **Task-Specific Models** – Task-specific language models are models fine-tuned on specific NLP tasks. While pretrained models like GPT and BERT provide a strong foundation, task-specific fine-tuning helps optimize the models for specific tasks such as sentiment analysis, named entity recognition, question-answering, and more.

All these LLMs have revolutionized the field of NLP by pushing the boundaries of what is possible in language understanding and generation. They have demonstrated the ability to understand context, generate coherent text, perform complex language-based tasks, and provide valuable insights into human language.

Examples of Large Language Models

LLM have revolutionized the ML techniques and capabilities of machine to learn, manipulate, and generate suitable responses against the input data in the form of natural language that humans speak. The modern NLP applications are mostly based on these models. A few of the most important ones are as follows[149]:

- **Generative Pretrained Transformer** – The GPT series of LLMs, including GPT-3, developed by OpenAI, are among the most well-known LLMs. The GPT models are trained using unsupervised learning on massive datasets and have shown impressive performance in a range of NLP tasks, including text generation, translation, summarization, and more.

- **Text-to-Text Transfer Transformer** – The T5, developed by Google, is a versatile language model that is trained in a text-to-text framework. It excels in various NLP tasks and achieves state-of-the-art results by fine-tuning on specific datasets.

- **Bidirectional Encoder Representations from Transformers** – This LLM is developed by Google. It introduces the concept of pretraining language models on large amounts of text data in a bidirectional manner. It has been influential in advancing NLP tasks, including question-answering, sentiment analysis, and named entity recognition.

- The names of other major models used in different applications by many big IT organizations are as follows:
  - Turing-NLG – By Microsoft Corporation
  - XLM-RoBERTa – By Meta
  - NeMo LLM – By NVIDIA
  - BLOOM – By BigScience
  - LaMDA – By Google Corporation

What Is the Large Language Model Dataset?

LLM uses large corpus of training data to train the ML model. The data that is used for training the ML models is known as LLM dataset. These datasets consist of a vast amount of diverse and representative text from various sources, including books, articles, websites, forums, social media, and more. They are designed to provide a rich and comprehensive training environment for language models to learn the intricacies of human language. Large language datasets are crucial for training language models with high capacity and the ability to generate coherent and contextually relevant text. They enable models to learn grammar, syntax, semantics, and even nuanced linguistic patterns by exposing them to a wide range of linguistic contexts and structures.

The size of large language datasets can range from several terabytes to petabytes, containing billions or even trillions of sentences or tokens. The larger the dataset, the more linguistic diversity it can capture, enhancing the model's ability to generalize and generate human-like text. Examples of large language datasets used in training state-of-the-art language models include Common Crawl, which is a vast web crawl dataset, Wikipedia dumps, books from Project Gutenberg, news articles, and other publicly available text corpora. These datasets are carefully curated and cleaned to ensure quality and to remove biases or inappropriate content.

Main Types of Large Language Datasets

Datasets are used for training the LLMs. The training of LLM models can be either supervised or unsupervised ML. In certain cases, both supervised and unsupervised training is used for training the models. The datasets are formed from a wide range of data sources and types of data. The most important categories or domains from where the data is taken to form datasets for the training the models are as follows:

- **General Text Corpus** – This category of datasets consists of a wide range of text from various sources such as books, articles, websites, and other publicly available written material. Examples include the Common Crawl dataset, Wikipedia dumps, and the BookCorpus dataset.

- **Social Media Content** – A very powerful domain in which huge volumes of data is created every hour in different forms and formats. These datasets focus on text data from social media platforms like Twitter, Facebook, Reddit, and Instagram. They capture informal language, user interactions, and trending topics. Examples include the Twitter Sentiment Analysis dataset and the Reddit Comments dataset.

- **Question–Answer Datasets** – This is another special-purpose domain of data to form datasets for ML projects. These datasets are designed specifically for question-answering tasks and contain pairs of questions and corresponding answers. Examples include the Stanford Question Answering Dataset (SQuAD), MS MARCO, and Natural Questions.

- **Dialogue or Conversation Content** – Communication based on conversational or dialogue data is another very strong domain from where the datasets can be created for ML projects to train on. Dialogue datasets consist of conversational exchanges between two or more participants. These datasets are valuable for training conversational agents and chatbots. Examples include the Persona-Chat dataset, Ubuntu Dialogue Corpus, and the OpenSubtitles dataset.

- **Translation Content** – The content in the form of translation datasets contains parallel texts in multiple languages, with corresponding translations. These datasets are used to train machine translation models. Examples include the WMT (Workshop on Machine Translation) datasets and the Multi30K dataset.

- **Medical Data** – These datasets focus on text data from the medical domain, including clinical notes, research articles, and patient records. Examples include the MIMIC-III dataset, i2b2 Medical Records dataset, and the PubMed dataset.

- **Legal Textual Content** – Legal text content contains legal documents such as court cases, statutes, regulations, and legal opinions. Examples include the Legal-GPT dataset, Caselaw Access Project, and the United States Code dataset.

- **Scientific Content** – It is another main area from where the data can be taken to form datasets for machine training. These datasets contain scientific literature from various fields such as physics, chemistry, biology, and computer science. Examples include the ArXiv dataset, PubMed Central (PMC) dataset, and the ACL Anthology dataset.

The availability of all these types of data or content is huge on both online and offline platforms. The online platforms are the most flexible and easy to access and use for the formation of datasets by taking them in digital forms and ingesting that data to the machine for learning purposes. The offline or traditional sources of content is a bit difficult to collect, manage, process, and use for building the datasets. The most important datasets extensively used in modern ML-based NLP projects like ChatGPT, BERT, and others are as follows:

- Wikipedia Text Corpus
- Web Page Text Corpus
- Books Text Corpus

Let us have a look into the details of all the corpuses or corpora (technically, both terms may be used as plural) listed above to make those topics more understandable and clearer.

Wikipedia Text Corpus

Wikipedia text corpus is one of the most reliable and vast sources of data pertaining to numerous domains, areas, businesses, and academics. This corpus is available for free to use for numerous ML projects. Many existing projects such as ChatGPT and others have also used this source for building datasets for ingesting into the NLP projects. The following are the most important areas covered through Wikipedia corpus[150]:

- General knowledge
- Modern business domains
- Science and technology
- Research and development
- History and social sciences
- Engineering and medicines
- Geography and geology
- Arts and culture
- Society and biographies
- Personalities and places

Wikipedia corpus is based on the Wikipedia dump based on the 2006 information. The data is continuously updated by adding more and more information regarding both topics and languages. The Wiki-corpus is available in three main languages and counting. The main languages supported by the Wikipedia corpus include English, Catalan, and Spanish. The present count of languages is larger than this cited number of languages. The present size of the Wikipedia corpus consists of about 586 million pages by September 2022. The size at that point of time was about is about 21.23 GB compressed text without any multimedia and other content.[151]

Wikipedia is a collaboratively edited and constantly evolving knowledge base that covers a wide range of topics in multiple languages. The Wikipedia text corpus is often used as a valuable resource for NLP tasks and language model training. The articles are typically written in a formal style and undergo revisions and updates over time to ensure accuracy and quality. The Wikipedia text corpus is widely used in NLP research and applications because of its vast coverage, availability, and richness of information. It provides a large-scale dataset for training language models, conducting information retrieval tasks, performing text classification, and other NLP-related tasks. Researchers often preprocess the Wikipedia text corpus to clean and tokenize the text before using it for various purposes.

Web Page Text Corpus

Web page text corpus is another very important source of data for NLP applications or projects to train the machine leaning models on. The web page corpus is the combined repository or environment in which the text is extracted from across the World Wide Web (WWW) network. The web page text corpus does not include the HTML tags or any other form of content such as scripts, multimedia, and other types of content other than text. This corpus covers a wide range of domains, areas, businesses, and field such as history, society, politics, personalities, places, science and technology, engineering, research and development, business domains, information technology and computers, natural languages and linguistics, all types of academics areas, and much more. The web page text corpus is the largest text corpora available in the world with a whopping size of 7.2×10^{11} words that is over ten times bigger than English Giga Word Corpus.[152] The following are the most important components of web page text corpus:

- Blogs and articles
- News and reviews
- Products and services descriptions
- Press releases and how-to guide
- Questions and answers
- Technical concepts and research reports
- Technical specifications and explanatory topics

Webpage text corpora are valuable resources for training language models, information extraction, sentiment analysis, topic modeling, web scraping, and other text analysis tasks. Creating a webpage text corpus involves crawling and scraping web pages to extract the desired textual content. Web scraping involves programmatically extracting information from web pages using tools or libraries that can parse HTML and extract text. The extracted text is then stored and processed as a corpus for further analysis. It is important to note that during scraping web pages for creating a corpus, one should respect legal and ethical considerations, including website terms of service, robots.txt files, and any copyright or licensing restrictions. The other main limitations and challenges of using online web page text corpus that may lead to very unreliable results in any type of NLP projects are as follows[153]:

- Grammatically incorrect sentences
- Incomplete sentences and other structural issues
- Advertisements and other commercial content that are mostly biased in terms of building an NLP application neutrally
- Large volume of repetitive content on all types of websites such as menus, services, top menus, legal clauses, disclamation, and others
- Availability of huge volumes of text snippets
- Spams and other types of biased text

A special care is required to avoid any misleading results by building incorrect or biased datasets for the NLP projects for training purposes through web page text corpus.

Books Text Corpus

Books text corpus is the most reliable and feature-rich text content extensively used for the training of NLP projects to achieve major objectives such as text classification, text categorization, sentiment analysis, language modeling, and a few others. The collection of text from books of all kinds and domains is known as the text corpus. The book text is extracted not the images or other multimedia or other types of content. The book text corpus is considered as the most reliable and accurate source of text for building NLP datasets due to numerous reasons:

- **Diverse and Rich Content** – Books cover a wide range of topics, genres, and writing styles. They provide a diverse set of language patterns, vocabulary, and contextual information for training language models or analyzing textual data.
- **Helpful Linguistic Complexity to Teach ML Models** – Books often contain more complex and nuanced language compared to other types of text, making them valuable for studying grammar, syntax, semantics, and discourse analysis. More complex text with greater reliability makes the NLP projects learn more complex concepts perfectly.

- **Reliable Cultural and Historical Context** – Books provide insights into different cultures, historical periods, and societal perspectives. They enable language models to learn about specific contexts and enhance their understanding of cultural references.

- **Well-Structured Text** – This corpus offers more structured and reliable text compared with many other sources of text data. Books typically have well-organized chapters, paragraphs, and sentences, making it easier to preprocess and analyze the textual data. The structured nature of books makes them suitable for various NLP tasks.

The process of building book text corpus is a little difficult and costly due to numerous activities and processes. Creating a books text corpus involves compiling and digitizing books into a machine-readable format. This can be done through various means, including manual digitization, scanning, or accessing existing digital libraries. Some popular books corpora are constructed using publicly available books, while others are created through collaborations with publishers or digital libraries. Books text corpora can be created for specific purposes or can encompass a broad range of genres and subjects. Some examples of books text corpora include the Project Gutenberg corpus, which comprises thousands of public domain books, and various collections of contemporary fiction, scientific literature, poetry, or academic publications. The example of a typical book corpus available online for getting text data for different NLP projects is BookCorpus. It is also known as Toronto Book Corpus. This is a form of dataset comprising as many as 11,000 unpublished books that have been scrapped from the Internet and have been parked in this library for building datasets for NLP ML projects.[154] This text corpus was also the most important source of dataset-building for ChatGPT application developed by OpenAI. This dataset consists of over 985 million of words from a wide range of books pertaining to different fields such as fantasy, fictions, technology, romantic stories, history, culture, scientific fiction, and many others.

Other Corpora

The main text corpora used in the NLP ML projects have been described above. Other than those three major types, there are many other text corpora that also play crucial roles in the development of reliable datasets for NLP projects. A few of those important text corpora are as follows[155]:

- **GloVe** – It is another very useful text corpus. The Global Vectors for Word Representation (GloVe) corpus is derived from a large collection of web documents. It provides pretrained word vectors that capture semantic relationships between words, making it valuable for tasks like word embeddings and semantic similarity.

- **Common Crawl** – The Common Crawl corpus is a vast collection of web pages from across the Internet. It provides a large-scale dataset for training language models, conducting information retrieval tasks, and performing various NLP analyses.

- **IMDb** – Associated with the entertainment domain, IMDb is another very important dataset building text corpora. The IMDb dataset contains movie reviews and associated ratings. It is often used for sentiment analysis tasks, where the goal is to determine the sentiment expressed in a given text.

- **SQuAD** – It is a reliable domain-specific text corpus named as Stanford Question Answering Dataset (SQuAD) that consists of question-answer pairs based on passages from Wikipedia articles. It is frequently used for training and evaluating question-answering models.

- **Medical Literature Datasets** – Various datasets contain text data from medical literature, such as clinical notes, research articles, and patient records. Examples include MIMIC-III, i2b2 Medical Records, and PubMed, which are utilized for medical NLP tasks.

- **Reddit Social Media Text** – Reddit datasets comprise text data from the popular social media platform. They offer conversational exchanges, discussions, and various sub-Reddits, making them suitable for training conversational agents and analyzing user-generated content.

- **Twitter Datasets** – Twitter datasets capture the language used in tweets, including informal language, user interactions, and trending topics. They are employed for sentiment analysis, topic modeling, and studying social media trends.

The above-mentioned corpora are just a few examples of the main text corpora used in NLP projects. Depending on the specific task or domain, researchers and practitioners may also use specialized corpora, such as medical text corpora, legal text corpora, social media datasets, dialogue datasets, and more, to cater to their specific needs.

Architecture of Different Versions of GPT

GPT is an AI model for NLP and other applications. It is based on transformer architecture. The transformer is a neural network–based structure for powering the AI applications for a wide range of use cases such as generating human-like conversation, understanding the human conversation, and manipulating the input in the form of natural language and producing the output in the form of natural language. The most important example of GPT architecture is ChatGPT, which is capable of generating human-like text, images, and voice based on the text input in natural language.[157]

The main purpose of developing GPT models is to enable machines to understand and generate human-like text automatically with the help of only ML process through which the machines are trained on large corpora of text data with different types of ML methods with or without any human intervention. The key concept behind transformer architecture of GPT is based on the concept of self-attention. As already mentioned, the concept of self-attention was introduced by Vaswani et al. in 2017. Transformers are DL models that use self-attention mechanisms to process sequential data, such as text. They excel at capturing long-range dependencies in the input and have been highly successful in various NLP tasks.

GPT models are "pretrained" on massive amounts of text data from the Internet. During pretraining, they learn to predict the next word in a sentence or fill in missing words, gaining an understanding of grammar, context, and semantics. This unsupervised pretraining helps the models develop a broad knowledge base of language. After pretraining, GPT models can be "fine-tuned" on specific downstream tasks, such as text completion, summarization, translation, question-answering, and more. Fine-tuning involves training the model on a narrower dataset with labeled examples to specialize its behavior for a particular task. GPT models have gained significant attention due to their impressive text-generation capabilities.

Other salient features and characteristics of GPT architecture are as follows[156,157]:

- Transformers are also types of neural network models that use self-attention mechanism for fine-tuning and improvements of the model.

- They are text prediction models based on the transformer to perform a wide range of activities such as content generation, text summarization, automated question-answering, language translation, and many others.

- They are trained on the billions of words and parameters and text datasets through different ML models.

- The modern GPT architectures are capable of multimodal features through which it can generate not only text but also other types of content such as images and voices.

Since the building of GPT models in 2017, numerous models of GPT have been released and new areas of applications are being explored. A few of the most important applications based on the transformer include ChatGPT, BERT, and others. A few very important versions of GPT architecture are as follows[156]:

- Version GPT 1.0
- Version GPT 2.0
- Version GPT 3.0
- Version GPT 3.5

These GPT architectures with all their features and capabilities are described in the following sections.

Version GPT 1.0

GPT-1 is the first or initial model of ML, especially for NLP applications based on transformer neural network architecture. It was released in 2018, just one year after the introduction of concept of self-attention by Vaswani et al..[156]

The GPT-1 architecture had 12 transformer layers and was trained on a large corpus of text data from the Internet. The model's primary objective during pretraining was to predict the next word in a sentence, allowing it to learn grammar, context, and semantic relationships. Through this process, GPT-1 developed a strong understanding of language patterns and was capable of generating coherent and contextually appropriate text. One of the key features of GPT-1 was its ability to handle diverse language tasks, including text completion, question-answering, and summarization. The model demonstrated impressive language-generation capabilities and showcased the potential of large-scale transformer-based models for various NLP applications.

The advancement and enhancement in the architecture continued with the passage of time. The newer versions of GPT were released very soon after the launch of GPT-1 with advanced capabilities and deeper understanding of the NLP and allied techniques. The GPT-1 architecture was later replaced by GPT-2. The main features and capabilities of GPT-1 are as follows:

- GPT-1 version of this transformer architecture was developed by OpenAI.
- It is a kind of LLM for transformers.
- The first version of GPT was trained on over 117 million parameters with huge corpora of text datasets online.
- The amount of text data used for training of GPT-1 was about 40 GB compressed text.

- GPT-1 consisted of 12 layers of the decoder stack for processing the entire NLP subprocesses.
- The fine-tuning of GPT-1 was accomplished for achieving the following objectives:
  - Question-answering
  - Semantic similarity
  - Natural language inference
  - Text classification
- The completion of GPT architecture for deploying it consisted of two main phases:
  - Training phase on large corpora of text for general purposes
  - Fine-tuning on large corpora of text for specific domains
- GPT-1 laid the foundation for subsequent advancements in the GPT series and contributed to the development of more powerful language models.
- The main components of GPT version 1.0 architecture are as follows:
  - **Transformer Layers** – The GPT-1 architecture consists of a stack of transformer layers. Each layer performs a series of computations on the input data. The model usually has multiple layers to capture hierarchical representations of the text.
  - **Self-Attention Mechanism** – The core component of the transformer architecture is the self-attention mechanism. It allows the model to weigh the importance of different words in the input sequence while generating representation of those words. This mechanism helps the model capture long-range dependencies and contextual relationships between words.
  - **Feed-Forward Neural Networks** – Within each transformer layer, there are two feed-forward neural networks. These networks apply nonlinear transformations to the representations obtained from the self-attention mechanism, helping to refine the features learned by the model.
  - **Layer Normalization** – Layer normalization is applied after each sublayer (self-attention and feed-forward network) in the transformer layer. It helps in normalizing the values and stabilizing the training process.
  - **Positional Encoding** – Since transformers do not inherently possess positional information, GPT-1 incorporates positional encoding into the input representation. Positional encoding provides information about the relative positions of words in the input sequence, allowing the model to understand the sequential order of the text.

- **Vocabulary Embeddings** – The GPT-1 architecture uses learned embeddings to represent the words in the input text. These embeddings capture the semantic relationships between words and are updated during the training process.
- GPT-1 architecture is encoder-only setup in which the input text is converted into contextually aware representation.
- After generating contextually aware representation, numerous other downstream tasks such as summarization, text completion, and question-answering are performed.

Version GPT 2.0

GPT-2 is the advanced version of GPT-1 released by OpenAI. Like GPT-1, it is a LLM based on transformer neural networks. This version was released in February 2019. Compared with previous version, it represented a significant advancement in terms of model size, capacity, and performance compared to its predecessor GPT-1.[158]

The GPT-2 architecture gained attention for its impressive language-generation capabilities and its ability to generate coherent, contextually relevant text. It showcased the potential of large-scale transformer-based models in NLP tasks. The main features of GPT-2 architecture are as follows[158,159]:

- It has 1.5 billion parameters, making it much more powerful in terms of modeling capabilities.
- Like GPT-1, GPT-2 employs a stack of transformer layers.
- The transformer layers consist of self-attention mechanisms and feed-forward neural networks that capture contextual dependencies and refine representations.
- The GPT-2 architecture, like other GPT models, is pretrained on a large corpus of text data from the Internet. During pretraining, the model learns to predict the next word in a sentence, gaining an understanding of language patterns, grammar, and semantics.
- GPT-2 excels at understanding the context of a given text. It can consider the surrounding words and sentences to generate coherent and contextually relevant responses.
- It has impressive language-generation capabilities. Given a prompt or input, it can generate human-like text responses that are coherent and contextually appropriate.
- This version of transformer architecture can be fine-tuned on specific tasks by training it on narrower datasets with labeled examples. This fine-tuning process allows the model to specialize in various downstream tasks such as text completion, translation, summarization, and more.

- The GPT-2 architecture gained attention for its impressive language-generation capabilities and its ability to generate coherent, contextually relevant text. It showcased the potential of large-scale transformer-based models in NLP tasks.
- The parts or components of GPT-2 are almost similar to the GPT-1. The architecture of GPT-2 version consists of the following components or parts:
  - Transformer layer
  - Self-attention mechanism
  - Feed-forward neural network
  - Layer normalization
  - Positional encoding
  - Vocabulary embeddings
  - Decoding and sampling
- The main steps involving the workflow of GPT-2 architecture are as follows:
  - **Pretraining Phase** – GPT-2 undergoes a pretraining phase on a large corpus of text data. During pretraining, the model learns to predict the next word in a sentence or fill in missing words. It develops an understanding of language patterns, grammar, and semantics. This pretraining process is unsupervised and helps the model build a broad knowledge base of language.
  - **Model Architecture Building and Configuration** – The GPT-2 model architecture is set up with a specific number of transformer layers, hidden units, attention heads, and other hyper parameters. The size and configuration of the model may vary based on the specific variant of GPT-2 used (e.g., small, medium, large).
  - **Fine-Tuning** – After pretraining, GPT-2 can be fine-tuned on specific downstream tasks. Fine-tuning involves training the model on a narrower dataset that is relevant to the target task. This dataset typically contains labeled examples, allowing the model to specialize its behavior for specific applications like text completion, translation, summarization, or question-answering.
  - **Input Encoding** – When using GPT-2 for inference, the input text is tokenized and converted into numerical representations suitable for processing. This involves breaking the text into tokens (e.g., words or sub-words) and mapping those tokens to their corresponding indices in a vocabulary.
  - **Contextual Representation** – The input text is passed through the GPT-2 model's layers to generate a contextual representation. Each transformer layer refines the representation by considering

the contextual relationships between words. The model attends to different parts of the input sequence and updates the representation accordingly.

- **Text Generation Phase** – GPT-2 uses the generated contextual representation to generate text. It employs decoding and sampling techniques to produce words one at a time. The model conditions its predictions on the previously generated words and samples from a probability distribution to determine the next word. This process continues until the desired length or stopping condition is reached.

- **Output Decoding** – The generated text is decoded from the model's numerical representation back into human-readable text form. This involves reversing the tokenization and mapping the numerical indices back to their corresponding tokens.

- **Post-Processing and Evaluation** – Depending on the specific task and requirements, post-processing steps may be applied to the generated text. Evaluation metrics or human judgment may be used to assess the quality, coherence, and relevance of the generated output.

- GPT-2 architecture is pretrained on the BookCorpus of text dataset consisting of over 7000 unpublished books related to art, culture, fiction, science, and other genres.

- The GPT-2 version full release later in 2019 was trained on over 1.5 billion parameters.

- Both GPT-1 and GPT-2 are open-source transformer models. The later versions are not released under open-source code license.

- The transformer architecture of GPT-2 version consists of 48 layers and training size of text equal to 40 TB from different sources on the Internet.

The GPT-2 architecture gained attention for its impressive language-generation capabilities and its ability to generate coherent, contextually relevant text. It showcased the potential of large-scale transformer-based models in NLP tasks.

Version GPT 3.0

GPT version 3 has revolutionized the NLP technology with numerous additional capabilities and features. This is the advanced version of GPT released by OpenAI. The architecture and capabilities of GPT-3 significantly expanded the range of tasks and applications that could benefit from large-scale language models. Its immense size and capacity allowed for impressive language-generation capabilities and breakthroughs in various NLP tasks. This architecture was released in June 2020 with numerous advanced features, capabilities, capacities, and performance. The main features and capabilities of GPT architecture are as follows[160]:

- It is an advanced version of GPT-2 architecture based on LLM.
- It is a decoder-only deep neural network transformer model.
- GPT-3 architecture uses 2048 token long text for training.
- This architecture is trained under a huge number of 175 billion parameters.
- The total size of the data that the GPT-3 model is trained on is 800 GB.
- This model supports the capabilities of zero-shot and few-shot learning.
- Zero-shot learning refers to the ability of a model to perform a task or make predictions on classes or data it has never seen during training. In the context of NLP, zero-shot learning allows a language model to generate outputs or make predictions for categories or topics that were not explicitly part of its training data.
- Few-shot learning is a ML approach that deals with the problem of learning from a small amount of labeled data, typically with only a few examples per class. In traditional ML, models require a large number of labeled examples to learn effectively. However, few-shot learning aims to enable models to generalize and make accurate predictions even when the available labeled data is limited.
- The GPT-3 architecture was released in June 2020 in beta version.
- The foundation of ChatGPT is based on this architecture with a little enhancement or improvement. This architecture is also referred to as foundation transformer model.
- It was also developed by OpenAI.
- It is considered as the state-of-the-art next-generation language model in the field of AI, especially for NLP domain.
- As many as eight different models of GPT-3 architecture have been released by OpenAI, starting from GPT-3 small through GPT-3 175B.
- It supports the concept of self-attention mechanisms, which allow the model to focus on different parts of the input sequence when encoding and decoding text, enabling it to capture contextual relationships effectively.
- It consists of a vast number of neural network layers and parameters, allowing it to learn complex patterns and generate high-quality text.

- GPT-3 is trained using unsupervised learning on a diverse range of Internet text, providing it with a broad understanding of language.

- It generates text by predicting the most probable next word or sequence of words given the input context.

- The architecture of GPT-3 combines the power of the transformer model with massive-scale and extensive pretraining to deliver state-of-the-art language-generation capabilities.

- The model is designed to perform a wide range of NLP tasks, including language translation, text completion, question-answering, summarization, and more.

- During pretraining, the model learns to predict the next word in a sentence, which helps it understand grammar, syntax, and semantic relationships.

- GPT-3 demonstrates strong generalization capabilities, allowing it to perform well on a wide range of NLP tasks without task-specific fine-tuning. It can handle tasks like text completion, question-answering, summarization, translation, and more.

- GPT-3 excels at generating human-like text based on the given prompt or context. It can generate coherent and contextually appropriate responses, articles, stories, summaries, answer and much more.

- The GPT-3 supports multiple languages, allowing it to understand and generate text in various languages.

- It can also engage in interactive and dynamic conversations, simulating chat-based interactions.

- The work flow of GPT-3 architecture is based on the following phases:

  - The first phase of GPT-3 architecture is data processing. You need to process data in line with the requirements of specific tasks; for that purpose, you need to tokenize the text into smaller units (such as words or sub-words), encoding the text into numerical representations, or format the input in a specific way based on the API requirements.

  - Once the data processing is accomplished, you need to choose and configure the right model as per your requirements. Choosing the right GPT-3 variant suitable for your requirements such as gpt-3.5-turbo, gpt-3.5-turbo-turbo, etc. They differ in terms of their capabilities and cost. Configuring the model by specifying parameters such as the maximum length of generated text or the temperature value (which controls the randomness of the generated output).

  - The next step is fine-tuning. It involves training the model on a smaller dataset specific to your task, which helps the model adapt and perform better on that task. Fine-tuning is optional and may require additional labeled data and training time.

- Text generation is the next phase after fine-tuning. The input can be a prompt, a sentence, a question, or any relevant context depending on the task. GPT-3 will generate a response or continuation of the text based on its understanding of the given input and the context it has learned during training.

- The last phase is known as post-processing. This could involve filtering or refining the output, extracting relevant information, or formatting the text for better readability.

- This workflow may vary slightly in terms of variation in the implementation of APIs and selection of domain-specific applications.

Version GPT 3.5

GPT-3.5 is a fine-tuned version of previous version, i.e., GPT-3. This model is also released by OpenAI in March 2022. Numerous fine-tuning and improvements were achieved by incorporating different techniques in the foundation platform of this series, i.e., GPT-3. The main improvements, compared with the previous version of this series, include the following:

- Elimination of certain toxic outputs
- Self-learning capabilities through reinforcement learning

The main difference between the foundation GPT-3 and the advanced version of this series GPT-3.5 is the domain- or task-specific features and capabilities that can help achieve the focused objectives in the output, especially the text generation output functions:

- Text generation
- Text summarization
- Contextual learning of text
- Creating and debugging computer code
- Answering the prompted queries

Other than the above-mentioned differences and capabilities of GPT-3.5, a few other features and characteristics are as follows[161,162]:

- GPT-3.5 is an advanced or a fine-tuned version of the foundation version of GPT series architectures, referred to as GPT-3.
- It is also referred to as InstructGPT version.

- The present ChatGPT platform is based on this fine-tuned or improved architecture GPT-3.5.
- This uses a feedback system for continual improvement in the quality of the created text. For this purpose, a reinforcement learning algorithm known as reinforcement learning with human feedback (RLHF) is incorporated in the foundation architecture GPT-3 to take the user feedback and make corresponding improvements.
- The following are the most important models of GPT-3.5:
  - Code-Davinci-002
  - Text-Davinci-002
  - Text-Davinci-003
- The previous versions of GPT series such as GPT-2 and GPT-3 had one model, while the GPT-3.5 has three models.
- It has three versions of parameters such as 1.3B, 6B, and 175B versions.
- The overall output of GPT-3.5 is state-of-the-art text with fewer toxic outputs.

SAMPLE QUESTIONS

1. What is transformer model, and how does it work in ML?
2. What does a pretrained system mean in ML, and why is it important for building models?
3. What makes LLMs unique, and where do we commonly use them?
4. Outline the main types of large language datasets used in NLP.
5. Explain briefly the differences in the architecture of various GPT versions.
6. How do GPT architectural differences affect how well the GPT models work in real-world situations?

6

Fundamentals of ChatGPT Training

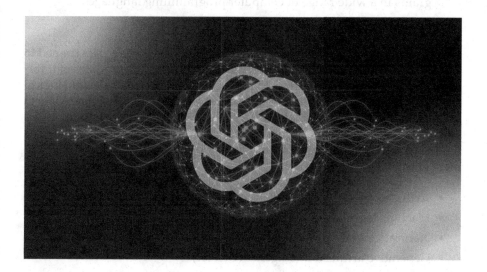

Introduction

Before introducing the fundamentals of training process of ChatGPT platform, let us have an overview of this promising online machine learning (ML)-based application that deals with the natural language processing (NLP) field and generates the text similar to that the humans understand. It is also capable of understanding the communication in the form of text, images, and voices when either prompted or fed through other automated sources of input to the application. This promising application was launched in November 2022 and took the world by surprise within a few days with millions of users registering with this phenomenal application. This application is able to interact with the human through different sources of input and provides the suitable response to the communication in an interactive and impressive way. It can perform the following tasks easily:

- Understanding the queries put to it (apparently)
- Manipulating the input queries in terms of meaning, context, and other parameters

DOI: 10.1201/9781003474173-6

- Generating the suitable response to the queries put up to the platform in natural language that humans use for communication
- Translating the text from one language to another language
- Correcting text in terms of grammar and other writing issues
- Converting text into voice, and vice versa
- Creating the suitable code for developing different software programs in a wide range of computer programming languages
- Debugging the computer code effectively

All those tasks are performed by ChatGPT platform because it is trained to do so through numerous ways and with numerous types of sources of information or data. The core of this program is the architecture or technological stack that handles the training of the machine so that the machine is able to learn from the large corpora of data in such a way that it can manipulate the data by processing the text it ingests for training and testing purposes. The following are the main models and technologies involved in the development of ChatGPT[163]:

- Artificial intelligence (AI)
- Machine learning
- Natural language processing
- Generative artificial intelligence (Gen-AI)
- Generative pretrained transformer (GPT) architecture
- Artificial neural networks (ANN)
- Self-attention mechanism
- Reinforcement learning from human feedback (RLHF)

The training of ChatGPT is a continual process for achieving the improved outcome through different ways. But the most fundamental training of developing ChatGPT consists of the phases or stages through which it passes and gets verified. The most fundamental stages of ChatGPT training are divided into two categories[163]:

- Language modeling or pretraining phase
- Fine-tuning phase

During the pretraining phase, a language model is trained on a large corpus of publicly available text from the Internet. The model learns to predict the next word in a sentence based on the context of the preceding words. The specific architecture used in pretraining or language modeling is a transformer neural network, which is a type of deep learning model that excels at processing sequential data. The fine-tuning stage follows pretraining and involves training the model on more specific data with a narrower domain. In the case of ChatGPT, the fine-tuning process includes demonstrations and comparisons. Human AI trainers provide conversations where they play both the user and an AI assistant and have access to model-written suggestions to compose their responses. They also have access to model-generated completions to help them craft their replies. This dataset is then mixed with other sources like the InstructGPT dataset, which includes transformed prompts from users. The fine-tuning process helps make the model more useful and safe by incorporating human feedback and guiding it to provide appropriate and helpful responses. This iterative process helps in refining the model's behavior and reducing biases or harmful outputs.

The basic phase of training is accomplished through unsupervised ML in which the data is fed into the model without any explicit programming or labeling of the data fed into the model. However, other forms of machine training are also involved at different stages and levels such as training, testing, and real-world interaction of the ChatGPT platform. The following are the main types of ML used at different stages of ChatGPT development:

- Unsupervised ML
- Supervised ML
- Semi-supervised ML
- Reinforcement learning (RL)

The training of ChatGPT has been accomplished through a large number of sources of large data corpora available online. The following are the main sources of those large corpora of text data on which the ChatGPT platform is trained:

- Books and eBooks
- Articles and blogs
- Websites and webpages

The most important source of ChatGPT training is the publicly available repository of websites or web pages known as Common Crawl. This dataset pool consists of billions of websites and multi-billion datasets. The other sources used by ChatGPT for language modeling phase training included Wikipedia, online articles and news, and books. The ChatGPT is based on the fundamental architecture released by OpenAI, i.e., ChatGPT-3. The additional improvements are made based on a few additional mechanisms or algorithms; but the core of this model is based on GPT-3. The training process of GPT-3 model consists of two phases as described earlier and numerous sublevels. Those sublevels of GPT-3 model training used in the ChatGPT are as follows:

- **Data Collection** – A vast amount of publicly available text data from the Internet is collected. This corpus of text is used as the basis for training GPT-3, which is the fundamental foundation of the entire architecture of ChatGPT application.

- **Data Preprocessing** – The collected text data undergoes preprocessing steps such as tokenization and cleaning. Tokenization involves splitting the text into individual tokens such as words, sub-words, or characters to create a vocabulary for the model. Cleaning involves removing any irrelevant or noisy data from the corpus.

- **Pretraining of Model** – ChatGPT application is pretrained on the processed text data using transformer architecture. The transformer model consists of multiple layers of self-attention mechanisms and feed-forward neural networks. The model learns to predict the next word in a sequence based on the context of the preceding words.

- **Language Modeling Objective Maximization** – During the pretraining phase of ChatGPT, the objective of the platform is to maximize the likelihood of predicting the next word accurately, given the context provided by the preceding words. This process helps the model learn language patterns, grammar, facts, and some level of world knowledge from the training data.

- **Fine-Tuning of Application** – As we know, the ChatGPT application is based on GPT-3 and the fine-tuned version of GPT-3; therefore, after the pretraining phase, it undergoes a fine-tuning process. In this stage, the pretrained model is further trained on a specific dataset or task to adapt it for specialized use. Fine-tuning involves training the model on a narrower domain or task-specific data to improve its performance and behavior.

- **Fine-Tuning of Dataset** – The fine-tuning of dataset is typically generated with the help of human AI trainers. These trainers provide demonstrations and comparisons, playing both the user and an AI assistant. They have access to model-written suggestions to compose their responses and can also use model-generated completions to aid in crafting their replies. This dataset, along with other relevant sources, is used to fine-tune the model.

- **Continual Repetitive Refinement** – The fine-tuning process often involves multiple iterations and refinements to improve the model's performance, address biases, and ensure safety. Feedback from AI trainers and continuous evaluation of the model's outputs play a crucial role in iteratively improving the model.

Another part of the training of mechanism involved in ChatGPT is the training process taking place in every layer of the transformer architecture because ChatGPT platform is based on pretrained transformer based on neural network. The neural network consists of numerous layers which involve numerous training processes:

- **Input Embedding** – The input text is first transformed into numerical representations suitable for processing by the model. This is typically done using an embedding layer, which maps each token in the input sequence to a continuous vector representation.

- **Positional Encoding** – Since transformers do not have inherent positional information, positional encoding is added to the embedded tokens to provide the model with a sense of sequence order. This sense of sequence order allows the model to understand the relative positions of words in the input sequence.

- **Encoder Layers** – The encoder layers form the core of the transformer architecture. Each encoder layer consists of two sublayers:
  - **Self-Attention Mechanism** – The self-attention mechanism allows the model to weigh the importance of different words in the input sequence when predicting the next word. It captures dependencies and relationships between words in a sequence, enabling the model to better understand the context.
  - **Feed-Forward Neural Network** – After self-attention mechanism, the output of the process is passed through a feed-forward neural network for applying nonlinear transformation. This network accomplishes nonlinear transformations to the input, through different mathematical theorems introducing more complex interactions between the tokens.

- **Decoder Layers** – If the transformer is designed for sequence-to-sequence tasks, such as machine translation, it incorporates decoder layers in addition to the encoder layers. The decoder layers have similar components to the encoder layers but with an additional attention mechanism that attends over the encoder's outputs. This allows the decoder to generate the output sequence based on both the input sequence and previous predictions.

- **Output Layer** – The final layer of the transformer model is the output layer. It typically consists of a linear transformation followed by a soft-max activation function. This layer outputs the probabilities of each token in the vocabulary being the next word or the predicted token for sequence generation tasks.

This entire process of training of ChatGPT takes place within the algorithms and models of this application and is not visible to the external process. The external components applied to the model consist of training content types and datasets. The details of training content types are mentioned in the following section.

Training Content Types

At the time of writing this book, ChatGPT has not yet disclosed the details of the training processes, techniques, and other parameters pertaining to the training of the model but one thing has been announced publicly that it is based on the GPT-3 version of GPT and fine-tuning of its versions such as InstructGPT. The following are the most important types of content used for the training of the ChatGPT platform:

- Text content
- Image content
- Voice content

The text content constitutes the major area of the content used in the training of ChatGPT. The learning of the natural language and responding in the natural language is mostly based on the text input as training datasets. The creation of codes against the prompts delivered in the natural language spoken by humans is also ingested through text format of the datasets. Thus, we can say that the main areas of training content relate to the text in different forms and formats available in the public domain for building training datasets. The training of ChatGPT is done through large corpora of text data and the main domains of text sources are as follows:

- Articles
- Books
- Webpages

Let us have a deeper insight into those large corpora of text datasets used for the training of ChatGPT platform separately.

Articles

The online articles such as news reports, blogs, and other public domain articles were one of the most important sources of getting text for training the ChatGPT platform. As we know, the data required for training a machine is extensively huge. The larger the volumes of data ingested to the system, the more accurate and reliable the results are expected from the model. The large corpora of data collected for ChatGPT included articles. The articles were used for building volumes of datasets ingested for unsupervised ML in the language model training phase. The following are the most important sources of articles[164]:

- Academic journals
- News reports
- Popular magazines

Those articles covered all domains of knowledge such as politics, science, current affairs, psychology, engineering and technology, societal matters, governments, and others. The majority of the articles are taken from the publicly available sources such as Wikipedia and other similar types of sources.

Books

It is very important to note that the details of the training of ChatGPT platform have not been disclosed in public (at the time of writing this book). It may be that in future it would be available. The generic information has been provided that the training datasets were created from articles, non-copyrighted eBooks, and other scraped books on different platforms that have not been published to fall under the jurisdiction of copyright infringement. This topic is being discussed on different legal and moral platforms whether the training datasets for ChatGPT were built from the copyrighted books or not.[165]

One thing is very clear that a large number of books from a wide range of fields and domains have been used as the source of data for building the ChatGPT training datasets. As per the public information available, the following are the main types of books used for training purposes for building training datasets for the platform:

- Freely available books
- Non-copyrighted books
- Scraped books
- Open Educational Resources (OER)

Webpages

The most commonly used webpages by OpenAI for training their ChatGPT platform were those that are called as Common Crawl websites. The content of those websites is available for many types of uses publicly under common category of copyright. The Common Crawl is a huge repository of websites and webpages available for public use. It contains a very large number of webpages, i.e., billions of pages of websites for building training datasets and other applications.

Other Sources

The other sources on which the ChatGPT was trained include numerous customized, self-generated content and other sources of their business partners and community. The following are the most important of those sources:

- Technological journals
- Newspapers and social media
- Entertainment and arts content
- Marketing content and campaigns
- Healthcare and science magazines

Training Models

ChatGPT was trained through large language models (LLMs), which are very prominent training models used in the ML domain. Other than the LLMs, the GPT model and RL through human feedback are also used for training and fine-tuning of ChatGPT. The most important training models that are based on AI neural networks are LLMs.

Large Language Models

LLM is a type of AI model that is based on ANN to impart training to a wide range of AI platforms used for generating human-like text by learning the input prompts in human-like natural language by the opposite person or an intelligent machine. LLMs have found applications in various fields, including natural language understanding and generation, chatbots, content creation, language translation, sentiment analysis, and more. They have the potential to significantly impact how we interact with technology and automate various language-related tasks.

The following are the main features, capabilities, and characteristics of a LLM:

- It accomplishes the pretraining process of ML systems based on ANN with the help of mass training datasets.
- After pretraining, this model is also capable of fine-tuning the training imparted to the ML models with the help of more domain-specific and more specialized training datasets and procedures.

- It is also able to generate the human-like text in natural language against the prompts from a given input or prompt. This text generated by the LLMs is very correct and relevant contextually and coherently.

- It enables learning of the input text in the form of datasets such as training datasets, texting datasets, and queries in the form of prompts.

- These types of models are also capable of providing highly creative and versatile content through its creative abilities.

Techniques Used in Training Models

Numerous types of techniques have been used in the ChatGPT platform, which is based on LLM and generative pretrained architecture. The list of those techniques is described below to provide you an overview:

- Tokenization technique
- Transformer architecture technique
- Masked-language modeling (MLM) technique
- Next-token-prediction (NTP) technique
- Attention mechanism
- Positional encoding technique
- Evaluation and human feedback techniques

Let us now know about some of the most important techniques from the above-mentioned list.

Masked-Language Modeling Technique

MLM is a type of technique used in pretraining of the ChatGPT platform. This technique is also used in other AI generative applications. This technique is used to teach the model how to predict missing or masked words in a sentence. It is a fundamental part of the pretraining phase for these models and helps them learn about syntax, grammar, semantics, and contextual relationships between words. MLM is particularly effective in helping the model learn contextual relationships between words and understand the structure of sentences. It encourages the model to learn about the relationships between words and their roles in different contexts, which contributes to its ability to generate coherent and contextually relevant text. The following are the most important functions and activities performed by this model:

- Positional encoding and bidirectional context
- Tokenization and random masking
- Training signaling and others

Next-Token-Prediction Technique

NTP technique is a type of tokenization technique that is extensively used in the ML models based on the auto-generative models like generative pretraining architectures or transformers. This technique is used to train models to generate coherent and contextually relevant text by predicting the next token in a sequence given the preceding tokens. The main objective of this technique is to predict the next token in the sentence that is accomplished by the following steps:

- Autoregressive and sequential generation
- Cross-entropy loss and teaching-the-model
- Building sampling strategies and others

The NTP technique trains the model to understand and generate coherent text by learning the relationships between words and their context. This technique is foundational to autoregressive language models like GPT, which generate text by predicting the most likely next token at each step based on the tokens generated before.

ChatGPT Training Process Simplified

The training process of ChatGPT is based on huge volumes or data corpora and numerous types of techniques working in collaboration and coordination to make the models learn from the natural language input and make a decision to generate a response against the given prompt or query. The ChatGPT training process is in reality very complex and highly technical because of its involvement of substantial intervention of human feedback and automated learning through different techniques and models by ingesting huge volumes of text data from a wide range of sources. This entire process is simply described with a few main steps and models[166]:

- Long short-term memory (LSTM) model
- Supervised fine-tuning (SFT) model

- Reward model
- Reinforcement learning model (RLM)
- Model evaluation

Long Short-Term Memory Model

There are several steps in the training of ChatGPT platform. The first step is pretraining, which involves numerous models such as LLMs, generative-pre-trained transformers, and others. The second main stage of ChatGPT training is the sequential prediction or generation. In this step, the sequence of the data or text is handled. For handling the sequential data in the ChatGPT model, the LSTM model is commonly used. It is a recurring neural network (RNN) and was introduced to address the vanishing gradient problem that traditional RNNs faced when trying to capture long-range dependencies in sequences. LSTMs are capable of learning and remembering information over long sequences, making them particularly useful for tasks involving sequences with long-term dependencies. The newer techniques used for sequential data handling are more powerful and consolidated, such as trans-formers and LLMs.

This model consists of three main components:

- Cell state
- Gates
  - Input gate
  - Output gate
  - Forget gate
- Hidden state

These models have been widely used for various NLP tasks, including language generation, machine translation, sentiment analysis, and more. They are effective at capturing long-range dependencies and handling sequences with complex patterns.

Supervised Fine-Tuning Model

SFT technique, precisely referred to as SFT model, is a ChatGPT model for fine-tuning the learning after the pretraining process. The fine-tuning of ChatGPT-3 is performed with the help of supervised datasets created by the data labelers to build predefined output datasets against the input data. In this technique, the prompt data from the real-world users for GPT was collected and labeled for the predefined output. Thus, the entire process of fine-tuning is based on the supervised datasets. In other words, the SFT refers to a process where a pretrained model, which has learned general features from a large dataset, is further tuned or adapted using labeled or supervised data specific to a particular task. This process is often employed to make the pretrained model perform well on a specific task, by leveraging the knowledge it has gained during its pretraining phase. Specifically speaking, the SFT model is designed for fine-tuning the prompt responses in ChatGPT and other generative platforms.

Reward Model

The second step of fine-tuning of generative platform ChatGPT is the reward method in which the model is trained with a series of prompts and their respective responses as input to the model. The output of that input data is generated in the form of a scaler value known as *reward*. The following are the main characteristics and features of this reward model:

- It is a type of reinforcement ML.
- It focuses on training agents for interaction with the environments for generating the desirable certain objectives.
- It is a type of feedback learning system.
- This method is based on agent-environment interaction.
- It consists of reward functions, reward signals, and types of reward functions such as sparse and dense reward functions

Developing and designing an appropriate reward model is crucial for the success of RL algorithms. A well-designed reward function guides the agent to learn desired behaviors and achieve the intended goals. However, defining reward functions can be challenging as they need to accurately represent the task's objectives and avoid unintended side effects or prevent incentivizing undesirable behavior known as reward-hacking effect.

Reinforcement Learning Model

RLM uses the policy of the model. The policy of the model is learned in the second step of fine-tuning known as reward modeling. The most commonly used reward policy is referred to as proximal policy optimization (PPO) in modern versions of ChatGPT. In this step or technique, the input is again the prompts which are taken randomly and the response is generated based on the policy of the model. This entire process of RL from the human feedback is also named as RL from human learning, precisely referred to as RLHF model in ChatGPT. This is the combination of RL and the feedback or input review regarding the service from the human users.

Model Evaluation

Model evaluation is the last process in which the entire training process is checked and verified for the desired level of output or outcome. It is important to note that the training of ChatGPT platform is based on three main phases:

- Pretraining of the model
- Fine-tuning of the model
- Evaluation of the model

The first two phases have already been described in this chapter, and the remaining process – evaluation of the model – will now be studied. Before discussing about the evaluation of the model, let us have an overview of the previous two phases of this generative model based on the LLM and GPT transformer.

The first phase of ChatGPT model is pretraining phase that includes the training of the model on large data corpora. The main objective of this phase is to equip the model with the real-world knowledge and its processing methods to learn from the data and make decisions based on that data and learning. The following are the main techniques used in the pretraining or training phase of the model:

- **Transformer Architecture** – The core architecture used in models like GPT is the transformer architecture. Transformers are designed to handle sequential data, like text, by using self-attention mechanisms to weigh the importance of different words in relation to each other. This allows the model to capture long-range dependencies and context.
- **Pretraining and Fine-Tuning** – ML models like ChatGPT undergo two main phases: pretraining and fine-tuning. In the pretraining, the model is trained on a large corpus of text to learn grammar, syntax, semantics, and world knowledge. Fine-tuning involves training the pretrained model on a more specific dataset related to the desired task, such as generating conversational responses.
- **Tokenization** – In this process, the text is broken down into smaller units called tokens, which could be words, sub-words, or characters. Tokenization helps in representing text in a format that the model can process effectively.
- **Masked-Language Modeling** – During pretraining, models are often trained to predict missing words in sentences. This is called masked-language modeling. The model learns to predict the masked tokens based on the surrounding context.
- **Attention Mechanisms** – This type of mechanism has been incorporated into the transformer architecture that allows the model to

weigh the importance of different words or tokens in a sentence relative to each other. This helps the model capture relationships and dependencies across the text.

- **Positional Encodings** – It is important to note that GPT transformers do not inherently understand the order of tokens; therefore, the positional encodings are added to the input embeddings to convey the positions of tokens in the sequence.

- **Data Augmentation** – A wide range of techniques are used to increase the diversity of training data, such as adding noise to input text, paraphrasing, or introducing variations in input prompts.

- **Prompts and Conditioning** – In the case of ChatGPT, models are conditioned on prompts or initial input. The generated output is influenced by the input provided, allowing for controlled and contextually relevant responses.

- **Temperature and Top-k Sampling** – During text generation, techniques like temperature scaling and top-k sampling are used to control the randomness and diversity of generated responses.

- **Evaluation and Human Feedback** – GPT models are often fine-tuned using RLHF. Human reviewers evaluate and rate model-generated responses, and the model is updated based on this feedback to improve its performance over the time of operation.

The second phase of ML generative models like ChatGPT is known as fine-tuning. The fine tuning of ChatGPT is achieved through different techniques as described in this chapter. The summary of those techniques and processes is as follows:

- Prompt data collection
- Human reviewing or user reviewing
- Iterative feedback to the model through prompts
- Model updates through human feedback outcomes
- Taking safety measures for generating relevant and accurate response
- Controlling and customization of the model
- Continual improvement strategies

Once the fine-tuning of the model is done, the last phase or step of GPT model development, like ChatGPT model, is the evaluation of the model to verify that the results provided or generated by the models against the prompts or queries are correct and under the desirable criteria or tolerance. This process is described now.

It is important to note that the evaluation of the model is completely separate from the training dataset verification during the course of ChatGPT pretraining and testing with the help of testing datasets. The evaluation is a completely separate process. This is done based on the following criteria:

- **Truthfulness** – This is achieved by using the Truthful QA dataset. In this criterion, the tendency for illusion produced by the PPO policy is checked.
- **Helpfulness** – The helpfulness of the output generated by the model is checked in this process of evaluation of the model.
- **Harmlessness** – Any kind of derogatory, inappropriate, or denigrating tendency of content creation of the model is checked through this criterion.

SAMPLE QUESTIONS

1. What are the various types of training contents?
2. How is training model defined in ML?
3. What techniques are commonly used in training ML models?
4. Provide an overview of the LSTM model and its functionalities.
5. What is RLM and its applications in ML?
6. Define the SFT model and its applications within specific contexts.

7

Using ChatGPT Like a Pro

Introduction

ChatGPT is getting huge traction in all domains of industries, especially in the field of information technology, content writing, language translation, voice-to-text conversion, and similar fields. The results of generative text astonish the users due to their noticeable accuracy, clarity, and conciseness. Many industries are changing the way they deal with the content creation, computer programming, and other software development and management tasks and trying to pave the way for the use of ChatGPT for increasing their productivity and efficiency by reducing the human resource charges used on the costly hiring of manpower.

Many experts and domain specialists fear making a great reshuffle and changes in the job markets, especially in the field of content creation and software development. The effective use of ChatGPT may be very helpful for different roles in a wide range of industries across the globe in the modern era

DOI: 10.1201/9781003474173-7

of businesses. It can be possible only when the use of ChatGPT is done properly like a professional to achieve the best results that are highly desirable in different domains or fields. Using ChatGPT like a professional depends on numerous useful tips that help the users achieve the most customized, personalized, and specific answers to their respective queries. The following are the most important tips to achieve the most reliable and personalized results of the prompts you provide to the platform[167–169]:

- **Clear Input** – Start with a clear and concise input. You need to clearly state your question or prompt, so that the model understands what you are asking for.

- **Prompt Engineering** – Experiment with different prompts to see what gets the best results. You can provide context, set the tone, or even pretend to be a specific character to guide the model's responses.

- **Setting Right Temperature Parameter** – Temperature controls the randomness of the generated responses. Higher values (e.g., 0.8) make the output more diverse and creative, while lower values (e.g., 0.2) make it more focused and deterministic.

- **Max Tokens Setting** – This parameter limits the length of the generated response. You can set it to a specific number to ensure that the response does not exceed a certain length. This parameter is set in the number of characters and words.

- **Iterative Refinement of Response** – If the initial response is not exactly what you need, you can iterate by providing more context or asking for clarification. This can help guide the model to provide a more accurate response.

- **Provide More Specifics and Details** – If you're looking for a detailed answer or specific information, be explicit in your request so that the platform understands the context and the domain of your queries. For example, instead of asking, *"Tell me about space"*, ask, *"What are the latest discoveries about black holes?"*

- **Make Prompts as Clear as Possible and Avoid Ambiguity** – Ambiguous questions might lead to vague or irrelevant answers. Make sure your prompts are well-structured and clear. The clearer the queries, the accurate the answers you get.

- **Setting the Desired Formatting and Response Structure** – ChatGPT offers you with the feature to set the desired structure and format of the response you want to get from this platform against the query prompts. You can guide the model to produce organized and structured content by specifying the format you want. For instance, you can ask for bullet points, pros and cons, step-by-step instructions, etc.

- **Continual Fact-Checking** – ChatGPT provides responses that are very accurate and reliable but still the chances of inaccuracy remain.

To overcome this problem, you need to be very careful. While ChatGPT can provide a lot of information, it is always good to fact-check the responses, especially if the information is critical or you are using it for important decision-making.

- **Playing with Your Creativity** – Humans are highly creative in their respective ideas. Hence, you should not hesitate to experiment with different approaches and phrasings to see what yields the best results for your specific use case. Playing with your prompts provides you options to learn more from the responses and catch the best one.

- **Adapt to Fair Use Policy Always** – Remember that ChatGPT generates responses based on the data it was trained on. It is important to use it ethically and avoid generating harmful, inappropriate, or misleading content. Always try to use your creativity positively for the betterment of this artificial intelligence (AI) platform and other users or community.

- **Learning and Feedback Provisioning** – Over time, you will learn how to better interact with the model. Pay attention to its strengths and weaknesses, and adjust your approach accordingly. Providing feedback on both good and poor responses can help improve the model's performance. It is the moral responsibility of users to provide the continual feedback on the responses they get against their queries on the ChatGPT. This will help the AI platform to improve the performance continuously.

- **Collaborative Use of Other Tools** – You can use ChatGPT as part of a larger workflow in collaboration with numerous other conformable and complementary tools to increase the effectiveness of the content created by ChatGPT. For example, you can use it to brainstorm ideas, generate content, or answer questions, and then refine and polish the output using other tools available on the market.

- **Choosing the Right Value for Top-p (Nucleus) Sampling** – The selection of the top-p nucleus sampling makes the OpenAI ChatGPT to choose the closeness or likeliness of the words in the response. For example, a high value like 0.8 restricts the sampling to the most likely words, while a lower value like 0.2 allows for a wider range of words.

- **Choosing the Correct Tones and Styles** – You can use ChatGPT like a professional to get the most desirable level of accuracy and relevancy in the generated response from the platform. You can do it by setting different criteria for tones and styles of the generated text in the form of numerous values or parameters.

- **Integrate ChatGPT in Your Browser** – Like many other complementary applications, you can integrate the ChatGPT platform into your browser for faster access to this platform at any time you want to.

- **Properly Understand the Features and Capabilities of ChatGPT** – If you do not understand all features and capabilities of ChatGPT, you would not be able to make most of it. Thus, you need to properly go through all interfaces, windows, panes, links, setting options, and other associated capabilities to achieve the most desirable responses.

- **Evaluating Tools and Interfaces Associated with ChatGPT** – There are numerous tools and web interfaces or APIs (Application Programming Interfaces) that offer options for users and developers to work with ChatGPT with more capabilities and power like a professional user. For example, OpenAI playground is very user-friendly web interface for the developers to make most of this platform. This interface enables users to integrate ChatGPT into a wide range of web applications. You can also explore numerous other options for better results.

- **Make All Additional Configurations Properly** – There are numerous other configurations and settings that help you achieve the most desirable and personalized or even more specific answers or responses from this platform. You need to do all those configurations and settings properly by following different procedures as mentioned in the next section.

Important Tasks to Use ChatGPT Like a Pro

How to Register for ChatGPT?

To use the service of ChatGPT AI platform, you need to register with this platform. To register, take the following simple steps:

- Visit https://chat.openai.com/auth/login page. The registration page appears (Figure 7.1).

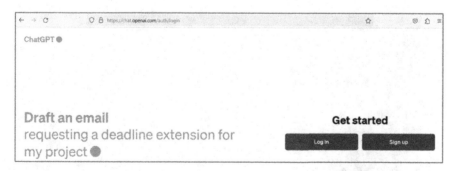

FIGURE 7.1
ChatGPT registration page.

- Click the *Sign up* link (see Figure 7.2). Sign-up page will appear with different options to register with the ChatGPT platform.

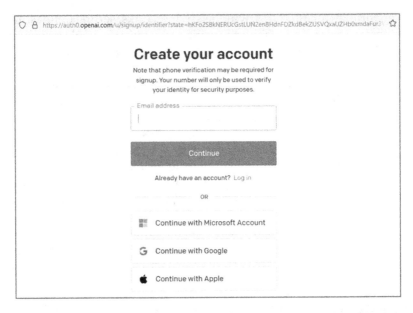

FIGURE 7.2
Sign-up page with different options.

- Choose the most suitable option from the list, as shown in the Figure 7.2. For example, choose the *Continue with Google* option. Choose the Google account that you want to use for registering with ChatGPT and hit the enter button. The registration is done with the welcome page, as shown in Figure 7.3.

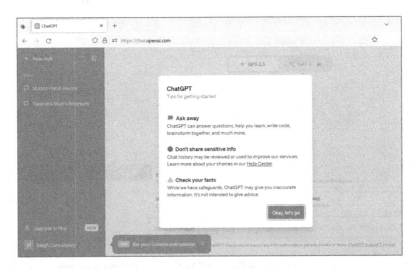

FIGURE 7.3
Screenshot of the registration process.

- Read the tips carefully, click the *Okay, let's go* button. You have been successfully registered with ChatGPT now.

How to Login ChatGPT?

If you are already registered with the ChatGPT AI platform, you need to just login to the application to use it. For logging in, take the following simple steps:

- Visit https://chat.openai.com/auth/login page. The registration/ login page appears. Click the Login link.
- Choose the correct option that you selected for registering with ChatGPT from the list that appears on the page. For example, you registered by using your email.
- Put the email address in the field and click the *Continue* link. Password insertion page appears, as shown in Figure 7.4.

FIGURE 7.4
Password insertion page.

- Enter the password and click the *Continue* link. You are logged into the ChatGPT service successfully.

Overview of ChatGPT Interface

ChatGPT interface is very simple and intuitive to use without any steep training. The interface consists of numerous sections, which have their own functions. Let us have an overview of the main interface of ChatGPT, as shown in Figure 7.5.

FIGURE 7.5
Main interface of ChatGPT.

- The left pane of the interface consists of numerous things, as high-lighted in Figure 7.6 and explained in the descriptions.

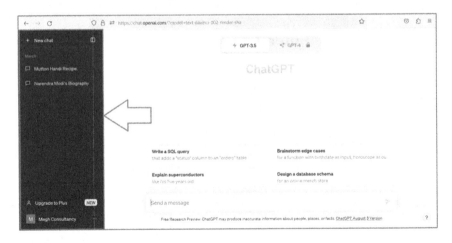

FIGURE 7.6
The arrow pointing to the left pane of the main interface.

1. **New Chat and Show/Hide Side Pane Option** – The New Chat option allows you to start over a new discussion that is out of the context of the present discussion. This is important to note that ChatGPT uses context of your discussion and queries for the next queries if you do not change the chatting option by using the next chat link. Moreover, the side page hide/show option is used to either hide the sidebar or show the sidebar.

2. **Chat History** – The left pane of the interface also keeps the record of the queries that you made in a particular chat while using the ChatGPT in the past. The record is saved under the categories of months and week.

3. **Account Details and Settings** – This is another option in the left pane of the interface that shows you the details of the account that is being used for using ChatGPT and also the options to upgrade your free account of ChatGPT-3.5 to ChatGPT-4. This area provides you with a link to configure or manage your account under the hood of *Settings*.

- Right pane of the main interface of ChatGPT consists of numerous other options, as shown in Figure 7.7 and described in the sub-bullets. The most important area that displays the results of the queries is also located in this pane. The other options on this pane include the query/message send field, regenerating options, feedback options, versions change, etc.

FIGURE 7.7
The arrow pointing to the right pane of the main interface.

- The right pane of the interface of ChatGPT consists of different options as shown in the following bullet points:

1. **Send a Message Field** – This is the field where you put your question or query to ask ChatGPT about doing something for you. You type your question and click the arrow located at the end of the field.

2. **ChatGPT Versions** – If you have not entered any new query since you used it a few days back, the version options appear at the top of the right pane. You can choose ChatGPT-3.5 or ChatGPT-4. If you have already received a response from ChatGPT in the ChatGPT response area, you can use the *Upgrade to Plus* option available on the left pane.

3. **Help and Support** – There is a "?" symbol located at the bottom of the right pane of the interface. It is the link to the support and read resources. Click it to open the technical resources and support content.

- Additional options appear once you start querying the system and getting the response from ChatGPT, as shown in Figure 7.8, which includes numerous additional options that are not visible on the maiden interface.

  1. **Existing Version and Sharing Options** – At the top of the right pane, you can see the option for sharing the response generated by the ChatGPT platform. The version of ChatGPT you are using is also shown in the same line, as depicted in Figure 7.8, highlighted with a rectangular box.

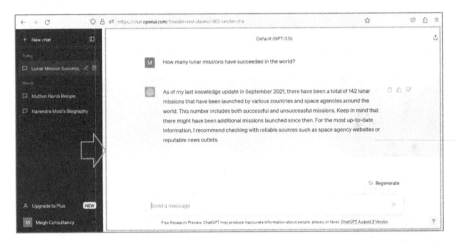

FIGURE 7.8
Highlighted part of the right pane.

2. **Feedback and Copy Text Options** – In this main interface of ChatGPT, you can see the thumbs-up and thumbs-down along with *copy the text* or *response* option (see Figure 7.9). You can choose any of those options to provide additional feedback and copy the content generated by ChatGPT.

FIGURE 7.9
Feedback options.

3. **Prompt Area** – Prompt that you provided ChatGPT to generate a response appears on the top of the response area in the right pane of the interface.

4. **Response Area** – This is the portion of right pane of the main interface of ChatGPT in which the response generated by ChatGPT against your prompt is displayed. This is the largest area of this page or interface.

5. **Regenerate Option** – It is a link sitting just above the *send a message* field. This option is used to change the response that ChatGPT generated against your existing query or prompt. If you are not satisfied with the response, you can choose this option to revise or rephrase the response.

Getting Started with Your First Query

You have been introduced with the interface of ChatGPT with full details. Now, it is time to get started talking with ChatGPT through prompts. To get the response of your first prompt, take the following steps:

- Open ChatGPT application.
- Add the desired query or prompt in the *"send a message"* field and click the green-turned arrow located at the end of the prompt insertion field. The response is generated by ChatGPT, as shown in Figure 7.10.

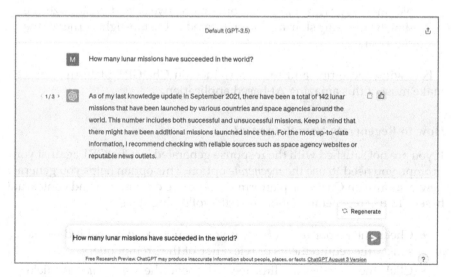

FIGURE 7.10
ChatGPT's response for a query.

- The response is produced in the ChatGPT response area with feed-back options and the prompt is stored in the prompt area.

Overview of Using ChatGPT

Till now, registering and logging into ChatGPT and the details of ChatGPT interface with the first query prompt to generate response has been covered. The sequential steps of using ChatGPT like a professional are mentioned herein to provide you with a clearer way to use ChatGPT effectively:

- While using any prompt, you need to be very creative, innovative, and specific so that you get the most reliable and accurate response.
- Read the response generated by ChatGPT carefully and make sure the content is relevant to your prompt query.
- If you are not satisfied with the quality, accuracy, or relevancy of the response, you can choose the regenerate option as many times as you like to generate the most desirable response you want to. This is very important to note that you should provide feedback if you are not satisfied with the response. This will help ChatGPT improve the response and context in the future to provide better and relevant responses.
- If you want to share the response with anyone through any social media or other forms of communications, you can click the copy icon located along with thumbs-up and thumbs-down icons.
- Sharing directly with links with other users of ChatGPT is very simple and easy with additional options to tweak and customize the sharing by using sharing button located at the top-right corner of the right pane.

Following these tips and to-do activities on ChatGPT platform, you can make most of this amazing AI-based application.

How to Regenerate New Response?

If you are not satisfied with the response generated by ChatGPT against your prompt, you need to use the *regenerate* option. This option helps you generate new response on ChatGPT platform that is more customized and contextual based. To use regenerate option, take the following steps:

- Check the response carefully, if you do not like it or feel it does not satisfy the requirements or relevancy of the prompt query.
- Click the *"Regenerate"* link located above the *send a message* field. ChatGPT generates a revised response, as shown in Figure 7.11.

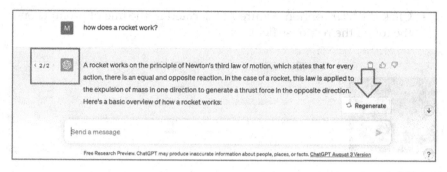

FIGURE 7.11
A revised response sample.

In Figure 7.11, you can see the content created second time is highlighted with the box showing (2/2), after using the *Regenerate* option.

How to Copy and Share Response?

Copying and sharing the generated response can be accomplished in two ways. To accomplish this task in both of those ways, take the following simple steps:

- Use the copy link located along with thumbs-up and thumbs-down icons. The response is copied to the clipboard. You can paste that copied content to any other source such as email, WhatsApp chat, or any other communication source, as shown in Figure 7.12.

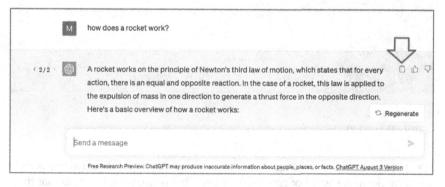

FIGURE 7.12
Copy response option.

- You can also share the link of your entire chatting with ChatGPT with any other users through different source of communication.

- Click the *Share* option (Figure 7.13) located in the line of prompts on the top of the response field.

FIGURE 7.13
Share option.

- The *"Share Link to Chat"* pop-up window appears as shown in Figure 7.14.
- Choose the *"Copy Link"* option (Figure 7.14) to copy the chatting. The entire chatting will be copied to the clipboard for further sharing.

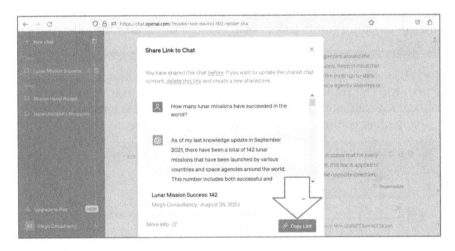

FIGURE 7.14
"Copy Link" option.

- Share the entire chatting with ChatGPT copied on the clipboard through any desired source of communication. This is important to note that the link shared to another person should be ChatGPT user too.

How to Give Feedback to ChatGPT?

ChatGPT is designed to ingest data input in the form of training and continual improvement through feedback provided by the users in two main forms.

This communication or learning of ChatGPT is governed by Reinforcement Learning through Human Feedback (RLHF) model of machine learning. It is a type of reinforcement learning, which uses the formula of reward and punishment for generating the correct and wrong responses.

To provide feedback to ChatGPT against each response you get, you need to follow the simple steps:

- Insert a query or prompt into the *"Send a message"* field and click the arrow to generate a response against that particular query or question.
- Read the response carefully and make your mind to give any type of feedback. If you are satisfied with the response, you can choose thumbs-up icon and if not satisfied with the response, you can choose the thumbs-down icon located at the top-right corner (Figure 7.15) of the response field along with the option to copy the text.

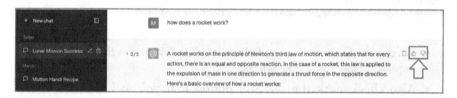

FIGURE 7.15
Location of the thumbs-up and thumbs-down icons.

- Click the thumbs-up icon. The *"Provide Additional Feedback"* pop-up window appears as shown in Figure 7.16.

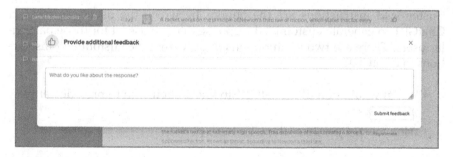

FIGURE 7.16
Pop-up window to provide additional feedback.

- Provide the additional feedback in natural language in the field, *"What do you like about the response?"*

- Click the *Submit feedback* link once you are done with writing feedback. Your feedback has been submitted successfully.
- To provide negative feedback, you need to click on the thumbs-down icon. The "Provide additional feedback" pop-up window appears as shown in Figure 7.17.

FIGURE 7.17
Pop-up window to provide additional feedback (for negative input).

- Fill out the feedback in the field named as *"What was the issue with the response? How could it be improved?"*
- Also check-mark the relevant option that you feel matches your response from other three options available on the feedback pop-up window.
- Finally, click the *"Submit Feedback"* option. Your feedback has been sent successfully.

How to Add Customized Instructions?

Customized instructions are the options by which the users can instruct ChatGPT to generate customized response that are useful for those particular users. There are two main options of providing the customized instructions to ChatGPT:

- What would you like ChatGPT to know about you to provide better responses?
- How would you like ChatGPT to respond?

Both customized types of instructions are provided through natural language a human being uses for daily conversation. As we know, ChatGPT is also trained to take, learn, decide, and generate content against the human prompts or input exactly (or, somewhat) the same way like the humans do. Therefore, it takes the customized instructions in natural language. This is important to note that both the instruction options are given on the same form or page.

To provide the customized instructions to ChatGPT for producing the most relevant and desirable response, take the following steps:

- Login to the ChatGPT application to show main interface of the platform.

FIGURE 7.18
ChatGPT's main interface with the left pane's additional options.

- Click the "..." sign located at the left-bottom of the page in the left pane of the main interface. A list of more options will appear, as shown in Figure 7.18. The list of options is highlighted inside a box.
- Click the *Custom Instructions* option from the list. The pop-up window to instruct ChatGPT appears, as shown in Figure 7.19.

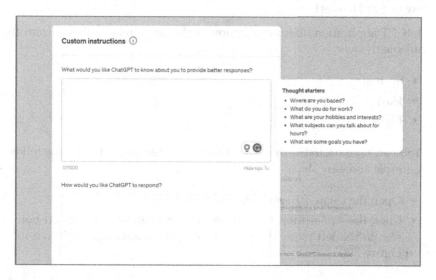

FIGURE 7.19
Custom Instructions window.

- In the first field, you can provide instructions to ChatGPT up to 1500 words. In this input you can instruct different things:
  - Where are you based?
  - What do you do for work?
  - What are your hobbies and interests?
  - What subjects can you talk about for hours?
  - What are some goals you have?
- Write down all instructions in expressive and clear way so that the most desirable responses can be achieved.
- In the second field named as *"How would you like ChatGPT to respond?"* on the pop-up window, you can add numerous types of instructions in 1500 words:
  - How formal or casual should ChatGPT be?
  - How long or short should responses generally be?
  - How do you want to be addressed?
  - Should ChatGPT have opinions on topics or remain neutral?
- Turn on the option for *"Enable for new chats"* if you like it or close this radio button.
- Click the *Save* button. Your custom instructions have been submitted to the ChatGPT platform to customize your response accordingly.

How to Set Themes?

ChatGPT application offers you option to choose a suitable theme from the available themes:

- System
- Dark
- Light

You can set a desirable theme on ChatGPT interface by taking the following simple and easy steps:

- Open the ChatGPT application main interface.
- Click the "..." option located beside the username at the left-bottom in the left pane. A list of more options appears, as shown in Figure 7.20.

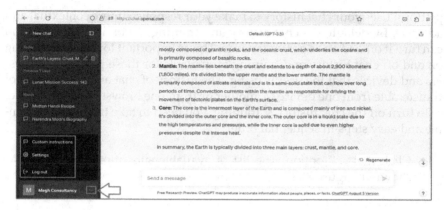

FIGURE 7.20
More options beside the username on the left pane.

- Click the *Settings* option from the list. The *Settings* pop-up window appears, as shown in Figure 7.21.

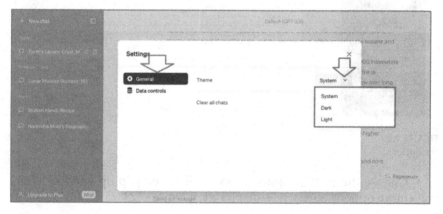

FIGURE 7.21
Settings option.

- Click the *General* setting option and then the dropdown list of themes, as shown in Figure 7.21. The list of available themes appears as shown with the box on the figure.
- Choose the desired theme from the dropdown list. The new theme is successfully applied to your ChatGPT interface.

How to Turn-Off/On Your Chat History?

Turning off and on chat history saving is a useful option offered by ChatGPT application. It allows you to save the chat history for unlimited time, if you turn it on; otherwise, the data history is stored for only 30 days. After that duration of time, the chat history will be deleted automatically. The ChatGPT platform uses your chat history to make your responses more contextual and accurate. By default, the chat history and training option is turned on. You can turn it off and on as per your needs. This is important to note that turning on and off chat history and training is available for those particular browsers and devices that the user is using. The history of chat and training is not transferable from one device to another or from one browser to another one.

To turn off the chat history & training, you need to take the following simple and easy steps in sequential order:

- Click the "..." option. The list of available suboptions appears, as shown in Figure 7.22.

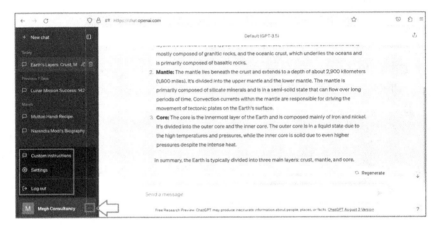

FIGURE 7.22
Suboptions.

- Choose the *Settings* option from the list. The pop-up window with more options appears, as displayed in Figure 7.23.

FIGURE 7.23
Settings option that pops up.

- Click the "Data Controls" option on the pop-up window. More options appear including the *Chat history & training* option.
- Turn the slider button off. The *Chat history & training* option has been disabled and the disabled history link appears on the main page, as shown in Figure 7.24.

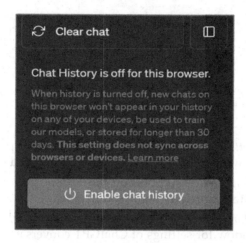

FIGURE 7.24
Screenshot showing chat history is off for the browser.

Now, the chat history is disabled. If you need to enable the chat history, you need to click on the *"Enable chat history"* soft button that appears on the left pane of the main interface. The *Chat history & training* option will be enabled successfully.

How to Manage Links for Sharing Chats?

ChatGPT offers you an option to share your chatting with any other friend through a shared link. You can create multiple shared links through a simple process in which the link creation is done through the "share chat" icon located at the top of the main page at the end of prompt line. You need to just click on that icon; the chat data is copied in a link and saved on the clipboard. You can manage those links by taking a few simple steps:

- Click the "..." located beside the username on the left pane of the main interface of ChatGPT platform. The list of additional options appears, as shown in Figure 7.25.

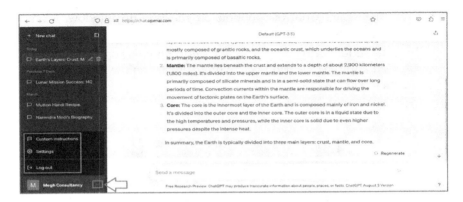

FIGURE 7.25
After clicking the "…" located beside the username on the left pane.

- Click the *Settings* option from the list. The *Settings* pop-up window will appear with more options for configuration and settings.
- Click the *Data Controls* option on the *Settings* page. More options related to a few more functions would appear.
- Click the *Manage* link located against the *Shared Links* option on the pop-up window for settings of ChatGPT conversation, as shown in Figure 7.26.

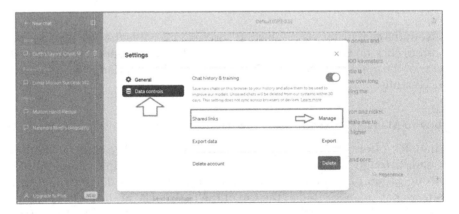

FIGURE 7.26
Shared Links option.

- The *Shared Links* pop-up window will appear as shown in Figure 7.27 with the list of saved links on the clipboard.

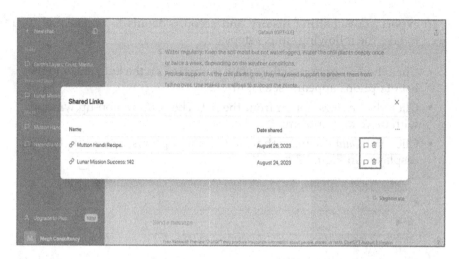

FIGURE 7.27
Pop-up options window for Shared Links.

- Every link has two options – *view source chat* and *delete chat* – as shown in Figure 7.28.

FIGURE 7.28
View source chat and delete options.

- By clicking on the view source chat link, you can see the details of the chat history that you saved on the clipboard for sharing.
- Click the delete icon to remove the desired link from the list.

How to Export Chat Data?

Another very important option provided by the ChatGPT platform is the ability to export the chat data to your designated email that you used for registering with ChatGPT. ChatGPT processes your entire chat history and your account details into a downloadable file and sends it to the email registered with ChatGPT. A downloadable link will be shared by ChatGPT in the email. The active time of that link is 24 hours. You need to use that link to download the chat data and save somewhere on your computer for future use.

To export your chatting history and account details to your email, you need to take the following simple steps:

- Click the "..." option against your username on the left pane and the list of options appears (see Figure 7.25).
- Click the *Settings* option from the list. The *Settings* pop-up window with more tabs appears.
- Click the *Data Controls* tab to show more options under this tab, as displayed in Figure 7.29.

FIGURE 7.29
Data controls option.

- Click the *Export* link located against the *Export data* option on the data controls tab as shown in Figure 7.29. The data export request confirmation pop-up message appears with more information about this function, as shown in Figure 7.30.

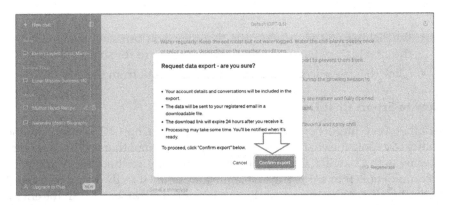

FIGURE 7.30
Confirming exporting of data.

- Click the *"Confirm Export"* button to allow ChatGPT to process your request and send the link to downloadable file in an email sent to your email that you registered with the ChatGPT platform as your user credential. An email will be received in your inbox with a link to downloadable file active for next 24 hours. You can download the data within that duration of time and save it on your computer for further sharing or archiving.

How to Log Out of Your ChatGPT Account?

Logging out of ChatGPT account provides you with additional security and privacy on your device. It is more useful function when multiple users are using a device in a home, office, or other common place. To log out of your account, take the following simple steps:

- Click the *"..."* option in the left pane against your username at the bottom of the main ChatGPT page. The list of available options appears, as shown in Figure 7.31.

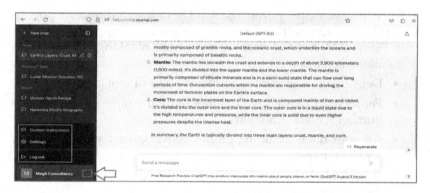

FIGURE 7.31
Options available after clicking "...".

- Click the *Log out* option from the list. The system will automatically log out you from the ChatGPT service.

How to Delete Your ChatGPT Account?

Deleting an account with ChatGPT will mean that you will not remain a registered user with ChatGPT service. To use the services, you will need to register afresh from scratch. If you want to delete your account with ChatGPT anyway, you need to follow a few simple steps:

- Click the *"..."* option located at the left-bottom of the page of the ChatGPT interface. A list of more options appears, as shown in Figure 7.31.
- Click the *Settings* options. The pop-up window with two tabs appears.

- Click the *Data Controls* tab. A list of other options will appear, as shown in Figure 7.32.

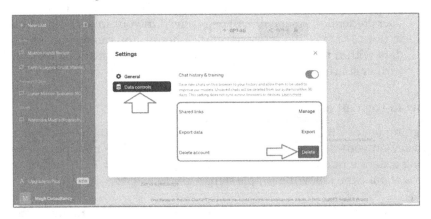

FIGURE 7.32
Delete account option under "Data controls" option.

- Click the *Delete* option from the list. The delete confirmation pop-up window named as *"Delete account – are you sure?"* appears, as shown in Figure 7.33. A list of warning and results of taking this action are mentioned on a list:
  - Deleting your account is permanent and cannot be undone.
  - For security reasons, you cannot reuse the same email or phone number for a new account.
  - All your data, including profile, conversations, and API usage, will be removed.
  - If you've been using ChatGPT with the API, this access will also be deleted.

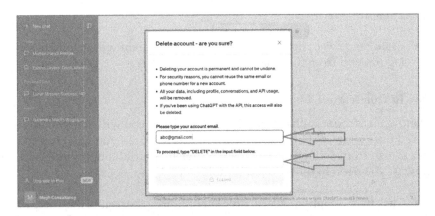

FIGURE 7.33
Delete account option's warning messages.

- Fill in the email address that you used to register with ChatGPT and type the word "DELETE" in the text field to confirm that you are okay with the above-mentioned conditions and you want to delete your account.
- Click the "locked" to confirm that you want to delete your account anyway. The account will be deleted permanently.

Upgrading to ChatGPT-4

If you are using the freemium version of ChatGPT application named as ChatGPT-3.5 and want to upgrade to the premium version of ChatGPT known as ChatGPT-4, you can enjoy numerous additional and advanced features and capabilities. The premium version is a paid service that offers a range of features and capabilities[170]:

- ChatGPT-4 is powered by Engine GPT4.
- It is capable of processing images along with text due to the characteristics of multimodal it possesses.
- It is much more powerful than freemium version, which is based on Engine GPT3.5.
- The output or results of ChatGPT-4 are more contextual and nuanced.
- Offers greater accuracy and reliability.
- Higher creativity and innovative characteristics.
- It is lesser prone to illusions or hallucinations.
- Many other additional features that are not offered by the ChatGPT-3.5 version.

If you want to purchase or upgrade to the advanced (premium) version of ChatGPT, you need to take the following few steps:

- Login to ChatGPT 3.5.
- Click the *Upgrade to Plus* link located in the left page above the username of the main interface of ChatGPT platform. An upgrade pop-up window appears.

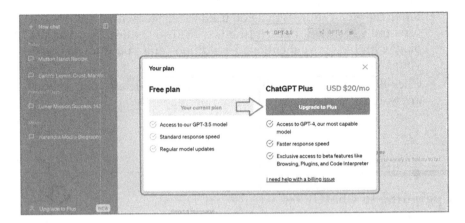

FIGURE 7.34
"Upgrade to Plus" button.

- Click the *Upgrade to Plus* plan on the pop-up window, as shown in Figure 7.34. The billing and contact information page appears, as shown in Figure 7.35.

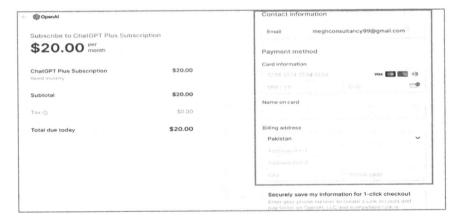

FIGURE 7.35
Billing and contact information window.

- Add *email address, payment method, card name,* and *billing address* in the given fields on the billing page.

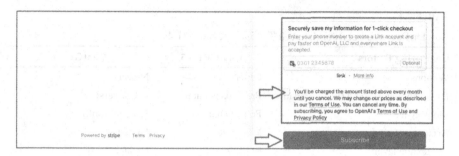

FIGURE 7.36
The checkout window.

- Add confirmation by adding your phone number and other information for one-click checkout in the future, as shown in Figure 7.36.
- Click the *Subscribe* button once the form is completed. You would be upgraded to ChatGPT version 4 with the subscription fee charged on your account or card.

Difference between Different Versions of ChatGPT

Both ChatGPT 3.5 and ChatGPT 4 are AI-based models for creating content such as text, image, and voice. Both are regenerative models based on transformer architecture that use the most advanced AI technologies for creating the most reliable and accurate content exactly like the human does. In fact, both of those platforms are two different versions in terms of capabilities, features, and charges; but the main purpose of both platforms is to generate text in natural language like the humans do. ChatGPT 3.5 is a freemium version while the ChatGPT 4 is an advanced premium version that is available for some monthly fee. Despite numerous similarities, there are certain differences between the two versions. OpenAI ChatGPT has explained this in terms of different comparing parameters, as mentioned in Table 7.1.[171-174]

TABLE 7.1

Key Differences between ChatGPT 3.5 and ChatGPT 4

Comparing Factors	ChatGPT 3.5	ChatGPT 4
Versions	Older	Newer
Large language model (LLM) versions	Previous version	Latest version
Monthly fee	Free of charge	$20 per month
Accuracy of results	Moderate	Higher
Contextual level	Moderate	Greater
Level of hallucination	Low	Lower
Smartness in prompt responses	Average	Greater
Capability to handle complexity of question	Low	High
Support to mathematical complex problems	Low	High
Level of advanced attributions and capabilities	Standard	Ten times higher than ChatGPT 3.5
Power to nuance distinguishing	Average	Higher
Coherence in responses	Average	Higher
Numbers of parameters supported by each platform	175 billion parameters	About 100 trillion parameters
Modality support	Single-modal	Multimodal
Content supported	Text	Text and image
Short-term memory capabilities	About 8000 words	About 64,000 words
Support for automatic text extraction from website or URLs	No	Yes
Supported languages	A few	Over 25 languages
Steer ability and control features	Lower	Higher
Training or search capability	Limited up to September 2021	Limited up to September 2021 with additional capability to search through search engines
Number of supported plugins	Few	Numerous
Exam results accuracy	Normal	40% higher than ChatGPT 3.5
Speed and efficiency	Faster due to support for less complex issues	Slower due to support for complex issues
Supported length of prompts	Smaller	Longer
Type of model	Text to text model	Data to text model
Token-handling capability	About 4000 tokens	About 8192 tokens (twice)

With the passage of time and release of newer versions, the advancements in the features, capabilities, performance, accuracy, reliability, and other characteristics will keep improving.

Advanced Features of ChatGPT 4

ChatGPT 4 is the advanced version of ChatGPT 3.5; therefore, it is very natural that it will possess numerous advanced features and capabilities compared with its previous version ChatGPT 3.5. The most important advanced features of ChatGPT 4 compared with the older version ChatGPT 3.5 are as follows:

- Ability to handle highly complex questions and mathematical expressions in queries with greater accuracy
- Powered by latest large language model (LLM)
- Capable of handling over 64,000 words in short-term memory, which is many times larger than the previous version
- Offers higher accuracy, reliability, and context in responses
- Trained on over 100 trillion parameters, multiple times higher than the previous version
- Supports direct text and image data from online websites, URLs, and live images
- Supports numerous languages

How to Use ChatGPT in Software Development?

ChatGPT platform is developed to learn from real-world training, make decisions, and respond to the input queries or prompts in the way humans do. It is designed to create text in response to the queries provided through prompts. The advanced version of ChatGPT can also take the text and image from the online sources as well as from the manual input and process it for the desired output. The text can be in natural language or in the computer codes for building a software website, application, or any other product.

ChatGPT is trained on not only large corpora of natural language text but also on the computer programming languages to generate the suitable response in a particular computer language against a written text-based queries regarding a software function or module. A software engineer can use the capabilities and features for performing a wide range of functions and activities related to the software development. The following are the most important ways for a software developer to use this advanced AI-powered platform for software development[175,178]:

- **Coding Support** – This can be accomplished in two ways:
  - **Code Generation** – You can use ChatGPT to generate code snippets for specific tasks. Describe what you need, and the model

can provide you with code examples in various programming languages.

- **Code Review** – It can assist in reviewing code by pointing out potential issues or suggesting improvements based on the code you provide.

- **Problem-Solving** – The solution to any problems in the software development field is one of the most brain-stretching, creative, and cumbersome activity. With the help of ChatGPT, finding the solution to the problems is very easy and effective. When you encounter a tricky problem or error in your code, describe the issue to ChatGPT. It may provide insights, solutions, or debugging tips.
  - Abridges the gap between technical and nontechnical staff
  - Predicts the suitable outcome
  - Gives insight into possible problems
  - Identifies correct solution to the issues

- **Learning Software Concepts** – Learning through search engines is very long and complex. ChatGPT has made it very simple and easy. ChatGPT can help explain complex programming concepts, algorithms, or frameworks in a simplified manner, aiding your learning process.

- **Generating Documentation** – It can also assist in generating documentation for your software projects, including API documentation, README files, and comments. It can help you save huge costs on hiring technical writers for creating and managing software development technical documents.

- **Software Project Planning** – Another major support you can get in your software development projects is the project planning with the help of ChatGPT. Use ChatGPT to brainstorm project ideas, create project plans, or outline the architecture of your software.
  - Accurate workflow development
  - Correct workhour estimation
  - Effective communication among teams
  - Better collaborative mechanism
  - Efficient change management

- **Bug Tracking and Resolution** – If your code gets buggy, you need to track it. Programmers know how complex it can be in some cases. ChatGPT has made it very simple and fast to track the bugs. Describe a bug or error, and ChatGPT can assist in identifying potential causes and suggesting debugging steps. The solution offered by ChatGPT is very reliable and accurate to save your huge time and efforts.

- **Code Refactoring** – You do not need to worry about the maintainability and clarity of the codes now. ChatGPT can provide suggestions for code refactoring to improve code readability, maintainability, and performance.

- **Stack Overflow and Forum Assistance** – When you are stuck on a specific coding problem, you can use ChatGPT to draft questions for Stack Overflow or other programming forums, or even help you search for existing solutions.

- **Application Interaction through Natural Language Interfaces** – Build natural language interfaces for your software using ChatGPT, allowing users to interact with your application using text or speech.

- **Automated Software Code Testing** – Software code testing is one of the most crucial areas in the software development, which defines the quality, consistency, security, and reliability of the software application or code. A huge time was required to be spared for testing in all types of code developments. ChatGPT has made it more effective and easier for the developers. You can use ChatGPT to generate test cases or test scripts for your software to improve test coverage:

  - Supports test case generation
  - Analyzes logic structures
  - Covers numerous code paths and edges
  - Builds test case documentation
  - Has provision of short descriptions of test cases
  - Makes prediction of test outcomes
  - Defines test fail and pass conditions

- **Support for Integration of Code Generation Tools** – Software development is a comprehensive process or activity that comprises numerous activities that are accomplished through different types of tools. ChatGPT is capable of integrating a wide range of tools used in the software development field. Integrate ChatGPT into your development environment or tools as a plugin or extension for on-the-fly code generation.

- **Faster Code Completion** – By using the suggestive feature, you can improve the speed of code generation through suggestive capabilities of ChatGPT.

- **Wider Area of Languages** – You can use ChatGPT platform for numerous supported computer programming languages. Thus, you get a wider scope of coding with the help of the amazing platform for many applications and projects.

- **Elimination of Typos and Other Human Errors** – The automated coding system by ChatGPT help you improve the productivity and efficiency by eliminating the chances of typos and other similar kinds of human errors during the course of coding. Thus, you can improve your coding productivity greatly. ChatGPT is also capable of numerous repetitive tasks and formatting of codes to save your huge time.

- **Code Translation** – It is an amazing capability of ChatGPT to translate the code of a project or product into multiple languages supported by it. Thus, you can enjoy a greater flexibility and freedom in computer coding.

- **Effective Narrow Down Support** – You can sharpen your coding by using the knowledge and domain-specific knowledge of ChatGPT with the help of your wisdom effectively. The functions and routines that you have decided with your wisdom can be completed in just a blink of an eye with the help of ChatGPT.

- **Efficient Library Exploration** – You can explore a wide range of tools, platforms, and libraries without any huge time and efforts through ChatGPT while coding your diverse projects in multiple language paradigms.

- **Implementation of Good Practices** – Programmers can use ChatGPT for the implementation of good practices in software development. Eventually, it helps in perfect software coding.

How to Use ChatGPT for Effective Text Generation?

Initially, ChatGPT was designed to generate text in natural language like the humans do. It has been trained on large corpora of data so that it can learn from the real-world data on how to take and process communication messages received from any human through prompt and understand the objectivity behind that particular prompt and make response in the form of text in natural language that the humans understand. As the time passed, the capabilities have increased and the latest version of ChatGPT can generate text by taking simple prompts in the form of text as well as in the form of images. It can process the messages to generate a suitable response in the form of text as well as images. Remember that while ChatGPT is a powerful tool, it may not always generate perfect responses. It is important to review and refine the output as necessary to ensure that it aligns with your requirements. To generate the most effective text through ChatGPT, you need to take care of numerous things while interacting with this platform. There are a few most important things that are required to use (like tips) so that ChatGPT can provide you with the best answers in the form of text.

To generate the text responses, you need to follow some simple and easy-to-follow steps:

- **Open ChatGPT Interface** – To generate the most effective text through ChatGPT, first of all, access the main interface where you can input the prompts and receive the suitable responses generated by ChatGPT.

- **Input Your Text** – Start by typing your message or question into the text input box. The question should be well-refined and clear.

- **Generate Response** – It is an automated response from ChatGPT. After you provide the input, ChatGPT will process it and generate a text response. The response will be based on the input you provided.

- **Check Text and Refine** – Read the generated response carefully. If the response is not exactly what you were looking for or needs refinement, you can iterate by tweaking your initial input or asking for clarification.

- **Carry on the Conversation** – You can continue the conversation by providing more input. Ask follow-up questions or provide additional context to guide the conversation in the desired direction.

- **Use Innovative Approaches and Experiments** – Feel free to experiment with different prompts and instructions to see how ChatGPT responds. You can use it for a variety of tasks, such as drafting content, brainstorming ideas, programming help, and more.

- **Keep Refining and Repeating** – If the response is not meeting your needs, do not hesitate to make further adjustments to your input. ChatGPT learns from your guidance, so refining your prompts can lead to better results.

- **Feedback ChatGPT for More Improvements** – Providing the detailed feedback on every bad response would increase the accuracy, reliability, and relevancy of the response for you. So, always keep providing feedback responses.

It is important to note that ChatGPT generates the text based on patterns it has learned from its training data. While it can provide helpful and coherent responses, it might not always be accurate or perfectly aligned with your expectations. It is a good practice to review and refine the generated content to ensure that it meets your needs. To review and generate more relevant responses, you should take care of the following important tips and good practices:

- **Input Clear and Specific Prompts** – The most important thing for the ChatGPT platform to produce the most relevant and accurate response is clear prompt. Be clear in your prompts and provide specific details. This helps guide the model in the right direction and ensures that the generated text is relevant to your needs.

- **Break Down Complex Requests into Simple Parts** – For maintaining the accuracy and relevancy, you need to provide simple prompts, which increase the level of clarity and simplicity for the ChatGPT platform to understand it properly. If you have a complex question or request, consider breaking it down into smaller, simpler parts. This makes it easier for the model to understand and generate accurate responses.

- **Use Complete Sentences** – Avoid using short keywords and fragmented sentences like we use in search engines. Frame your prompts as complete sentences to make the ChatGPT understand the motive and context behind your question. This makes it easier for the model to comprehend your request and generate coherent responses.

- **Choose the Right Options to Provide Context** – When starting a conversation or asking a question, give some context about the topic. You can provide this through either custom instructions or choosing the suitable tabs at the start of the ChatGPT application interface. This helps the model understand the context and generate more relevant text, which is more useful and desirable for you.

- **Ask for Step-by-Step Explanations** – You can request or revise the text that you feel is complex and it should be in the form of simple steps or bullets by asking the platform to generate step-by-step explanation of the procedure. If you are seeking explanations or instructions, ask the model to provide step-by-step guidance. This can help ensure the generated text is organized and easy to follow. You can also add more details by asking a specific question about a point or bullet that is looking a bit complex.

- **Play with Different Prompts and Questions** – The more you play with the ChatGPT application, the more you understand about the effective use of it. Do not hesitate to experiment with different ways of phrasing your prompts. Sometimes a slight rewording can lead to better responses that are more relevant and useful.

- **Effective Use of System Messages** – ChatGPT is an NLP-based machine learning model powered by numerous system mechanism to take input from the users. You can use system-level instructions to guide the behavior of the model. For example, you can introduce yourself as an expert in a particular domain to start with.

- **Repeat and Refine** – The more you iterate your inputs, the more diverse options of text you get. If the initial response is not perfect, refine your prompt and ask for clarifications or elaborations to improve the text generated in subsequent interactions. Using ChatGPT for innovative and repetitive questions offers better responses.

- **Always Remain Patient and Ethical** – If the initial responses are not exactly what you are looking for, do not get discouraged. Iterative conversations and slight adjustments to your prompts can lead to better outcomes. Keep improving and repeating your queries. Remember that ChatGPT generates text based on patterns in its training data, so always review and ensure the content aligns with ethical guidelines and accuracy standards.

- **Edit and Modify Text Manually** – ChatGPT is evolving its capabilities with the passage of time. It is a great idea to check and edit the text generated by ChatGPT to give a natural touch to it. Feel free to edit and modify the generated text to match your preferences or needs. ChatGPT is a tool to assist you, and your input can help shape the final output. The combination of machine and man makes the response highly effective. Use ChatGPT as a starting point and then apply your own creativity and expertise to refine and expand upon the generated text.

By following the above-mentioned tips while using the ChatGPT platform, you can generate the most reliable, accurate, and effective responses that are highly beneficial in a wide range of text creation fields.

What Are the Benefits of Using ChatGPT?

ChatGPT is emerging as the most disruptive technology in the present-day global marketplace. Numerous businesses and industries are repositioning their strategies by transforming many of their processes that involved content as the core components such as marketing, education, training, printing, blogging, book writing, software development, text editing, grammar correction, proofreading, software testing, code debugging, and many others. The main reason behind this huge transformation in processes is driven by a wide range of benefits offered by ChatGPT and similar types of AI text generative models.

The following are the most important advantages of using ChatGPT[179–181]:

- **Cost-Saving** – One of the most fundamental advantages ChatGPT offers is the cost-saving in numerous areas across the domains of industries. It can save substantial amount of cost in different areas:
  - Replacing costly human resources with ChatGPT for different roles such as technical writers, content creators, coders, testers, and others
  - Faster creation of text in all domains of technologies and society

- Replacing the costly content creation with no charges or with a very small fee
- Substituting costly editing and proofreading services with ChatGPT services
- Using ChatGPT in place of code testers and quality assurance professionals in the field of software development

- **Time-Saving** – The automated generation of text in natural language and coding in a wide range of computer programming languages saves you huge time compared with the manual creation of text and codes, respectively. The time-saving provides you with the additional benefits that result in increased revenue and reduced cost.

- **High Quality** – ChatGPT enables the professionals to create high-quality content with greater level of accuracy and reliability and free from all types of mistakes made by a human known as human errors. ChatGPT is trained on large corpora of data from across the domains and areas of technologies and other field of our day-to-day life. The machines get the information accurately without any skipping. The response generated is based on the huge information or knowledge that ChatGPT is trained on; therefore, the output generated by this amazing platform is surprisingly great.

- **Accuracy and Reliability** – The accuracy and reliability of the text generated by ChatGPT is significantly high because of its wider training on almost all types of knowledge and information available in the world. If a proper prompt or query is provided to the ChatGPT platform, it comes up with highly accurate and reliable response.

- **Efficiency and Productivity** – Overall efficiency and productivity of a professional or a business has increased significantly due to the power of ChatGPT used in their respective activities and processes, respectively. Multiple processes are performed by a single professional in software development and content creation fields. This increases cost-efficiency as well as the performance of the professionals and business processes significantly. The performance of regular roles such as writers, editors, news reporters, lawyers, bloggers, teachers, students, and others have increased many times due to automated creations of content through highly efficient platform of ChatGPT.

- **Greater User Experience** – The creation of great user experience in ChatGPT service users is another main advantage.

- **Greater Level of Automation** – By integrating ChatGPT with numerous online applications such as customer support, technical support, customer relationship management processes, chatbots, and others, you achieve a higher level of automation in business processes and activities across the verticals of industries.

- **Effective SEO Optimization** – The optimization of the content will get pace due to faster development of unique text and other content for the future. The capability of ChatGPT to generate unique content for all types of writings is a big deal indeed.

- **A Comprehensive Platform for All Types of Needs** – ChatGPT has merged a wide range of AI-powered services into one unified platform which is trained for everything. It offers a unified platform for searching any kind of knowledge and programming skills across the fields. It is comprehensively beneficial for all types of peoples and professionals:
  - Researchers and scholars
  - Editors and writers
  - Marketers and managers
  - Teachers and students
  - Trainers and apprentices
  - Journalists and scientists
  - Engineers and doctors
  - And many others

- **Creative Writing and Entertainment** – This is an amazing capability of ChatGPT in which it provides you with the creative ideas, entertainments, and arts. For instance, you can ask ChatGPT to create a story based on a few hints or plot. It is also able to create you a poem or other literature items. You can create numerous types of memes, dramas, stories, games, puzzles, and much more. It is also able to generate a wide range of arts, images, sounds, videos, and other types of arts from simple text as input.

- **Solution Provisioning** – ChatGPT is able to provide you with solutions to a wide range of problems in all major domains of industries, businesses, and technologies such as computer programming, project management, complex mathematical derivations, measurements and scales, and many others.

- **Cybersecurity Improvement** – ChatGPT is very helpful in providing you with support for enhancing cybersecurity. With the help of this, you can preempt the emerging cybersecurity threats such as fraudulent activities, phishing, spamming, and others.

- **Transformation Force** – ChatGPT is emerging as one of the most powerful processes and activity transformational forces in all domains or areas of modern business ecosystems. This is a very critical platform that is redefining the positions and orientation of all types of businesses, industries, and processes.

Other than the above-mentioned notable advantages, newer areas of upsides of using ChatGPT are emerging with the passage of time. All of those benefits are achieved due to the increasing number of areas and domains where the use of ChatGPT is becoming important. In fact, the advantages are achieved due to the following technical features, characteristics, and capabilities of ChatGPT[180,182,183]:

- **Effective Learning with Explanation** – Learning has become so easy and comprehensive under one single roof. ChatGPT can explain complex concepts in a simplified manner, making it a helpful learning aid in all domains of educations. It can provide explanations for academic subjects, technology, science, and more.

- **Versatile Content Generation** – ChatGPT can help you generate creative and engaging content for articles, blog posts, marketing materials, and more. It is a valuable tool for overcoming writer's block and getting your ideas flowing. You can create highly versatile and unique content every time you use it.

- **Drafting Proofreading and Editing** – This is another revolutionary capability of ChatGPT in which it can assist in drafting emails, reports, and other written documents. It is also useful for editing and proofreading to catch errors and improve readability.

- **Innovative Idea Generation** – It is a human-like capability of ChatGPT. When brainstorming ideas for projects, products, or creative endeavors, ChatGPT can provide fresh perspectives and suggestions to inspire your thinking.

- **Unified Programming Support** – Some people say, it will replace the programmers. However, in our view, at this time, it is a great support for computer code developers. If you are a programmer, ChatGPT can assist with coding questions, debugging, and providing code examples (which may not be always accurate but as time passes, it can be better). It is like having a programming mentor available in numerous computer programming languages commonly used in modern coding. However, replacing human programmer completely would not be possible. In fact, a human has to interact with, edit, check, modify, and operate with ChatGPT generated codes after all!

- **Social Interaction Capabilities** – Owing to highly professional-level abilities for social interaction, ChatGPT can be used for social interaction and companionship, especially for those who may be looking for conversation partners.

- **Professional Language Translation** – ChatGPT is emerging as a big challenger for language service platforms such as grammar checkers, text editors, translation services, and others. You can use ChatGPT to help translate text between languages, aiding in communication and understanding across linguistic barriers.
- **Creative and Artistic Writing** – Whether you are working on a novel, a screenplay, or poetry, ChatGPT can provide creative input, generate dialogue, or even help with character development. It can create smaller pieces of literature writings and art to make a bigger creation very fast.
- **Deep Research and Exploration of Topics** – ChatGPT is leading in comprehensive research and exploration of a wide range of topics from across the domains under one single roof. If you are curious about a particular subject or want to learn more about a topic, ChatGPT can provide explanations and information.
- **Customer Support Capabilities** – ChatGPT can handle routine customer inquiries, providing quick and accurate responses to frequently asked questions on websites and platforms.
- **Perfect Support for Accessibility** – ChatGPT can help individuals with disabilities by providing information, reading text aloud, or assisting in communication.
- **Natural Simulation of Conversations** – ChatGPT can simulate conversations with historical figures, fictional characters, or even your favorite celebrities, allowing for creative and entertaining interactions.
- **Personal Assistant Abilities** – You can use ChatGPT as a virtual personal assistant to set reminders, make to-do lists, and manage your schedule.

It is very important to note that the efficiency, capabilities, features, and advanced characteristics are continually improving in ChatGPT with every newer version. ChatGPT 3.5 is much lesser capable than the present ChatGPT 4. The advancements are continuing to enable more and more capabilities to this amazing platform in the future.

Limitations of ChatGPT

ChatGPT has been designed to learn from the training provided through ingestion of data in the form of text and images without any explicit computer programming to learn from that data. It learns like human brains do from the raw and unstructured data. It has become a very attractive and useful platform across all the domains of businesses as well as our daily lives. It is on the track to transform numerous processes, functions, activities, and roles in the modern business and technological ecosystem. Despite such huge potential scope of ChatGPT, there are certain limitations of this platform too. Let us explore the limitations here[184,185]:

- **Lack of Common Sense and Contextual Understanding** – ChatGPT may sometimes struggle to understand the context of a conversation, leading to responses that are off-topic or nonsensical. It lacks the common sense that a human possesses. The responses generated by ChatGPT are based on the information it got from training.

- **Limitation in Generating Complex and Structured Long Responses** – When this platform encounters complex and long prompts, it gets confused.

- **Generating Incorrect Information** – The model might generate text that sounds plausible but is factually incorrect or misleading, as it generates responses based on patterns in its training data.

- **Chances of Creating Sensitive/Offensive Content** – The responses of ChatGPT are learned from a wide range of Internet text, which means it might unintentionally produce content that is biased, offensive, or inappropriate.

- **Biased Response** – Sometimes, it can generate biased responses because ChatGPT generates response based on the information fed during the training.

- **Excessive Use of Certain Phrases** – The model might repetitively use certain phrases, leading to responses that sound formulaic or unnatural.

- **Unrealistic Creativity** – While creativity is strength, ChatGPT might generate creative but unrealistic scenarios or ideas.

- **Inability of Multitasking** – ChatGPT is not able to handle multiple tasks at a time. You need to work on one single task at a time on ChatGPT.

- **Inconsistency Responses** – The model's responses might vary between different prompts or interactions, and it could contradict itself within a single conversation.

- **Limited Cutoff Knowledge** – The knowledge used by ChatGPT is based on data available up to September 2021 (while writing this book in 2023), so it might not have information on events or developments that occurred afterward.

- **Complete Dependency on Input** – The quality of the output heavily relies on the quality of the input. Vague or poorly phrased prompts might result in suboptimal responses.

- **Not a Substitute for Human Interaction** – While ChatGPT can simulate conversation similar to the way human does, it cannot replace genuine human interaction, empathy, or emotional understanding.
- **Fine-Tuning Is Still Required** – ChatGPT responses are not perfect, you need to fine-tune them to use in the professional activities.

SAMPLE QUESTIONS

1. Enumerate key tasks where ChatGPT finds significant utility.
2. Examine the limitations inherent in the application of ChatGPT.
3. Detail effective strategies for utilizing ChatGPT in text generation processes.
4. Highlight distinctions among various iterations of ChatGPT and their respective features.
5. Explore the integration of ChatGPT in software development and its practical applications.
6. Analyze the advantages associated with the utilization of ChatGPT.

8

Using Different Versions of ChatGPT

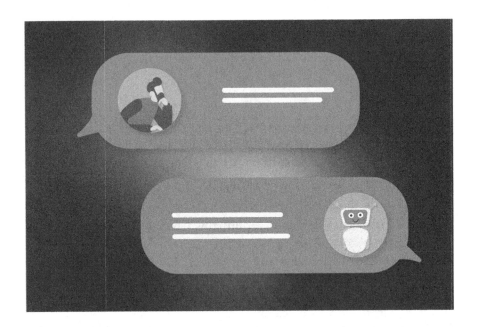

Introduction

ChatGPT has evolved from its foundation artificial intelligence (AI) structure or architecture known as generative pretrained transformer, precisely referred to as GPT. The main purpose of building GPT model was to process the natural language and enable machines to intake, understand, decide, and generate response like the human brain does. It is a natural language processing or NLP model. The NLP is a part of machine learning (ML) technology that deals with the processing of natural language that humans use for their interaction and communication. This fundamental model of ML has passed through an evolution from its first version, GPT-1 through GPT-4. The first version was trained with smaller volumes of data and parameters. The training level and capabilities were continuously increased by adding more parameters and processing capabilities. This is important to note that all those versions

DOI: 10.1201/9781003474173-8

or models were developed by OpenAI LLC. The following are the most important versions of GPT used in the development of modern ChatGPT platform[186-188]:

- Generative pretrained GPT-1
- Generative pretrained GPT-2
- Generative pretrained GPT-3
- Generative pretrained GPT-3.5
- Generative pretrained GPT-4

The first version of GPT was launched early 2018. This was the original version of the GPT model, introduced by OpenAI in 2018. It had 117 million parameters and demonstrated the potential of large-scale unsupervised pretraining for natural language understanding and generation tasks. The second version of it was released in 2019. GPT-2 was a larger and more powerful version of the model with 1.5 billion parameters. Due to concerns about its potential misuse for generating fake news and deceptive content, OpenAI initially withheld the full release of the model, providing only smaller versions. The third one known as GPT-3 was released in 2020. GPT-3 marked a significant advancement with a staggering 175 billion parameters. It demonstrated impressive performance on a wide range of NLP tasks, often achieving state-of-the-art results with just a few examples or prompts. The submodel of GPT3 referred to as GPT-3.5 was launched in 2022. This version had a few tweaks and refinements over the previously released model version GPT-3. Finally, the advanced version of GPT-4 was released in March 2023 (this is the version available at the time of writing of this book). The latest version of GPT is used in the modern multi-modal ChatGPT 4 platform, which is capable of processing not only text but also other forms of content such as image and others. The ChatGPT service based on GPT-4 model is commercially known as ChatGPT Plus. The GPT-4 model can handle numerous complex processes such as mathematical expressions, image data, conversion of image data into text and vice versa, and much more.[189]

Use of the Main Versions of ChatGPT

Different versions of GPT architecture were used for training the application to an advanced level and for the advanced uses. The first two versions – GPT-1 & GPT-2 – were not launched commercially for general public uses. But the later versions of GPT such as GPT-3, GPT-3.5, and GPT-4 were used in different AI services for generating responses in text as well as in other content such as images and other mathematical expressions.

There is a very little difference between GPT-3 and GPT-3.5. For the first time, GPT-3 was used in the launching of InstructGPT platform. This platform is based on the ML model, which uses the human feedback for learning or fine-tuning the responses that it can generate against the prompts. The InstructGPT is a fine-tuning model that is integrated beneath the GPT-3 model to generate more reliable, relevant, and accurate response powered by the human feedback module working at the bottom of this application known as ChatGPT. The combination of the features of InstrcutGPT and GPT-3 model is broadly considered as the ChatGPT 3.5 model working to realize the objectives of ChatGPT basic version.[190] These models were used for the first commercial AI-based text generating application named as ChatGPT.

There are two main AI platforms launched in the form of a web application by OpenAI for all types of users publicly:

- ChatGPT 3.5
- ChatGPT 4

Both the above-mentioned services of OpenAI LLC have become so popular that they are setting new trends and orientations in modern business ecosystems of life. There are numerous powerful uses of these two main models or online commercial services that can be utilized to transform the existing business and daily life processes and activities across all domains of industries, societies, governments, and business ecosystems. Let us discuss the use of these two major versions of ChatGPT services separately with main focus on different uses in different domains of industries and their respective impacts on modern ecosystems of business and technology.

Using ChatGPT 3.5

ChatGPT 3.5 is based on the GPT-3.5 model, which is a tweaked form of GPT-3 version of transformer architecture designed for generating human-like text against the prompts provided by a human through an input question. The first version of ChatGPT-4 service was also based on this model until the latest model named as GPT-4 was launched recently in 2023. Thus, we can say that the ChatGPT3.5 platform is powered by the GPT-3.5 version for providing service in both freemium and premium services commercially launched by OpenAI.

Main Features and Uses

The following are the most important uses, features, capabilities, and characteristics of ChatGPT 3.5:

- The fundamental service was commercially launched by OpenAI in November 2022.
- It is not a multimodal application, which means it is not able to handle content in any other form other than simple text in natural language.
- It is lesser reliable, creative, and relevant result producer compared with the advanced version of OpenAI ChatGPT-4.
- It has lesser creativity and intelligence compared with the advanced version.
- It is prone to misleading or hallucinating responses.
- Reasoning errors are possible in this application.
- Underlying AI model or architecture can support up to 175 billion parameters.
- It is extremely useful in creating coherent text for almost all areas of knowledge, businesses, and technologies available in the world.
- ChatGPT 3.5 is capable of generating unique content for every new prompt regarding the same question.
- Creation of text through ChatGPT-3.5 can be used for diverse purposes:
  - General-purpose articles
  - Political and social articles and editorial
  - Research papers and market researches
  - Thesis and dissertations
  - Emails and business communication
  - Marketing and advertisement content
  - Poetry and other creative writings
  - Business and material forecasting
  - Website contents and technical writings
  - Customer services and support chatbots
- The following are the main industries where the use of ChatGPT3.5 can revolutionize the underlying processes, functions, and activities:
  - Education, training, and research industries
  - Software development industry
  - Content creation industry

- Editing and proofreading sector
- Technical documentation and writing sector
- Entertainment and art industry
- Gaming and social media sectors
- It has capability of comprehensive explanations for very difficult concepts in all domains of learning and education.
- It can also be used for the following purposes[191]:
  - Creating customized résumés and cover letters
  - Creating business letters and contracts
  - Coding software functions and modules
  - Testing and debugging the software codes
  - Translation of text into multiple languages
  - Text correction through proofreading and editing
  - Creating recipes and cooking procedures
  - Creating poetry, writing music, jokes, and stories
  - Solving mathematical complex problems in a step-by-step way
  - Getting advice on different types of relationship maintenance and building new ones
  - Answering to almost every question in your minds
- ChatGPT 3.5 version is available for free in freemium subscription to the subscribers through a simple email instantly.
- There is no word or prompt limits to use this astonishing web application based on AI model for generating a wide range of text

Using ChatGPT 4.0

Using ChatGPT-4 offers you with numerous advanced features, capabilities, and benefits for creating text as well as image and voice from all those supported types of content inputs. It is an advanced version of ChatGPT3.5, which is free and has been already discussed in the above sections. For using ChatGPT-4, you need to upgrade your subscription to ChatGPT Plus. This advanced version of ChatGPT launched by OpenAI is designed to support not only text but also other forms of content such as image and voice. Like ChatGPT 3.5, it also offers application programming interface (API) for developers to develop applications in which ChatGPT can be integrated.

Main Features and Uses

The following are the most prominent features, capabilities, uses, and characteristics of ChatGPT-4:

- It is a multimodal platform that supports image and voice input along with the basic text input that was the only supported input in ChatGPT-3.5.
- You can upload excel worksheet to ChatGPT-4 or any other mathematical complex graphs or any other presentation for processing. ChatGPT-4 is capable of processing those types of file and their content to generate a text-based as well as image-based detailed report or analysis of that data as desired.
- It can perform all the activities that were performed by its predecessor version ChatGPT 3.5.
- The quality of the output provided by ChatGPT-4 is way better and reliable than the same provided by ChatGPT 3.5 freemium subscription.
- The underlying architecture in the modern ChatGPT-4 is Transformer GPT-4, which has been launched recently in March 2023.
- It offers API for software developers to create software applications with the help of this amazing version of ChatGPT.
- ChatGPT Plus offers highly advanced features compared with the previous version in terms of numerous characteristics[192]:
  - Accuracy and reliability
  - Greater contextual and sensible response
  - Highly creative and coherent texts
  - Higher programming and testing capabilities
  - Reduced biases and hallucinations
- It is less prone to errors in generating the response.
- It is capable of handling very complex prompts and problems to offer highly desirable solutions to those complex matters.
- It is available for users at a great speed even in peak usage hours.
- It provides regular updates, improvements, and advanced features without any delays.
- It provides additional knowledge beyond its last updated cutoff time, that is, September 2021. It uses Bing search engine to help users take the latest information from online resources and make comprehensive response suitable for the present time.

SAMPLE QUESTIONS

1. What are the principal versions of ChatGPT?

2. Highlight the key features characterizing ChatGPT 3.5.

3. Illustrate the main features distinguishing ChatGPT 4.0.

4. What are the primary differences between ChatGPT 3.5 and 4.0 versions?

5. In what ways does ChatGPT 4.0 differ from its predecessor, ChatGPT 3.5?

6. Outline the distinguishing features between ChatGPT 3.5 and the latest version, ChatGPT 4.0.

9

Future of ChatGPT

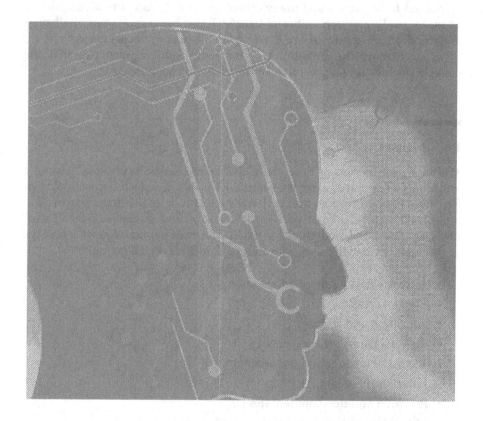

Introduction

Scientists have been striving for many decades to build a machine that have the capabilities to think and make decisions. Numerous fictitious and scientific concepts and ideas were experimented during the long decades of discovery and research. Today, one of the most advanced and highly capable tools powered by artificial intelligence (AI) is ChatGPT. It is a disruptive intervention that has disrupted numerous existing processes, activities, and function operational in modern business, industrial, and technological

DOI: 10.1201/9781003474173-9

ecosystems. After getting launched in November 2022, ChatGPT took the entire world by storm within a few weeks and months.

The prospects of this technology augur very well in the future. Many industries, companies, businesses, and professionals are exploring the effective use of ChatGPT in either modernizing or replacing the existing roles, functions, and processes. Within just a few months, many verticals of industries have already identified the processes and roles to transform with the help of ChatGPT and associated technologies and many others are in the process to accomplish it. These expanding opportunities of ChatGPT also bring numerous challenges and implications in our society as well as in the business ecosystems.[193]

Let us explore the possibilities, challenges, and implications that the ChatGPT is bringing all together in the following sections.

Possibilities

Within a short period of time, the global business environment is sensing a wide range of opportunities for the ChatGPT platform and similar technologies. The areas of opportunities are continually expanding as the time progresses in almost all areas and domains of industries and businesses as well as in all areas of societal life of the modern global world. The most important areas where the possibilities of ChatGPT usage are enormous include the following[193–195]:

- Software development and testing
- Content creation
- Education and training
- Customer support and services
- Technical writing and documentation
- Entertainment and creativity
- Research and development (R&D)
- Marketing and advertisement
- Virtual assistance and support
- Language translation and transcription
- Mental healthcare
- Counting

ChatGPT is a AI-generative technology which is used to generate responses against the prompts fed by humans or even other similar types of machines powered by AI. ChatGPT is not the single AI modal that is available in the marketplace; there are in fact numerous other similar types of models but ChatGPT has got the highest popularity due to its comprehensive qualities and capabilities. Also, the apparent accuracy of response has made the people somewhat crazy about it.

With the passage of time, the advancements in this natural language processing (NLP) technology are expected to emerge very quickly. The advancement of multimodal capability is also expected, which means the understanding of ChatGPT through different prompts such as text, image, voice, video, and other prompts. With the improvement in multimodality, the possibilities are expected to be more and would continue increasing.

Before the launching and successful traction of ChatGPT, many other similar types of applications were available on the market such as BARD from Google and BERT. All those applications were not drawing attention of the users properly; therefore, the companies behind those applications or platforms were also a bit reluctant to invest heavily on them. But with the popularity of ChatGPT, other applications are also being accepted at different levels and companies behind them are investing heavily to achieve the space in the expanding arena of possibilities of generative AI in the NLP areas.

The emerging possibilities will produce numerous desirable bottom lines for almost all types of business systems and industries. The most important results will include the following:

- Increased process and professional productivity
- Faster software development and updates
- Quicker and comprehensive solutions to complex problems
- Enhanced innovation and creativity
- Effective communication and collaboration
- Extensive automation in a range of processes
- Reduced operational and development cost
- Increased efficiency and quality of services and products
- Greater business margins and profits
- Effective cross-language communication
- Reduced human-related errors
- Efficient cross-content conversion
- Automation of time-consuming repetitive tasks

Challenges

As a natural process, any opportunity also brings some challenges along with it. With the increased opportunities for ChatGPT and related technologies, numerous challenges have also emerged for using the power of ChatGPT and other AI-generative models more effectively. The most important challenges faced by the industries or businesses include the following[196,197]:

- Generating unbiased content
- Creating 100% accurate content free from hallucinations
- Figuring out human errors in human prompts
- Understanding the most complex and longer issues in unstructured prompts
- Behaving emotionally like human does
- Understanding the body language or cues of users
- Catching the context of the question
- Maintaining robust security and privacy of users
- Removing ethical and legal concerns
- Maintaining security from user manipulation
- Addressing the concerns of inappropriate content generation
- Seamless adaptation across the industries and businesses

With the passage of time, more improvements will happen in ChatGPT platform to address the main challenges. The continual improvements are expected not only in ChatGPT but also for other similar types of AI-generative models based on NLP technology.

Implications

Any disruption in technology brings in numerous types of opportunities and excitement; at the same time, it brings numerous challenges and implications for the existing systems, technologies, and business ecosystems. ChatGPT is one of the most promising technologies in the field of AI that has started disrupting almost all the business processes and technological functions in the modern business environments. It is offering many options to replace or reduce a wide range of human professional roles through automated process of ChatGPT. At the same time, it is also impacting on numerous other areas of our modern as well as traditional domains of businesses and societal processes and activities[198–200]:

- **Social Implication** – The social impact of ChatGPT and related technologies is huge. It is going to leave a comprehensive impact on the society from multiple angles such as financial pressure on workers, loss of jobs, mental pressures, and others. As the ChatGPT platform or other similar types of AI-generative models get traction, the fundamental component of society is human or human resource. It starts getting influenced by the power of AI machines to compete with. A machine is highly efficient, fast, fatigueless, and easy to enhance its capabilities. Thus, less skilled human resource will be badly impacted in terms of mental health, financial power, social wellness, and other factors.

- **Legal Implications** – The legal implications relate to the copyright infringements of content used for the training of such AI models and also the unique creations of content without any understanding and research by the students or other scholars for developing thesis and dissertations, which will leave a big impact on the owners of the digital assets that are being compromised in terms of their legal ownership rights.

- **Security and Privacy Implications** – ChatGPT or other AI-powered generative NLP applications are evolving and have numerous drawbacks and downsides that leave serious impact on the security and privacy of the users. It is claimed by certain people in different countries that the social media content and users have been already compromised during the training of such platforms and in the future, the same is possible because there is no regulatory or any other authority to deal with the hidden training through artificial neural networks and their responses to the cyberattacks.

- **Learning and Creativity Implications** – This implication is specifically a point of concern for students, learners, trainers, teachers, researchers, and creative people. The use of ChatGPT or other similar types of software applications would lead to the inability of those people to learn from the real-world environments and previously done research work. They would be forced to skip striving themselves to create innovative and creative content or idea but rather would use readymade responses from such machines. Thus, their learning and creative abilities will be badly impacted due to ChatGPT and other AI-generative apps.

- **Other Implications** – Other than the above-identified main implications, there are numerous side effects of using ChatGPT like AI tools for performing a wide range of activities and functions automatically such as interpersonal skill reduction, human isolation, mental health issues, reduced writing skills, and many others.

SAMPLE QUESTIONS

1. Examine the potential applications of ChatGPT.
2. Discuss the hurdles and difficulties associated with the implementation of ChatGPT.
3. Explore the broader consequences and significance of ChatGPT.
4. What possibilities arise from the utilization of ChatGPT in various contexts?
5. Elaborate on the challenges inherent in the operationalization of ChatGPT technology.
6. How do the implications of ChatGPT extend to different domains and industries?

10

Top Use Cases of GPT-Based Tools

Introduction

According to the latest projections, the global market size of artificial intelligence (AI)-generative natural language processing (NLP) tools is expected to cross $200.73 billion by 2032 from just $10.63 billion in 2022 with a whopping growth rate of over 34.2% CAGR (compound annual growth rate) during the forecast period.[201] The growth from 2022 to 2023 is expected to reach US$14.26 billion with huge jump from the previous year. The most important driver of this jump is expected to be the traction of ChatGPT, which has taken the whole world by surprise and into *shock and awe* due to the highly accurate and reliable results produced by it.

AI-Powered Tools Similar to ChatGPT

Without any doubt, there has been a consistent approach among the scientists and investors to work on AI models, especially in the field of NLP for

DOI: 10.1201/9781003474173-10

developing a powerful ecosystem between human and machine with natural language. Many tools have already been developed in the market and many more are underway. But ChatGPT has revolutionized this field drastically in such a way that almost all major companies and businesses are focusing on this promising domain of AI. The most important of such platforms and tools are discussed below.[202,203]

ChatGPT

ChatGPT is based on the GPT-4 model developed by OpenAI, an American company. This application has left mindboggling impact on all types of businesses and professionals within a few months after its official launch in November 2022. It is capable of providing response to almost all types of queries ranging from a simple general-knowledge question to software development.[204] Whether the responses are accurate or meaningful in the true sense given a context (like a sane human being responds) is another issue left for discussion and further improvements. But, indeed, this is a tool that has surprised many.

Google BARD

Google BARD is another powerful AI-generative application developed for providing responses to a wide range of queries in a natural language that a human speaks. This also uses transformer model LaMDA. It is available in limited version and limited countries. The improvement work is going on at a very fast pace for this product to leave greater impression on the fiercely competitive marketplace. It is considered as the most powerful AI-generative tool after ChatGPT and is expected to compete with it in the future.[205]

Claude 2

It is a NLP-based AI application. It is developed by Anthropic company. The main objective of this AI model is to generate human-like text and computer coding. It is trained for offering highly reliable and accurate text for effective communication between human and AI-powered NLP machines. It is also capable of communicating in numerous natural languages as well as computer programming languages.[206]

DALL-E 2

It is a multimodal AI generative model designed for producing not only text but also other contents such as images and arts. This model is developed by OpenAI and is integrated into the ChatGPT Plus service. There are two main versions of DALL known as DALL-E and DALL-E 2. The latter one is the advanced version with additional capabilities and features. It can develop highly natural images from the text prompts as well as from the image inputs. It offers application programming interface (API) for software developers to work with DALL platform for software development.[207]

GitHub Copilot

GitHub Copilot is a highly powerful AI-generative tool that is developed by GitHub. The main purpose of this AI-based application is to offer help to the software developers for checking their codes, supporting the faster creations of codes, and providing advanced suggestions on software development through natural language communication. You can prompt the platform in natural language to provide you with the detailed code suggestions. This platform is trained on billions of lines of codes in multiple computing languages.[208]

SAMPLE QUESTIONS

1. Provide an overview of Google BARD and its functionalities.
2. Explain the features and purpose of Claude.
3. What does define DALL-E 2 and how does it operate?
4. Explain the role and capabilities of GitHub Copilot.
5. In what ways does Google BARD contribute to technological advancements?
6. Explore the applications and significance of DALL-E 2 in the field of AI?

Bibliography

1. https://www.techtarget.com/searchenterpriseai/definition/AI-Artificial-Intelligence
2. https://en.wikipedia.org/wiki/Artificial_intelligence
3. https://www.coe.int/en/web/artificial-intelligence/history-of-ai
4. https://www.statista.com/statistics/1365145/artificial-intelligence-market-size/
5. https://www.g2.com/articles/history-of-artificial-intelligence
6. https://www.simplilearn.com/tutorials/artificial-intelligence-tutorial/what-is-artificial-intelligence
7. https://www.techtarget.com/searchenterpriseai/definition/Turing-test
8. https://www.javatpoint.com/turing-test-in-ai
9. https://www.spiceworks.com/tech/artificial-intelligence/articles/what-is-ai/
10. https://www.elements-magazine.com/8-aims-and-objectives-of-artificial-intelligence/
11. https://www.javatpoint.com/goals-of-artificial-intelligence
12. https://www.javatpoint.com/reasoning-in-artificial-intelligence
13. https://www.techtarget.com/searchenterpriseai/definition/machine-learning-ML
14. https://www.javatpoint.com/reinforcement-learning
15. https://www.techtarget.com/searchenterpriseai/tip/4-main-types-of-AI-explained
16. https://www.javatpoint.com/what-is-the-role-of-planning-in-artificial-intelligence
17. https://explodingtopics.com/blog/data-generated-per-day
18. https://dataconomy.com/2022/11/07/big-data-and-artificial-intelligence/
19. https://gamco.es/en/types-of-artificial-intelligence-capacity-functionality/
20. https://www.javatpoint.com/types-of-artificial-intelligence
21. https://www.alturis.ai/post/4-types-of-artificial-intelligence-type-i-reactive-machines
22. https://www.bmc.com/blogs/artificial-intelligence-types/
23. https://machinelearningmastery.com/gentle-introduction-long-short-term-memory-networks-experts/
24. https://www.analyticsvidhya.com/blog/2021/03/introduction-to-long-short-term-memory-lstm/
25. https://www.expresscomputer.in/artificial-intelligence-ai/what-if-ai-becomes-self-aware/81828/
26. https://blog.techliance.com/types-of-artificial-intelligence/
27. https://codebots.com/artificial-intelligence/the-3-types-of-ai-is-the-third-even-possible
28. https://www.edureka.co/blog/types-of-artificial-intelligence/
29. https://www.tutorialspoint.com/artificial_intelligence/artificial_intelligence_agents_and_environments.htm
30. https://www.javatpoint.com/agent-environment-in-ai
31. https://www.geeksforgeeks.org/agents-artificial-intelligence/
32. https://www.section.io/engineering-education/intelligent-agents-in-ai/
33. https://www.electronicsforu.com/technology-trends/tech-focus/sensors-robotics-artificial-intelligence

34. https://www.javatpoint.com/agents-in-ai
35. https://www.analyticssteps.com/blogs/6-major-branches-artificial-intelligence-ai
36. https://www.webio.com/faq/what-is-the-difference-between-cognitive-computing-and-ai
37. https://www.techtarget.com/searchenterpriseai/definition/machine-learning-ML
38. https://www.mathworks.com/discovery/deep-learning.html
39. https://www.javatpoint.com/artificial-neural-network
40. https://www.sas.com/en_us/insights/analytics/computer-vision.html
41. https://www.ibm.com/topics/computer-vision
42. https://www.techtarget.com/searchenterpriseai/definition/natural-language-processing-NLP
43. https://www.ibm.com/topics/natural-language-processing
44. https://www.techtarget.com/searchenterpriseai/definition/expert-system
45. https://www.geeksforgeeks.org/what-is-reinforcement-learning/
46. https://deepchecks.com/question/what-are-the-four-key-components-of-reinforcement-learning
47. https://www.javatpoint.com/robotics-and-artificial-intelligence
48. https://aibusiness.com/verticals/robotics-and-artificial-intelligence-the-role-of-ai-in-robots
49. https://www.tutorialspoint.com/artificial_intelligence/artificial_intelligence_robotics.htm
50. https://www.includehelp.com/ml-ai/what-is-logic-in-artificial-intelligence.aspx
51. https://www.upgrad.com/blog/propositional-logic-foundation-of-ai
52. https://en.wikibooks.org/wiki/Artificial_Intelligence/Logic/Representation/Second-order_logic
53. https://medium.com/abacus-ai/an-overview-of-logic-in-ai-and-machine-learning-2f41ccb2a335
54. https://blog.re-work.co/the-difference-between-symbolic-ai-and-connectionist-ai/
55. https://www.wsj.com/articles/chatgpt-ai-chatbot-app-explained-11675865177
56. https://www.hellotars.com/blog/chat-gpt-vs-chatbot-whats-the-difference/
57. https://www.mckinsey.com/featured-insights/mckinsey-explainers/what-is-generative-ai
58. https://www.techtarget.com/searchenterpriseai/definition/generative-AI
59. https://onlinelibrary.wiley.com/doi/abs/10.1002/gamm.202100008
60. Xu, J., Li, H., and Zhou, S., "An Overview of Deep Generative Models," *IETE Technical Review*, Vol. 32, No. 2, 2015, pp. 131–139.
61. https://lilianweng.github.io/posts/2018-10-13-flow-models/
62. https://www.jeremyjordan.me/variational-autoencoders/
63. https://scikit-learn.org/stable/modules/mixture.html
64. https://analyticsindiamag.com/a-guide-to-hidden-markov-model-and-its-applications-in-nlp/
65. https://www.techtarget.com/searchenterpriseai/definition/generative-modeling
66. Chakraborty, U., Roy, S., and Kumar, S., *Rise of Generative AI and ChatGPT: Understand How Generative AI and ChatGPT Are Transforming and Reshaping the Business World*. BPB Publications, 2023. ISBN-10: 935551798X
67. https://www.marktechpost.com/2023/03/21/a-history-of-generative-ai-from-gan-to-gpt-4/
68. https://matthewdwhite.medium.com/a-brief-history-of-generative-ai-cb1837e67106

69. https://bloggerspassion.com/chatgpt-statistics/
70. https://explodingtopics.com/blog/chatgpt-users
71. https://nerdynav.com/chatgpt-statistics/
72. https://medium.com/@mlblogging.k/reinforcement-learning-for-tuning-language-models-how-chatgpt-is-trained-9ecf23518302
73. https://towardsdatascience.com/proximal-policy-optimization-ppo-explained-abed1952457b
74. https://towardsdatascience.com/trust-region-policy-optimization-trpo-explained-4b56bd206fc2
75. https://vitalflux.com/large-language-models-concepts-examples/
76. https://www.techtarget.com/whatis/definition/large-language-model-LLM
77. https://huggingface.co/blog/rlhf
78. https://en.wikipedia.org/wiki/Reinforcement_learning_from_human_feedback
79. https://www.datasciencecentral.com/how-to-use-chatgpt-in-cloud-computing/
80. https://elephas.app/blog/how-to-get-chatgpt-api-key-clh93ii2e1642073tpacu6w934j
81. https://www.section.io/engineering-education/hugging-face/
82. https://huggingface.co/docs/transformers/index
83. https://hackernoon.com/how-to-use-chatgpt-for-python-programming
84. https://www.toolify.ai/gpts/understanding-chatgpt-a-deep-dive-into-its-architecture-143894
85. https://medium.com/@fenjiro/chatgpt-gpt-4-how-it-works-10b33fb3f12b
86. https://www.orbitanalytics.com/exploring-chatgpt-and-natural-language-processing-nlp/
87. https://www.zdnet.com/article/how-to-use-chatgpt/
88. https://www.nearshoretechnology.com/insights/blog/conversations-with-ai-7-features-of-chatgpt/
89. https://amberstudent.com/blog/post/chatgpt-limitations-that-you-need-to-know
90. https://research.aimultiple.com/chatgpt-use-cases/
91. https://www.linkedin.com/pulse/tech-stack-used-chatgpt-kedar-dixit/
92. https://plainenglish.io/blog/chatgpt-system-design-a-technical-overview
93. https://www.intel.com/content/www/us/en/products/docs/processors/cpu-vs-gpu.html
94. https://cloud.google.com/tpu/docs/intro-to-tpu#how_a_tpu_works
95. https://en.wikipedia.org/wiki/High_Bandwidth_Memory
96. https://docs.nvidia.com/cuda/cuda-c-best-practices-guide/index.html
97. https://en.wikipedia.org/wiki/ChatGPT
98. https://www.techtarget.com/searchdatamanagement/definition/C
99. https://www.infoworld.com/article/3299703/what-is-cuda-parallel-programming-for-gpus.html
100. https://en.wikipedia.org/wiki/PyTorch
101. https://www.simplilearn.com/tutorials/deep-learning-tutorial/what-is-keras
102. https://www.simplilearn.com/keras-vs-tensorflow-vs-pytorch-article
103. https://www.tensorflow.org/learn
104. https://openai.com/research/infrastructure-for-deep-learning
105. https://www.geeksforgeeks.org/theano-in-python/
106. https://www.w3schools.com/python/numpy/numpy_intro.asp
107. https://www.anaconda.com/
108. https://huggingface.co/docs/huggingface_hub/index

109. https://learn.microsoft.com/en-us/azure/databricks/machine-learning/train-model/huggingface/
110. https://www.dominodatalab.com/data-science-dictionary/spacy
111. https://online.york.ac.uk/the-role-of-natural-language-processing-in-ai/
112. https://aws.amazon.com/what-is/nlp/
113. https://www.optisolbusiness.com/insight/the-5-phases-of-natural-language-processing
114. https://levity.ai/blog/how-natural-language-processing-works
115. https://www.oreilly.com/library/view/python-natural-language/9781787121423/3071c4c9-b4d7-4329-80fe-fa5b76c73b6a.xhtml
116. https://en.wikipedia.org/wiki/Natural_language_processing
117. https://datasciencedojo.com/blog/natural-language-processing-applications/
118. https://www.tableau.com/learn/articles/natural-language-processing-examples
119. https://www.analyticsvidhya.com/blog/2020/07/top-10-applications-of-natural-language-processing-nlp/
120. https://www.grandviewresearch.com/industry-analysis/chatbot-market
121. https://www.datarobot.com/blog/text-processing-what-why-and-how
122. https://dataprot.net/statistics/spam-statistics/
123. https://towardsdatascience.com/how-to-identify-spam-using-natural-language-processing-nlp-af91f4170113
124. https://monkeylearn.com/sentiment-analysis/
125. https://blogs.commons.georgetown.edu/cctp-748-spring2018/2018/05/05/intelligent-personal-assistant-and-nlp/
126. https://www.springboard.com/blog/data-science/nlp-use-cases/
127. https://www.nobledesktop.com/classes-near-me/blog/natural-language-processing-in-data-analytics
128. Bhirud, N.S., Bhavsar, R.P., and Pawar, B.V., "Grammar Checkers for Natural Languages: A Review," *International Journal on Natural Language Computing* Vol. 6, No. 4, 2017. doi: 10.5121/ijnlc.2017.6401
129. https://www.linkedin.com/pulse/how-nlp-enables-marketers-understand-customer-sentiment/
130. https://monkeylearn.com/blog/natural-language-processing-techniques/
131. https://www.projectpro.io/article/10-nlp-techniques-every-data-scientist-should-know/415
132. https://www.techtarget.com/whatis/definition/named-entity-recognition-NER
133. https://www.analyticsvidhya.com/blog/2021/06/nlp-sentiment-analysis/
134. https://medium.com/analytics-vidhya/text-summarization-using-nlp-3e85ad0c6349
135. https://www.projectpro.io/article/topic-modeling-nlp/801
136. https://www.analyticsvidhya.com/blog/2022/03/keyword-extraction-methods-from-documents-in-nlp/
137. https://www.analyticsvidhya.com/blog/2022/06/stemming-vs-lemmatization-in-nlp-must-know-differences
138. Vaswani, A., Shazeer, N., Parmar, N., Uszkoreit, J., Jones, L., Gomez, A.N., Kaiser, L., and Polosukhin, I., "Attention Is All You Need," 31st Conference on Neural Information Processing Systems (NIPS 2017), Long Beach, CA, USA, pp. 6000–6010.
139. https://machinelearningmastery.com/the-transformer-model/
140. https://www.dominodatalab.com/blog/transformers-self-attention-to-the-rescue

141. https://www.techtarget.com/searchenterpriseai/definition/transformer-model
142. https://www.topbots.com/ai-nlp-research-pretrained-language-models/
143. https://en.wikipedia.org/wiki/Transformer_(machine_learning_model)
144. https://aliissa99.medium.com/transformer-gpt-3-gpt-j-t5-and-bert-4cf8915dd86f
145. https://www.datacamp.com/blog/what-we-know-gpt4
146. https://towardsdatascience.com/use-cases-of-googles-universal-sentence-encoder-in-production-dd5aaab4fc15
147. https://towardsdatascience.com/understanding-t5-model-text-to-text-transfer-transformer-model-69ce4c165023
148. https://www.analyticsvidhya.com/blog/2023/03/an-introduction-to-large-language-models-llms/
149. https://research.aimultiple.com/large-language-models-examples/
150. https://www.cs.upc.edu/~nlp/wikicorpus/
151. https://en.wikipedia.org/wiki/Wikipedia:Size_of_Wikipedia
152. Bond, F., "The Web as Corpus," Department of Asian Studies, Palacký University, Lecture 7 PowerPoint slides. Available at: https://bond-lab.github.io/Language-Technology-and-the-Internet/pdf/wk-07-wac.pdf
153. https://www.sketchengine.eu/blog/build-a-corpus-from-the-web/
154. https://en.wikipedia.org/wiki/BookCorpus
155. https://en.wikipedia.org/wiki/List_of_text_corpora
156. https://iq.opengenus.org/gpt-3-5-model/
157. https://aws.amazon.com/what-is/gpt/
158. https://en.wikipedia.org/wiki/GPT-2
159. https://rowlando13.medium.com/everything-gpt-2-0-intro-a82e1dd040ae
160. https://en.wikipedia.org/wiki/GPT-3
161. https://www.linkedin.com/pulse/chatgpts-guide-understanding-gpt-35-architecture-heena-koshti/
162. https://lablab.ai/tech/openai/gpt3-5
163. https://www.edureka.co/blog/how-chatgpt-works-training-model-of-chatgpt/
164. https://d1gi.medium.com/chatgpt-training-the-list-of-news-orgs-and-articles-92910f641480
165. https://www.businessinsider.com/openais-latest-chatgpt-version-hides-training-on-copyrighted-material-2023-8
166. https://towardsdatascience.com/how-chatgpt-works-the-models-behind-the-bot-1ce5fca96286
167. https://www.analyticsvidhya.com/blog/2023/05/how-to-harness-the-full-potential-of-chatgpt-tips-prompts/#Using_ChatGPT_Like_a_Pro
168. https://cointelegraph.com/news/use-chat-gpt-like-a-pro
169. https://zapier.com/blog/how-to-use-chatgpt/
170. https://www.kommunicate.io/blog/chatgpt-4-vs-chatgpt-3-5-key-differences/
171. https://www.zdnet.com/article/gpt-3-5-vs-gpt-4-is-chatgpt-plus-worth-its-subscription-fee/
172. https://www.linkedin.com/pulse/chatgpt-35-vs-chatgpt-4-comparison-latest-gpt-based-chatbot-kunerth/
173. https://www.pcmag.com/news/the-new-chatgpt-what-you-get-with-gpt-4-vs-gpt-35
174. https://chatgpt.ch/en/differences-between-gpt-3-5-and-gpt-4/
175. https://apiumhub.com/tech-blog-barcelona/chatgpt-for-developers/
176. https://inclusioncloud.com/insights/blog/chatgpt-productivity-developer/
177. https://www.zdnet.com/article/how-to-use-chatgpt-to-write-code/

178. https://cult.honeypot.io/reads/how-can-chatgpt-help-developers/
179. https://medium.com/@gulomnazarov/18-important-benefits-of-chatgpt-for-humanity-a76f738288c1
180. https://www.sandipuniversity.edu.in/blog/what-are-the-advantages-of-using-chatgpt/
181. https://www.calendar.com/blog/the-advantages-and-disadvantages-of-chatgpt/
182. https://www.spiceworks.com/tech/artificial-intelligence/articles/what-is-chatgpt/
183. https://becominghuman.ai/10-features-of-chatgpt-unleashing-the-true-potential-of-this-ai-language-model-66a3cf1098c5
184. https://amberstudent.com/blog/post/chatgpt-limitations-that-you-need-to-know
185. https://www.forbes.com/sites/bernardmarr/2023/03/03/the-top-10-limitations-of-chatgpt/?sh=798fcdb08f35
186. https://www.pluralsight.com/resources/blog/data/ai-gpt-models-differences
187. https://www.makeuseof.com/gpt-models-explained-and-compared/
188. https://www.techtarget.com/searchenterpriseai/feature/ChatGPT-vs-GPT-How-are-they-different
189. https://www.zdnet.com/article/what-is-gpt-4-heres-everything-you-need-to-know/
190. https://fourweekmba.com/instructgpt/
191. https://www.makeuseof.com/things-you-can-do-with-chatgpt/
192. https://blog.enterprisedna.co/is-chatgpt-plus-worth-it/
193. https://aicontentfy.com/en/blog/future-of-chatgpt-predictions-and-opportunities-1
194. https://www.linkedin.com/pulse/future-chat-gpt-where-revolutionary-technology-vineet-khankriyal/
195. https://101blockchains.com/generative-ai-and-chatgpt-future/
196. https://www.makeuseof.com/openai-chatgpt-biggest-probelms/
197. https://www.educative.io/answers/what-are-some-limitations-and-challenges-of-chatgpt
198. https://www.teachertoolkit.co.uk/2023/07/06/chatgpt-education/
199. https://www.scribbr.com/ai-tools/legal-implications-chatgpt/
200. https://hgs.cx/blog/the-rise-of-chatgpt-implications-and-applications-of-conversational-ai/
201. https://www.polarismarketresearch.com/industry-analysis/generative-ai-market
202. https://www.simplilearn.com/tutorials/artificial-intelligence-tutorial/top-generative-ai-tools
203. https://www.marktechpost.com/2023/08/28/top-40-generative-ai-tools-2023/
204. https://chat.openai.com/
205. https://bard.google.com/
206. https://claude.ai/
207. https://openai.com/dall-e-2
208. https://github.com/features/copilot

Index

Printed in the United States
by Baker & Taylor Publisher Services